THE ART OF
MENTAL PRAYER

THE ART OF
MENTAL PRAYER

BY THE REV.
BEDE FROST

WITH A PREFACE BY THE
Rt. Rev. ABBOT DENYS OF NASHDOM

LONDON

S·P·C·K

1960

First Edition February 1931
Second Edition September 1931
Third Edition January 1932
Fourth, revised, Impression, 1932
Reprinted 1934
Reprinted 1935
New Edition, S.P.C.K., 1940
Reprinted 1948
Reprinted 1950
Reprinted 1960

PRINTED BY COMPTON PRINTING WORKS (LONDON) LTD.,

DEDICATED

TO

THE MOST SACRED HEART OF JESUS

PERFECT ADORER
OF THE ALL HOLY TRINITY
AND
DIVINE MASTER OF PRAYER
BY WHOSE SPIRIT
WE ARE TAUGHT AND LED
TO
PRAY TO THE FATHER IN SPIRIT AND IN TRUTH

PREFACE

THERE is a certain peculiar difficulty, half pleasure, half diffidence, which must attach to the writing of a preface to such a book as this. A 'religious' must needs look upon prayer as the most practical as well as the most important activity in life. Any book which can make the ways of prayer more frequented, which can guide the bewildered, and above all can assist the clergy in doing so (one of the most difficult as well as the most necessary of their tasks), cannot but be sure of a welcome from every religious. But for a religious Superior to commend a book which springs from his own Community is a more delicate matter, and requires a belief in the book's value which is not always necessary to the writers of prefaces.

The book would seem to me to be one that may be commended not only to the notice, but also to the careful and above all devout study, of those called upon to direct souls – and this on two separate grounds.

First, if one can judge, the book is timely. The Tractarians, great men of prayer as they were, were forced, by the very circumstances of the case in which they found themselves, to concentrate upon the one basic end of the recovery of Catholic dogma. The English Church seemed to be in a parlous state, and its most alarming symptom was that it could see it appeared to have discarded its appeal to the Early and Undivided Church, and to be in danger of becoming an isolated entity in itself. With the vision of the Church Catholic, whose commission was from outside time, whose strength and whose message were not her own, the English Church's hope revived, and slowly from that hope came confidence and fulfilment.

But this was only a first step. The laity—even that butt of the more worldly clergy, the ' ecclesiastically minded ' laity—do not absorb theology as a rule from reading it ; or, even if they do, its implications and corollaries are as a rule obscure to them. If the Oxford Movement was ever to become more than a clerical mental attitude, then there would inevitably be needed another restoration, the restoration of Catholic worship.

The battle for this was bound to be longer, because such a restoration was more practically startling to the plain mind than any abstract doctrinal emphasis. But we can roughly say that by the outbreak of the war the battle had been won in many parts of the kingdom, or at least was going successfully.

But the victory for Catholic worship produced in its turn a new need. The keynote of Catholic worship is *latria*, that prostrate adoration by the ' nothingness,' which is the human soul, of the supreme and ever-lasting ' All,' that is God – that adoration which Baron von Hügel called ' the heart of religion.' But once this conception of religion had been regained even to a slight extent, the old-fashioned ' pietism ' which the eighteenth century at its best had substituted for devotion was bound to be inadequate to the needs of souls.

The restoration of Catholic devotion inevitably had to wait until the preliminary steps of restoring Catholic Faith and Practice had been taken. Devotion is alike their fruit and their only guarantee of life. But to change the whole current of a soul's life, let alone that of a Church, is often enough a dangerous business. Certainly, even where it is most tranquilly accom-plished, there will be swirlings and eddies and some-thing of a backwash. In this case the process has been complicated to an indefinite extent by the simultaneous

impact upon the English mind not only of the Catholic
tradition, but of a number of other forces, racial, psychological, critical, and moral (or frequently anti-
moral), which, though they have arisen outside the
religious world, have their full effect upon it.

It is under such circumstances as these, when the
Catholic ' Mind ' of the Church in these provinces, at
many stages of development and swayed by a multitude of very different influences, seems to be groping
in bewilderment, that we have to regain for the children
of our Church that plain but often weary path to
sanctity which has been beaten out by the footsteps of
those whom we call Saints, after they have trodden it
to the end – the Catholic tradition of prayer, in which
Being and not ' Doing ' is the all-important thing.

And here, I think, comes in the other great merit, in
my eyes, of this book – the truly Catholic wideness of
its view. One cannot help feeling at times that the
Ignatian method is being over-pressed among us to-
day. In spite of its psychological excellences and its
splendid results under suitable conditions, it remains
what the great and wise Saint who drew it up always
intended it to be, rather a gymnasium for the spiritual
athlete than a universally applicable system.

The over-stressing of what after all is one very fruitful method is understandable. Once the method is
fully grasped, there are few souls who cannot profit by
it to an extent, many for whom it is excellently suited,
and even the best of all methods. But whether all
souls, or even the majority, necessarily get from it the
full graces of prayer which the Holy Ghost only waits
to shed abroad in their hearts is another question.
Other methods were little known among us, and of the
dangers of unregulated reading of ' mystical ' books
many a director could give painful examples. At all
events, from the sane, sober methods of St. Ignatius
there would not spring that ' mysticality ' which hides

God behind the foggy sentiments of the worshipper's own mind and self. And so many an experienced priest has come to rely, even if he vaguely knew that other methods did exist, upon the only one whose study was not necessarily a specialist's preserve.

It is, then – at least, so it would seem to me – the special value of this book that without decrying or neglecting the virtues of the Ignatian method, it does present in detail the methods of a number of guides to the spiritual life. It is a platitude that no two souls are quite alike in their approach to prayer. It is well to have more than one path along which to guide them to the single Goal of all prayer – God.

' Jerusalem, which is above, which is the Mother of us all,' has her twelve gates, and Saints have entered by them all. I would commend to directors the need we have of broadening our grasp of the methods of prayer. It is true that methods are not all. But they are something, and in the early stages of the prayer-life they are of great importance.

In conclusion, I would only say this – it is the vocation to real sanctity to-day which often seems most lacking among us, clergy, religious, and laity alike. Yet it is charity nourished by grace – that *inchoatio quædam beatitudinis* which alone can attract our weary wounded world, that seeks for beauty and cries out for perfection even in the frail tottering things of earth that have so often cheated it already. The vision of that Life ever old and ever new – born yet never age-ing – the eternal reconciliation of rest and realised omnipotence which is the blessed felicity of the Saints, dawns upon the eyes of charity even in this world. If the blind are not once more pathetically to lead the blind into the ditch, and even over the precipice, the eyes of our charity must be strengthened for that vision, and that can only be by prayer.

That this book may counsel anxious priests, may

guide some who have already started on the long road of prayer, and may lead many to set out upon the strangest adventure of human life that leads from human life to Life Himself, is the hope and earnest prayer of

DENYS,
Abbot of Pershore.

PREFACE TO SECOND EDITION

I WELCOME this opportunity of thanking all those who have done me invaluable service by the criticisms they have made upon this work, and also those who have kindly pointed out minor errors, especially to the Rev. Fr. Harton and Mr. J. P. Godwin, the latter of whom has corrected many mistakes in the Bibliography. Unfortunately, it has been found impossible to add, as I should have liked to have done, a chapter on Dominican methods and one, after the manner of French writers, answering some of the criticisms made. The favourable reception and rapid sale of the book is very gratifying as evidencing the increasing attention which is being paid to this important subject.

BEDE FROST.

Feast of St. Dominic, 1931.

PREFACE TO THIRD EDITION

IT is obviously difficult for an author to discern the causes of the success of his own work, but I venture to think that a third edition of this book would not have been so speedily called for but for the fact that it states the Faith in a clear and uncontroversial manner and illustrates it as reflected in the prayer-life of the saints who have lived most nearly in and by that knowledge of God which the Faith reveals and conserves. Men are tired, not only of vulgarised and diminished versions of the Catholic religion and of the constant stream of controversy in which they have been involved during the past few years, but also of the lack of foundation and content in so much present-day preaching and teaching. The world can only be won back to the Church by Christians becoming more Christian, as Peter Wust says, and this will only be in the degree that devotion is founded on a living faith, born of a contact with Divine reality. The work of the Church is to make Christians, and, as a writer in a recent number of the *Hibbert Journal* well says, to help ' people who are weary of fruitless striving and endless argument to find the goal of their spirits in prayer.' The very kind reception afforded to one's efforts in this direction may, perhaps, be taken as some indication of what men of goodwill are looking for to-day.

BEDE FROST.

Epiphany, 1932.

INTRODUCTION

THE purpose of this book is clear, definite and restricted. It is to give to the clergy, religious and devout laity who, for one reason or another, are unable to go to the sources themselves, a concise and as brief a treatment as the subject allows of the interior life of prayer in its early stages as it has been taught and practised by the great masters of the spiritual life. It covers all that need be known, apart from that actual personal experience which each one may gain only for himself and without which little can be done in guiding others in the paths of prayer. If it is asked why I begin with the early sixteenth century, with St. Ignatius, St. François, St. Teresa and St. Pedro de Alcantara rather than with Cassian, St Nilus or even with the Victorines, it is simply because it was then that the practice of mental prayer, which had ever been regarded as an essential to the normal Christian life, became an exact science, an art, was ' codified ' and enclosed within ' methods ' such as this volume deals with. That this was, as Dom Chapman says, ' an entire reversal of tradition ' (article on ' Mysticism ' in the *Encyclopædia of Religion and Ethics*, vol. ix., p. 100), I am not concerned to deny. In chapter iii. I endeavour to show that such a ' reversal,' or, as I should prefer to call it, a ' development,' was as desirable and necessary then as it is to-day. Yet it must not be inferred that methodic mental prayer was an entirely new thing in the sixteenth century. In the *Scala claustralium* of Dom Guigues of Chartreuse (1083–1137) we find that fourfold act of prayer which was to be developed in succeeding ages. The four degrees of prayer, says Dom Guigues, are reading, meditation, prayer and contemplation. 'Reading is an attentive study made by applying the mind to Holy Scripture. Meditation is a careful investigation, by the aid of the reason, of a hidden truth. Prayer is the elevation of the heart towards God in order to avoid evil and obtain good. Contemplation is the raising of the soul in God, ravished in the taste of eternal joys. . . . The ineffable sweetness of the blessed life is sought in reading, found in meditation, asked for in prayer, tasted in contemplation.' The rest of the book consists of an explanation of this manner of prayer. Dom Guigues du Pont (*d.* 1297), in an important treatise *De Contemplatione*, the first part of which was reproduced in the Prœmium to the *Vita Christi* of Ludolph of Saxony, and through him became known to St. Ignatius, describes the three ways of spiritual life, purgative, illuminative or union with Christ, and contemplative. In the first two, Christ is the centre of the soul's effort, which, being healed by the Divine medicine in the purgative way, seeks to be united to, to adhere to Christ. The means of this is meditation on the life of our Lord, which must be practised in order, one mystery being considered each day, and this, not as if we were considering some past or far-off fact, but as if we were actually taking part in it. By contemplation, Dom Guigues means what later writers style 'acquired contemplation,' that prayer to which meditation is the way and which may be attained by our own efforts aided by grace. Such contemplation, he says, contains three elements, prayer (*oratio*), appropriate matter (*materia*), and a method (*modus exercitandi*). He divides this contemplation into speculative and anagogical, the first of which is akin to later meditation, being largely an intellectual exercise requiring the three conditions of purity of heart, spiritual solicitude and piety which desires to taste and feel (*sentire*) the Lord 'in goodness and simplicity of heart.' Anagogical contemplation,

which is more like our ' affective ' prayer, at least in
its first two degrees, has three steps, or ' adhesions.'
In the first we attach ourselves by love to the Sacred
Humanity, daily meditating or contemplating the
mysteries of the human life of Christ, gradually passing
to the contemplation of His Divinity. In both these degrees the subject should be prepared in order that we may
have matter to occupy our mind and stir our devotion.
In the third degree, we pass beyond all consideration,
being immediately and directly united to God ' immediate se submittere divinæ bonitati ad recipiendum
anagogicas benedictiones accensiones et ascensiones.'

In the *De triplici Via* or *Incendium Amoris* of St.
Bonaventura, one of the most noteworthy treatises
of his age, we find attached to each way its own
kind of spiritual exercise, meditation, prayer, contemplation. Of the first, the Saint writes, ' In meditation
of this kind, our soul should employ itself entirely with
all its faculties, reason, synderesis, conscience, will.
The reason considers that which it is doing, the understanding judges and defines the case supposed, the
conscience bears its witness and suggests the conclusion,
the will chooses and decides. Do you wish so to meditate in the purgative way ? The reason will then search
that which a man must do who has violated the temple
of God ; the judgment replies that he ought to be
condemned or to repent ; the conscience cries, " This
man, it is thou, then, damnation or penitence " ; then
the will makes its choice, rejects condemnation and
freely decides with tears to repent.' St. Ignatius is
hardly more definite as to the need, use and manner of
mental prayer. Later authors continue the tradition
which in the sixteenth century was clarified, codified
and made popular.[1]

[1] For a full study of the history of methods of mental prayer see
P. Watrigant, ' Histoire de la meditation methodique,' *Revue d' Ascetique
et Mystique*, April 1922, January 1923. P. Pourrat gives a brief account in
vol. iii., pp. 6–22, of his *Christian Spirituality*.

I should like to emphasise one point which will be dealt with more fully later on. Most people do not know either the need of mental prayer or the way to practise it, and need to be taught : those who do practise it are frequently hampered by the fact that only one method is in any sense generally known, and that a method not suited to or meant for the majority. There are many other methods, but most of them are inaccessible to the ordinary reader ; and even those which are available, e.g. that of St. Pedro of Alcantara, entitled *A Golden Treatise of Mental Prayer*, of which an admirable edition is now to be had in the " Orchard Books " series, published by Messrs. Burns, Oates & Washbourne, are much less used than they deserve.

I have, therefore, endeavoured to supply what seems to be a need by gathering in one volume all the chief methods taught by those whom the Church has either canonised or regards as pre-eminent in the spiritual life, adding only certain chapters, themselves no more than a *résumé* of the teaching of the Saints, which seemed necessary to complete the book and make it, if not a complete, yet a sufficient guide to the subject. Those who wish to read further in the matter will find abundant material in the Bibliography, scanty as it is compared with the vast store from which it is gleaned. I have quoted largely, not only because the exact words of spiritual authors are of more value than any others, but also that my readers may be led to desire to know more of the great classics of the spiritual life.

BEDE FROST.

Christmass, 1930.

CONTENTS

PART I
PRELIMINARIES

CHAPTER I

The ' Gap ' in the Religious Situation of To-day

ANYONE who is at all familiar with the present position of Catholicism in the Anglican Communion – that is, in any or all of the provinces in communion with the see of Canterbury – must be conscious of the existence of a certain 'gap' in teaching and practice which, to a much larger extent than is generally recognised, nullifies and renders sterile all the considerable progress which has been, and is being, made.

That ' gap ' is the absence of insistence upon, and the practice of, mental prayer.

Whilst in almost every other way we have assimilated, carried on, corrected and developed the work begun by the Tractarian Movement, we have sadly failed in learning and reproducing that practice of the interior life of prayer and mortification in which our fathers trained themselves and their people. Lest this statement should seem to savour of exaggeration, I venture to call attention to three facts, chosen from amongst many, which substantiate it.

(1) Some time ago an English diocesan Bishop addressed a questionnaire to his clergy in which he asked for information as to their teaching about, and practice of, prayer. The question did not receive a single answer !

(2) A long and varied experience amongst nearly all classes, both at home and abroad, not only in ordinary parish work, but also in conducting missions and Retreats, has revealed the existence of an astonishing ignorance as to what Christian prayer is, and how it should be practised.[1] Only a very few, even amongst

[1] ' It is generally recognised that our people to-day hardly pray at all.' – Fr. Conran, S.S.J.E., in the *Church Times*, April 4th, 1930.

3

the clergy and laity who make Retreats, know of, and
actually live, lives of prayer, and, if they have attempted
to do so, they are usually in a very elementary stage,
making little or no progress for want of knowledge.
Most of them have never been taught clearly, and
imagine that mental prayer is a spiritual luxury reserved for an *élite* few, as well as being exceedingly
difficult. That it is neither I shall hope to show.

(3) A knowledge of the contents of the bookshelves
of the average modern priest reveals, to some extent,
the reason for this ignorance and neglect of mental
prayer. For, whatever may be found there, it is
comparatively rare to find any of those solid, enduring,
indispensable books on the spiritual life and the practice
of prayer which exist in so rich an abundance that it is
almost incredible that they should be so ignored. The
truth of this statement will appear to anyone who
compares the average priest's library with the Bibliography at the end of this book. I do not imply that
the absence of at least some standard books on prayer
means that a priest does not pray and teach his people
to pray, but it does normally afford the presumption
that he has not that regard for the subject which the
books he does possess indicate he has for others.

Now I would claim that it is precisely this absence
of the teaching and practice of mental prayer, with all
that it involves, which is the most serious thing in the
life of the Church to-day, which, more than anything
else, is ' holding up ' the true and necessary development of the Catholic Revival in our midst. For, despite
the fact of a great amount of organisation and activity,
more alarming than reassuring to many, there is a quite
perceptible pause, and something of a consequent
depression, existing to-day. Some words of Fr. Faber's
in a letter written in 1850 to Mr. Watts Russell about
the then state of Roman Catholicism in England have
an unpleasantly familiar sound to-day : ' We have all

been too *cocky* here in England, both old Catholics and converts. We have gone on as if the game were in our own hands ; we have run off to shows, pageants, functions, fine churches, gentlemanliness, publicity, and not corresponded to what God was doing for us outwardly by an increase of asceticism or prayer, or the practice of an interior life generally. We were getting more hollow and presumptuous daily. . . . Alas, the misery is that so few people take a supernatural view of things.'

We have seen, almost within the limits of a lifetime, the recovery of Catholic ideals, faith and practice in a country which more than any other had lost touch with the main stream of Catholic tradition and life ; we have familiarised the people of England, as no one else could have done, with doctrines they had forgotten, Sacraments they ignored, and practices they had been taught to abhor : we have got an appreciable number of them to Mass and the Sacraments and to some growing perception of the supernatural, yet we are, or should be, sadly conscious that something is yet lacking. There is ; and it is the realisation of the fact that the acceptance of the Faith, the hearing of Mass and the reception of the Sacraments are not all ; that Faith, Cultus and Sacraments need a background and reinforcing power. That background, that power, is the interior life of prayer.

For, amongst other reasons which will be dealt with in a later chapter, it is prayer alone which makes the grace of the Sacraments operative in our lives. For, although the grace of the Sacraments is given *ex opere operato*, it does not produce fruit without our moral assimilation and response, which is mainly the work of prayer. This is one reason why all the masters of the spiritual life teach that mental prayer is morally necessary to the acquiring and maintaining of even a low degree of holiness. We see people going regularly to Mass and the Sacraments for years, yet remaining in a mediocre and barren piety. It is because they do not really pray. That is the reason, referred to by Fr. Rawlinson at the First Anglo-Catholic Priests Convention (*Report*, pp. 79 ff.), why we do not produce ' heroic types of sanctity.' It is largely due to the fact that our direction in and out of the confessional is almost entirely moralistic, concerned more with sins than with sanctity, with the overcoming of temptation by strenuous, external efforts of our own rather than with the building up of the interior, spiritual life, of contentment with a well-drilled, mediocre piety instead of aiming at producing a desire for perfection.

In the course of the history of the Church there are some striking illustrations of her continuous appreciation of the supreme need of prayer in the Christian life. And by prayer, let it be said once for all, I mean much more than the term ordinarily conveys to-day. Not the recitation of ordinary, vocal prayers, mainly composed of petitions and intercessions, but that mental prayer which has been the continuous tradition and practice of souls from the earliest days of Christianity, the prayer of being with God, of attention to Him, of reflection upon spiritual realities, prayer which is, as says St. Nilus, ' an intercourse of the spirit with God ' (*de Oratione*, 3), ' an elevation of the soul to God ' (St. John Damascene, *De Fide Orthodox*, I. iii. 24), ' a friendly intercourse in which the soul converses alone with Him by Whom she knows that she is loved ' (*Life of St. Teresa*, chap. viii.), an act which 'places our understanding in the Divine Light, and exposes our will to the warmth of heavenly love ' (*Introduction to the Devout Life*, St. François de Sales, pt. ii., chap. 1).

In the Christian ages, most conspicuous, not only for striking examples of heroic sanctity, but for a very deep and widespread devotion amongst all classes, e.g. those of Syrian and Egyptian and Gallican monasticism, of early Benedictinism, the thirteenth and fourteenth centuries and the later sixteenth and seventeenth centuries in France, Spain and Italy, there is an *apparent* absence of emphasis, particularly in the earlier periods mentioned, on the reception of the Sacraments compared with that laid on prayer. This does not mean that the Sacraments were not esteemed ; on the contrary, one reason why so comparatively little is said about them is that they formed, where they could be had, so normal a part of Christian practice. Still, those ages were not *Sacramental* in the sense that ours is ; Confession and Communion were, with notable exceptions, infrequent ; St. Antony did not receive Holy Communion for some years ; in the earliest Benedictine monasteries Mass was only said and Communion given only on Sundays and the greater feasts, whilst the normal rarity of Communion, even amongst religious, in mediæval times, and indeed up to the Counter-Reform, is well known. Yet there was never a time when all alike, clergy, religious and laity, were not exhorted to the life of prayer, and that in its most advanced stages. Neither infrequent reception of the Sacraments nor any state of life was held to constitute any bar to the practice of mental prayer. Whatever else might be omitted, for one cause or another, this was absolutely necessary. Preaching to mixed congregations in the Lateran basilica, St. Gregory the Great exhorts all classes to strive after the highest states of prayer, as in his Pastoral Rule he clearly demands it of the clergy. The great teachers of the Middle Ages were no less insistent, and the immense work of the Counter-Reformation was founded on it. The reform and sanctification of clergy, religious and laity all depend upon this : to pray and to teach souls to pray – it is all. For given this, everything else will follow. It is as true to-day as ever. No duty is more incumbent upon the clergy than this. Unless they themselves learn how to pray, and centre all their efforts on teaching others to pray, their work is useless. For it is ignorance of this more than anything else which is the main cause, not only of the shallowness and mediocrity of modern piety, but of the general lapse from all Christian practice. It is not the difficulties of belief, the conflict between religion and science, or rather the camp-followers of science, the time-spirit or any of the many things at which the learned tilt ; it is primarily that our own people do not know how to pray and, not knowing, fall an easy prey to any temptation that besets them. It may be an article in the daily paper, or the fact, as I have seen it, of being suddenly placed in circumstances, e.g. in a foreign country, where all the normal surroundings of life are absent, where there is not only no church, priest or Sacraments, but a distinct absence of any moral or spiritual tone. For the man or woman habituated to prayer this would be hard enough ; for one who does not know how to pray it spells disaster. The average priest and well-disposed parent imagines that if a boy or girl is brought up to say vocal prayers twice a day (and how many do even this without fail any confessor knows), is confirmed and started off with a monthly Communion, it is enough.   It is not enough ; without mental prayer it is worth very little.

Nor should the teaching of prayer be confined to a select few – the faithful communicants or those who attend a week-night service. They need it, and we shall be surprised at the number who actually welcome it ; but so also will many who we have never suspected would respond to it – I mean those who seldom come to church at all. We complain about the exigencies of modern life which make it almost impossible for thousands even to fulfil their Sunday obligation or to receive the Sacraments frequently. But we have actually become so obsessed with the idea that the Christian life consists in going to church – 'a fond thing

vainly invented' by the Puritans of the seventeenth
century – that in dealing with ' outsiders ' we begin at
the wrong end by endeavouring to persuade them to
come to a ' mission ' service, a mothers' meeting or
Bible class, or even, daringly, to Evensong, or a Confirmation class. The general results are familiar
enough. If we succeed, they are usually more firmly
convinced than they were that religion is not for them.

Far better to face the truth that the Christian life
does not consist in ' coming to church,' that the great
majority of Christian people never have gone to church
with that frequency which we expect, and that if we
were in their places we should not do so either. It is
not modern conditions solely which account for our
empty benches, nor original sin. There never has been
a time when the vast majority of Christian people could
or did do much more than fulfil their Sunday obligation by attendance at a low Mass. Our mistake is that,
failing to get them to church, we give them up as hopeless and confine our attention to those who come, or
are likely to come. We need an Apostolate to the non-
churchgoers, an Apostolate, not of processions or open-
air preaching, still less of subsidiary attractions, but of
prayer. And by this I mean, not chiefly intercessory
prayer for this class, but the deliberate centring of
efforts on getting them to pray. Most of them still
retain one or two truths on which such an attempt must
be based. They believe in God, in some indistinct
way in our Lord and in prayer. It would not be
difficult to get many of them to same little practice of
prayer ; say, a simple act of adoration and offering
every morning, or a carefully recited Pater and Ave,
some little use of ejaculations and of offering their
work, etc., to our Lord, with Him, in Him and for
Him, a short evening prayer. It would require both
infinite care and patience, but in each soul who began
in the smallest way we should have implanted a Divine

seed of limitless possibilities, for once a soul really begins to pray, the way is open for our Lord to operate, desire for holiness grows, and the normal channels of grace are sought as well as the expression of the new life in Christian worship.

After this digression, which might seem to countenance laxity as to the necessary Christian obligations, though it does not nor is intended to do so ; after, too, what I have said about the less ' Sacramental ' ages of the Church, it may not be unnecessary to point out that the modern Sacramental movement is not to be viewed with suspicion. Brought about, as it largely was, by the insistence of the leaders of the Counter-Reform – Mother Blémur, writing of the reforms brought about in the Benedictine houses in France by the introduction of mental prayer, says that one of the results was an increased frequentation of the Sacraments,' car auparavant l'usage en était rare ' (Blémur, ii., pp. 121, 122) – checked for a moment by Jansenism, which had far more influence in England than is commonly recognised, reaching the full approbation of the Church under Pius X, it has already begun to bear fruit. What I am concerned with is not subtraction or substitution, but the combination of our Sacramentalism with the prayer life of the Saints. The Church is a living body, not a static institution ; a shrine of living realities, not a museum of relics. And, being a living body, she cannot be tied down or for ever bound within the particular limits of development reached in any one age ; to live is to move, *in motu vita*, to touch life as it is here and now. Thus the Sacramental Revival, both in cultus and communion, is the Church's answer, the answer of the Mind of Christ, Whose Body she is, to the materialism of our day, her deliberate way of combating the tendencies of the human spirit in our time.

In each age the Church, divinely guided by the Spirit

of Jesus, her Head, and despite much hindrance, not only from the world, but from the frailty of her members, carries on the mission of Jesus, opposing to the spirit of the world the spirit of the Gospel under new and varying forms, some of which persist, others of which do their work and pass away, never, however, without handing on some notable contribution to the life-total of the Body. In the first three centuries of her existence she met and conquered the world by the spirit of martyrdom, later by the institution of the eremitical and cœnobitic life ; Benedictinism was the salt and preservative during the Dark Ages, the Friars that of the time spirit of the thirteenth to the fifteenth centuries, a large part of the disaster of the Reformation being due to the failure of the Church to make any general and adequate response to their labours. The Counter-Reformation saved Catholicism in Europe, indeed it saved Christianity for the world. And in our day Sacramentalism in its varying forms, daily Masses, frequent and daily Communion (a return indeed to the ' early ' Church), the cultus of the Holy Sacrament, is our contribution to the age-long tradition of the Church, a contribution which seems about to lead to another wave of devotion in prayer and to the religious life. It must necessarily be so, for by no other means may faith be translated into living experience or grace become operative in human lives. No man's religion is safe, much less potent, until it has become in very truth his own. As Miss Evelyn Underhill says, ' No one, as a matter of fact, takes any real interest in the explanation [of the life of the Spirit] unless he has had some form of the experience ' (*Life of the Spirit and the Life of To-day*, p. 5). He must ' taste and see that the Lord is gracious,' and such taste and sight, sight because taste, comes, as St. Bonaventura says, ' of desire, not of intellect ; of the ardours of prayer, not of the teaching of the schools.'

One word more. Most of us do not sufficiently
recognise how much we have been and are handi-
capped by four facts in our history and development.

(1) The fact that for three centuries we have been
entirely cut off from the main stream of Christian
tradition, development and life. Only those who know
something of the interior life of the Catholic Church in
Europe as well as of her external labours during
that time can have any idea of its richness and
diversity, and in some part realise our own irreparable
loss.

(2) Added to this is the second fact that during this
time we have lived in an heretical atmosphere, an
atmosphere in which ' what was Christian in Christianity had largely disappeared ' (Tawney, *The Acquisi-
tive Society*, chap. ii., p. 13). Religion has become
merely a synonym for morality, philanthropy and self-
improvement ; Faith reduced to feelings ; the Christian life regarded as an activity rather than an act,
doing rather than being ; the intellectual and moral
side exalted to the exclusion of the spiritual and
affective ; nature opposed to grace ; a riot of con-
flicting and ultimately anti-Christian tendencies,
Lutheranism, Calvinism, Jansenism and Puritanism, a
spiritual malaria from which we still suffer.[1]

(3) A necessity of our peculiar and abnormal
circumstances has produced a third fact, that for the
past half-century our attention has been mainly riveted

---

[1] I must not be taken to be depreciating or criticising the lives or the
prayer of individuals who have held, in greater or less degree, Lutheran,
Calvinistic, Jansenistic or Puritanic tenets. I refer to them as systems of
doctrine and practice which, as such, are opposed to the teaching, spirit
and mind of the Catholic Church. The Lutheran doctrine of faith, the
Calvinistic conception of God, the Jansenist teaching on grace, the
Judaic-Manichean spirit underlying Puritanism, together with the
complete repudiation of the Church, the Hierarchy, the Sacraments of
fifteen hundred years, and the overthrow of moral principles which they
produced, are sufficient to justify the terms used here and elsewhere.
A system which produced or was produced by Luther, Calvin, Melanch-
thon, Beza, Knox, etc., and that which produced St. François de
Sales, St. Ignatius, St. Teresa and the innumerable Saints of the

on external things. The restoration of Divine worship,
the use of the Sacraments, the replacing of dogmatic
truth before the minds of our people, the recovery of a
liturgical and ceremonial sense – these and other things,
which had to be done, have so occupied our minds and
activities that we have had little time even to perceive
the need of something more. Thus we have evolved
a type of Catholicism which rarely gets beyond the
mediocre ; we have become content if people come to
Mass and the Sacraments more or less regularly ; we
have not, at least often, discerned their capability of and
our own responsibility for the awakening and development of a truly interior life.

(4) We have – and this becomes more marked daily
in both clergy and laity – neglected serious study of
and meditation upon the New Testament. We have
usually, following the wrong guides, given some attention to criticism, history, etc., of Gospel times, textual
revision and the like, but not to ' reading the Bible
biblically,' as the Dominican saying has it ; i.e. reading
the text itself and comparing one part with another.
Commentaries, ' ces gloses parasites qui coupent la
parole au Maître,' have been a snare and delusion to
us ; the word of God has been buried beneath a mass
of trivialities, the Divine Spirit has fled from our too
exclusive intellectualism.

Now all this has created and developed that
hard, unsupernatural, unspiritual and profoundly un-
Christian tone and habit of thought which is characteristic of our time. Pages could be filled with examples
of it. But it will suffice anyone to compare the ordinary
ideals of the parochial clergy or the spirit of the average

sixteenth and seventeenth centuries alone cannot be treated as if there
were no fundamental differences between them. It is precisely in funda-
mentals that they are different. But why waste time on ' disappearing '
religions in an hour of return to an ever-vital Catholicism? ' Calvinism
and Zwinglianism are disappearing from the map of Europe ' (Mr.
Arnold Lunn in *The Review of the Churches*, April 1903, p. 314).

Anglican book on religion with the New Testament, *The Spiritual Combat*, *The Devout Life* of St. François de Sales, or the *Royaume de Jésus* of St. John Eudes, to see the vast gulf between the spirit of one and the other. And ' it is the spirit which giveth life.' [1]

[1] Speaking at the 1930 Church Congress, Lord Eustace Percy said, ' The members of the Church speak, as St. Paul refused to speak, "in the words that man's wisdom teacheth " ; in loose phrases which may fit a dozen meanings, in terms which are indeterminate, and definitions which do not define. We no longer preach Christ crucified, but " the principle of the Cross " ; regeneration and redemption are swallowed up in " a process of spiritual development," the Gospel itself is converted into " the New Testament ethic." '

CHAPTER II

What is the Christian Life ?

IN order to appreciate the place which all the Saints and masters of the spiritual life give to mental prayer it is essential that we should have a right and clear conception of what the Christian life is and implies. For unless we have such a true conception it will be quite impossible for us to see why mental prayer is necessarily one of the strongest determining factors, if indeed not the strongest, of such a life.

The Christian life is the life of the first Christian, Jesus Christ, continued in the members of His Mystical Body, the Catholic Church.

To the explanation and development of this definition, this chapter will be devoted.

That the Sermon on the Mount is not, primarily, as is commonly supposed, a code of morality, may be inferred from more than one place, but it is sufficiently shown by the definite injunction, ' Be ye therefore perfect as your Father in heaven is perfect ' (Matt. v. 48). A similar word is St. Paul's : ' Be ye imitators of God as dear children ' (Eph. v. 1), where the lines of a mere morality are clearly passed, as indeed they are on almost every page of the New Testament. I am not discounting morality ; I am simply pointing out that it is not religion, certainly not Christianity. Yet nothing is commoner to-day than what M. Bremond, following Jean Baptist Nolleau, styles ' le crime d'avoir été religieux a la façon de l'honnête homme, mais non du chrétien ' (*Histoire littéraire du Sentiment Religieux en France*, vol. vii., p. 220).[1]

But to imitate God, to be perfect as God, surely this is impossible in any ordinary sense of the word. Must we not have in such words at least a touch of poetry, of Eastern mysticism, of analogy and so on ? To which I reply in the words of Cardinal Mercier, ' Sanctity consists in taking our Lord's words literally. We do Him a grave injustice and ourselves much harm when we do not do so.'

Further, the seeming impossibility is removed if we consider that an imitation is never the same thing as the original. The most perfect copy remains but a copy, even though it be the nearest possible approach to the original. And in the case of the Christian life, as we shall see, we are not merely invited to the copying of something external to ourselves; the Christian life is only an imitation because it is primarily a participation in that Divine Life which it is called to continue and reproduce.

We have, then, to consider what that perfection is with which we are to be perfect, and in this we can find no safer guide than St. Thomas Aquinas. ' We call that being perfect,' he says, ' which lacks nothing of the mode of its perfection . . . existence is the most perfect of all things, for it is compared to all things as that by which they are made actual ; for nothing has actuality except so far as it exists ' (*Summa Theol.*, pars. I., q. iv., art. 1).

[1] Compare the striking words of Cardinal Mercier addressed to his clergy on this point : ' It is incumbent upon us, priests and pastors, to preach the *Christian Life*. . . . The burden of our sermons and of the confessional is too much one of duty, of virtues, too little of supernatural charity poured out upon souls by the Holy Spirit. . . . It is the Christ whom it is necessary to give, His Gospel, the riches of His grace, His presence and that of the Holy Spirit in the soul, interior prayer, the peace and power of Divine union – it is this which needs to be preached. But you do not preach it, or but little, for it is dogma, and dogma, it seems, frightens you. And hence there grows up a generation of Christians whose ideal is an irreproachable honesty, the respectability of the gentleman with some practices of religion ' (*La Vie Intérieure*, pp. 457–460).

Now God is His own Existence, His Perfection is His own inalienable possession of infinite, inexhaustible life, of complete self-existence, and of the total possession of supreme good in Himself, so that He is in no way dependent upon, or has any need of, anything outside Himself, but is to Himself all in all. 'The perfection of no one thing is wanting to God . . . as is implied by Dionysius when he says that "God exists not in any single mode, but embraces all being within Himself, absolutely, without limitation, uniformly"' (*Summa Theol.* I. iv. 2).

St. Thomas says further, 'Things are perfect precisely so far as they have being after some fashion' (*ibid.*), and since our Lord declares that our perfection is to be, in some way, the perfection of God Himself, it is clear that this cannot be attainable merely by desire or imitation, but only by some communication of that Divine Life which is our perfection. For even if we could and did desire it, we are totally incapable of attaining to it by our own efforts, for, as the Apostle says, we 'cannot do the things that we would' (Gal. v. 17 ; cf. Rom. vii.). The possibility of a copied perfection may be dreamed of as Plato dreamed of painters 'who copy a Divine model . . . until to the best in their power they succeed in painting the lineaments of a human character as like to God as the matter will allow' (*Republic*, vi. 501), but it was no more than a dream, or, shall we say, a prophecy of what should become a sober actuality, not by men's efforts, but by the act of God.

For by two things is the creature separated from the Creator. First by the fact that God is 'other' than man, not merely in degree but in kind, so that, as St. Thomas says, 'Although it may be admitted that creatures are in some sort like God, it must in no wise be admitted that God is like creatures ; because, as says Dionysius, "a mutual likeness may be found between things of the same order, but not between a cause and that which is caused " and " The same things can be like and unlike to God : like, according as they imitate Him so far as He can be imitated, Who is not perfectly imitable ; unlike, according as they fall short of their cause, not merely in intensity or degree . . . but because they are not in agreement, specifically or generically " ' (*Summa Theol.* I. iv. 3).

Secondly, creatures are separated from God by the fact of sin. By an act and by repeated acts of his will, man has deserted God, the one Source and Principle of his being, and by those acts has rendered himself incapable of returning to God. The history of his repeated and continuous attempts is sufficient evidence both of his felt need for God and of his inability to attain to Him.

The gulf which exists between God and man can only be bridged by the act of God Himself ; in this as in all else He alone is the Prime Mover. Such an act He has willed to perform, and in doing so He has bestowed upon man not merely some gift external to Himself, but the gift of Himself, His very Life and Perfection, in order that He might make us, in the words of St. Peter, ' partakers of the Divine Nature ' (2 Peter i. 4). In the Incarnation of the Eternal Word of God we see the Divine Thought and Life made Flesh : ' Et Verbum caro factum est ' (John i. 14). By an ineffable act of Divine wisdom and power, the Nature of God is united to a created human nature, the Sacred Humanity, formed of Mary, appropriating in our full humanity the state of a Person at once human and Divine in the fullest and most literal sense of both terms.

' By this union, so inter-penetrating, so powerful and so permanent, God becomes man, truly, really and substantially, and man becomes God personally, God and man constituting but one and the same Person, which subsists in two natures infinitely Divine, lives in two states infinitely differing, experiences two conditions infinitely remote the one from the other. And yet these natures, these states, these conditions, for all this tremendous difference and inequality, are, according to the definitions of the holy councils, so divinely and intimately, so inseparably and indistinguishably united, that faith in two such different natures recognises and adores its God, and the spirit of man and angel loses itself in the unity in diversity of this most high mystery' (Bérulle, *Œuvres*, p. 938).

The Incarnation is the centre, the heart, the all of the Christian religion, and that for two main reasons. First, because the ineffable mystery of the Adorable Trinity, which is our Beginning and our End, our Sanctity and Perfection, our Beatitude and our Home, is only known to us in and through Jesus, the Word made Flesh. 'No man hath seen God at any time ; the only begotten Son Who is in the bosom of the Father, He hath declared Him' (John i. 18). 'He that hath seen Me hath seen the Father' (John xiv. 9).

Secondly, because by the Incarnation God not only reveals Himself to man, but *gives* Himself to man. The supreme purpose for which the Divine Life took our nature, was made visible to us, was not that we should see it, but that we should receive it. 'Factus est homo ut homo fieret Deus' (St. Aug., *Serm. CXXVIII., de Nativ.*),[1] 'God is made man that man may be made God,' a statement entirely justified by the New Testament, as is the frequent use of the term deification in early Christian writers.

'I am the Life,' says our Lord. 'This is the testimony that God hath given to us eternal life : and this life is in His Son ; he that hath the Son hath life, and

---

[1] This sermon is placed in the Appendix of 'sermones suppositiones' by the Maurist editors, but the thought is the saint's and may be paralleled by St. Athanasius. 'Αὐτὸς γὰρ ἐνηνθρώπησεν ἵνα ἡμεῖς θεοποινθιομεν' (De incarn. Verbi, 54).

he that hath not the Son hath not life' (1 John v. 11,
12). 'In this was manifested the love of God towards
us, that God sent His only begotten Son into the world
that we might live through Him' (*ibid.* iv. 9). It is
the centre of St. Paul's teaching, 'the hidden mystery'
which has now been revealed, 'Christ in you, the hope
of glory' (Col. i. 27). We are 'saved by His life'
(Rom. v. 10), an equivalent saying being that 'by
grace are ye saved' (Eph. ii. 8), grace being the communication of the Divine Life given not merely *for* us
but *to* us, to be continued, lived, exercised by us in the
sense of the Apostles : 'I live, yet not I, but Christ
liveth in me' (Gal. ii. 20).

'Why speak of imitation,' asks Fr. Prat, 'when the
Apostle aims at mystical identity?' (*Theology of St.
Paul,* ii. 344). In a footnote he adds, 'To put on
Christ (Rom. xiii. 14 ; Gal. iii. 27), to be transformed
into His image (2 Cor. iii. 18), to grow in Him (Eph.
iv. 5), to live in Him (Rom. vi. 11), are only different
expressions of the same thing. It is less the direct
imitation of Jesus than the effort to assimilate to ourselves always more and more the Divine nourishment
of grace which makes the Christian another Christ. St.
Paul is not afraid to propose to us Jesus Christ as a
model in His Divine pre-existence (2 Cor. viii. 9;
Phil. ii. 5–7). Why should he not do so, since he exhorts us to imitate God? (Eph. v. 1 : γίνεσθε οὖν μιμηταὶ
τοῦ θεοῦ).'

It is hardly any exaggeration to say that this whole
New Testament conception of the Christian life, a conception carried on and developed by the continuous
tradition of the Catholic Church, a conception which
is the source and background of Catholic 'spirituality,' is completely foreign to the average Christian
of to-day, who regards the Christian life as an attempt
which *we* make, and may expect God's help in making.

to model ourselves on the example and words, or rather on the adapted spirit of the example and words of Jesus Christ in much the same way as a Confucianist might model himself on the life and precepts of his master. Our Lord is regarded almost exclusively as a Teacher external to ourselves, not as a Saviour in the full, Christian sense of the word, nor as the Life destined to become our life. Little wonder, then, that men cannot understand the Catholic religion which makes this central, or that they say frankly and with truth that the life and precepts of Jesus are neither practicable nor even natural. They are right, for the Life and teaching of Jesus is altogether supernatural ; it is not the apex of human moral and spiritual *effort* but a ' *donum Dei*,' a gift of God coming down from heaven and bringing life, not merely a message, to the world. And the Christian life is not an external, human imitation of a life external to itself, but a participation in that Divine Life upon which human perfection depends and in which it rests. ' Be ye imitators of God *as dear children* ' (Eph. v. 1), that is, as possessing some real relationship, some real communication with the Life of God. ' The adoption of children of God resembles that participation in natural filiation,' says St. Thomas. We are able to imitate God since He has made that imitation possible by the gift of His own Life in and through Jesus Christ. ' To as many as received Him, to them gave He power to become the sons of God ' (John i. 12). ' The glory which Thou gavest Me I have given them ' (John xvii. 22). This is that eternal life of which our Lord speaks, not a future gift, still less a ' going on ' (the term eternal is the very opposite of succession or duration, *vide* St. Thomas, *Summa Theol.* I. x.) of our natural life under new and improved conditions, but a present possession by which we are made ' new creatures ' in Christ Jesus, so that we are, here and now, so united to Him, so filled with His Spirit,

His Mind, His Will, His Love, that our life is nothing less than a continuation of His Life.

Almighty God has created us of nothingness (*Summa Theol.* I. ii. 14), and as nothingness in ourselves, capacities for the reception of that true life which is Himself, the true substance of that ' shadow of life ' which we are in and by ourselves. ' Jesus is the accomplishment of our being, which subsists only in Him and is alone perfect in Him . . . we ought to regard our being as an emptiness . . . and Jesus our fulness . . . the perfect life of Jesus ought to be the excellence and perfection of our life . . . our first knowledge should be of our imperfect and defective condition : and our first movement ought to be to Jesus as to our accomplishment. For in that search of Jesus, in that adherence to Jesus, in that profound and continual dependence upon Jesus, is our life, our repose, our strength and all our power of being and doing ' (Bérulle, *Œuvres*, pp. 1180, 1181).

The initial bestowal of the Divine Life takes place in Holy Baptism, so that, once we grasp the greatness and the significance of the gift there given, the positive reality of the union it sets up between the soul and God, we can understand the tremendous place that Sacrament holds in the New Testament and in the Church. For ' baptised in Christ Jesus ' (Rom. vi. 3) we are actually incorporated into all the reality of His death and resurrection, made one with Him in the death to sin and a new life unto righteousness, ' saved by his life ' not by some merely external act done to us but by a radical change effected in us ' for ye are dead and your life is hid with Christ in God ' (Col. iii. 3). Thus the Christian becomes another Christ, his life is a continuation and extension of the Divine Human life of Jesus, who, as the Council of Trent says, ' communicates His own virtue to those who are justified.'

' The Christian life,' says St. John Eudes, ' is nothing

else but the continuation and achievement of the life of Jesus in each one of us . . . the true Christian continues and accomplishes by all that he does in the name of Christ all that the same Jesus Christ did during His life on earth.'

So real, so intimate and so perfect is this union accomplished by our moral response to Divine grace that, following St. Paul and St. John, St. John Eudes does not hesitate to say, ' The Eternal Father having done you the honour of receiving you into companionship with Himself by Baptism, as one of His children and members of His Son, He has obliged Himself to look upon you with the same eye, to love you with the same heart and to treat you with the same love with which He regards, loves and treats His Son.'

It is obvious that since the Christian life is nothing less than a continuation of the Life of Jesus Christ, its existence is incompatible with mortal sin, that is with a deliberate act, even in thought, which amounts to a rejection by the will of our Lord Himself. Since, too, the Christian life must always be a gift, it can never be attained purely from man's side, it must in the case of the sinner be a gift restored by God on the fulfilment of such conditions as He has laid down. Those conditions are again necessary, not arbitrarily, but on account of what the Christian life is, for a gift must be received, and this gift can only be received by penitence, renouncing the act which forfeited it and thus making possible its restoration. Here the Divine liberality, ' rich in mercy,' provides the Sacrament of Penance, wherein the penitent child is restored to the fulness of his Father's home, to which, however far he has wandered, he always belongs. ' Nor need we fear, lest there be no place whither to return, because we fell from it ; for in our absence, our home fell not — which is Thy eternity ' (St. Aug., *Conf.*, bk. iv. 16).

It is from the same Christian point of view that we

must continually regard Holy Communion, ' our daily super-substantial bread.' *Not* as a reward of virtue or a crown of our efforts, but as the source of our virtue and the principle of our efforts. There are no plainer or more significant words than ' As the living Father hath sent Me and I live by the Father : so he that eateth Me, even he shall live by Me ' (John vi. 57). The main purpose of the Most Holy Eucharist, considered as a Sacrament, is to make us more and more Christian by the transformation of our lives into the life of Christ. At the altar ' the guilty slave eats the body of his God,' and, as St. Chrysostom cries, ' is no longer mere dust and ashes, since he has tasted of the food of immortality,' for, in the exquisitely theological and beautiful words of Urban IV, ' This bread is eaten but not transmuted, it is nowise changed into the creature, but if it be worthily received, the recipient becomes like to it. This transformation is brought about by the streaming in upon us of the Spirit and Life of Christ. As a result, Christ liveth in us ; our thoughts, our impulses, our will and activity assume a resemblance to the hidden life of the Eucharistic Saviour and become Divine ' (Bull *Transiturus*). But this transformation of life is not effected by the most Holy Sacrament alone, as we shall see later. In his letter to Proba (No. 130) St. Augustine dwells on the fact that the secret of that happiness, the desire of which is inherent in our nature, can only be found in the possession of life in God. And to acquire this Divine life which is the complement and satisfaction of our nature should be the object of our prayer.

Baptised then, and so incorporated into the Mystical Body of Christ, the Christian carries on the life of Jesus Christ, reproducing that life in the particular way, form and manner determined by his vocation. The call and the grace of God constitute the initial as well as every successive step in that life. We do not begin it, and, having made some progress, arrive at a point where we must seek God's assistance. God is the author of the first movements, however slight and in whatever way they may manifest themselves, by which we are 'delivered from the power of darkness and translated into the kingdom of His dear Son' (Col. i. 13). 'We love Him because He first loved us' (1 John iv. 19). Our part is that of response to, and correspondence with, an act of God done for and in us, a response and correspondence deriving from the fact that we are both rational and free beings. God does not treat us otherwise than He has constituted us. But that response and correspondence is never purely a natural act of our own, but always an act suggested and aided by Divine grace. Thus the Apostle exhorts us, 'Work out your own salvation with fear and trembling,' as if, as St. Ignatius Loyola says, it were entirely dependent on ourselves, yet without any dependence on self but only on God, 'for it is God Who worketh in you both to will and to do of His good pleasure' (Phil. ii. 13).

Christian perfection is both a gift and an accomplishment. 'Baptised into Christ,' and so being made 'partakers of the Divine nature,' our part is one of continual, lifelong 'putting on of Christ,' of surrender to the Divine life of Jesus operating within our souls, of constant conformity to the Mind and Will of Christ, by all of which we are 'transformed from glory into glory,' growing up 'unto Him in all things,' as day by day we are 'renewed in the spirit' of our minds and 'put on the new man, which after God is created in righteousness and true holiness' by 'the spirit Who dwelleth in us,' 'till we all come

in the unity of the faith,
and of the knowledge of the Son of God
unto a perfect man
unto the measure of the stature of
The Fulness of Christ.'

CHAPTER III

The Object and Necessity of Mental Prayer

WHY, it may be asked, was it necessary, in a book on methods of mental prayer, to begin with such a sketch of the Christian life as I have just given? Mainly because it is not commonly seen, understood and followed by those who profess and call themselves Christians. The practice of the Christian life is not ordinarily and clearly seen as a practice of the life of Jesus Christ, a continuation of His life, interiorly and exteriorly, with a constant recurrence to Him as the one source and principle of all that we are and do, a life lived by Jesus, in Jesus, with Jesus and for Jesus. To compare the average modern view of what the Christian life is with that of St. Paul, notably in the Epistles to the Ephesians and Colossians, and of St. John in his Gospel and Epistles, will be proof sufficient of this.

But if our understanding of the Christian life be wrong, inadequate or distorted, it naturally follows that in like proportion and degree our prayer will be so. In fact, unless we see the Christian life as it is in Jesus Christ and is meant to be in us, we shall not see either the necessity or the end of mental prayer. Assuming, then, all that has been said or implied in the previous chapter, we shall now consider:

1. The object of mental prayer.
2. The particular need of it to-day.

But first a common fallacy must be dissipated. There is absolutely no justification for the very common idea that sanctity, perfection, is only required of certain

26

classes or individuals in the Church, that whilst it may
naturally be assumed that the clergy, religious and
certain of the laity should strive after the highest possible perfection, the ordinary layman or laywoman is
only expected to seek some lower degree of perfection.
This is not true ; the teaching of the New Testament
and the lives of the Saints absolutely negative such an
idea. There is but one Christian life, one Christian
sanctity, to which all Christians without any distinction
are called. 'Be ye therefore perfect' is addressed to each
baptised child of God ; so is 'called to be Saints,'
'this is the will of God, even your sanctification,' for
'without holiness no man shall see the Lord.'

There is no state or condition of human life from the
throne to the gutter from which Saints have not been
produced by the grace of God. The Church has
canonised thieves, murderers, harlots and beggars,
artisans and tradespeople, men in every rank of pro-
fessional life, women in every vocation; her calendar
has no restrictions of race, culture or condition, for
'with God there is no respect of persons,' nor any state
of life or action not sanctified by the life and actions
of Jesus.

Perfection consists in the loving union of the will
with God, a union, as we have seen, made possible by
a right use of His gifts. It is not, as Père Poulain points
out, to be regarded ' as a fixed and well-defined goal to
which we must attain under pain of having lost our
time,' but ' an endless road along which we continue
to advance' (*Graces of Interior Prayer*, xxiv. 27). The
words of Almighty God to Abraham, ' Walk before Me
and be perfect,' express clearly in what our perfection
in via is to consist.

To such perfection all are called, all are capable of it,
all must strive to attain it. It is not in the end or in the
general means by which the end is to be sought, but in
the particular use of the mea   by each individual

soul, that there are degrees in the manner of our progress. On these two points all the Saints speak with one voice. Fr. Baker admirably sums up their teaching in the first chapter of *Holy Wisdom.* ' Our duty in our present state and the employment of our whole lives must be constantly and fervently to co-operate with Divine grace, thereby not only endeavouring to get the victory over self-love, pride and sensuality, etc., by humility, divine love and all the other virtues : but also, not to content ourselves with any limited degree of piety or holiness, but daily to aspire, according to our abilities, assisted by grace, to the same perfection for which we were first created, to wit . . . a continual, uninterrupted union in spirit with God, by faith contemplating Him, and by love ever adhering to Him . . . for experience demonstrates that all the sublime exercises of contemplation may be as purely and perfectly performed by persons the most ignorant and unlearned (so they be sufficiently instructed in the fundamental doctrines of Catholic Faith) as by the learnedest doctors, inasmuch as not any abilities in the brain are requisite thereto, but only a strong, courageous affection of the heart.'

It follows, then, that whilst mental prayer is necessary for all as a chief means of perfection, any methods, much less any particular methods, are not necessary in the same sense, although, as we shall see, they are necessary in a large number of cases. But it should be remembered that where circumstances make any formal act of mental prayer in the ordinary sense of the word practically impossible, we must not cease to inculcate the vital necessity of the life of prayer and to suggest how it is possible for any soul to ' pray without ceasing.' Practically, the division runs between those who have or could make time and those who have not, but no height of prayer open to the former is closed to the latter. The Saints have been and are the busiest people in the world ; our feeble excuses falter upon our lips as we contemplate their practice of prayer.

1. ' This is Life eternal, that they might know Thee the only true God, and Jesus Christ, Whom Thou hast sent ' (John xvii. 3), and we cannot doubt that the knowledge of which our Lord speaks is not merely a knowledge of or about God, but such a know-ledge as will produce a right attitude toward God – that is, a knowledge of God and Divine things which will awaken, develop and perfect a life of love for God. For though it be true that eternal life is the gift of God, yet no less true is it that it consists, as St. John of the Cross says, in a union of the soul, transformed by love, with God, which is only verified when we realise in ourselves the resemblance of love – that is, when, by the exercise of the union accomplished in Baptism, we, who have been made ' partakers of the Divine nature,' realise that union by the moral response of our wills with the will of God.   This union, which is the end of our creation and in which consists our sole Beatitude, since, as Dame Julian saw, ' He is the Very Rest and willeth to be known, and it pleaseth Him that we rest in Him ; for all that is beneath Him sufficeth us not,'[1] is no Pantheistic absorption of the many in the one, with a consequent loss of individuality and creature-liness, but is essentially personal in character, a union of the creature, between God and whom there is an infinite difference in kind, not merely in degree, with the Creator by an act of the will moved by and responding to Divine grace.   It is a union based on knowledge, for we cannot desire or even think about that which we do not know, nor without such know-ledge as is possible to finite creatures could any real union with God be attained.   More, since it is pre-eminently a union of love, the kind of knowledge which

[1] *Revelations of Divine Love*, chap. v.

is required is that of friendship in the very highest sense of the word.[1]

How, then, is such a knowledge to be gained? The Saints and masters of the spiritual life, speaking from an experience verified by their lives, unanimously answer, by means of mental prayer. For ' prayer is an ascension of the soul towards God ' (St. Nilus), ' a familiar conversation with God ' (St. Ephrem), ' nothing else, in my opinion, but being on terms of friendship with God, frequently conversing in secret with Him Who we know loves us ' (St. Teresa), ' the uniting of the soul with God ' (Dame Julian), ' a familiar talk and an intimate union with God ' (St. Alphonsus). Speaking more exactly of the mental or reflective act in prayer, the Ven. Fr. Libermann defines it as ' a sensible application of the mind to a supernatural truth, in order to convince ourselves of it, and to be brought to love it by the help of divine grace ' ; and Cardinal Landrieux, Bishop of Dijon : ' We reflect in order that we may think aright, we think aright in order that we may desire aright, we desire aright in order that we may pray aright, we pray aright in order to obtain the grace of loving, willing and doing what is right.'

Let us consider all this a little in detail.

Only by thought, reflection, concentrated attention, are we able to gain a knowledge of any object. Real knowledge cannot be imparted, it must be gained ;

---

[1] St. Thomas, following Aristotle's doctrine of the identity created between the knower and the known, ' the power of perceiving the knowable is itself the possession of the knowable,' teaches that knowledge is the highest form of life, in that whilst desire tends toward the possession of life, the intellect actually achieves that possession in one indivisible act in which knower and known, lover and beloved are one. So Dante says of the blessed :

> ' And all are blessed even as their sight descends
> Deeper into the truth, wherein rest is
> For every mind. Thus happiness hath root
> In seeing, not in loving, which of sight
> Is aftergrowth.'
> (*Paradiso*, canto xxviii., Cary's translation.)

like a Sacrament, it requires the co-operation of the whole self; body, mind, will, must all set themselves to see, to enter into, to grasp and appreciate, and use whatever it may be we desire to know. The preliminary steps are never easy or pleasant; even when the subject is one which appeals to us, there is a necessary amount of drudgery to be gone through. But if – whether being compelled or attracted to a particular subject – we give our thought and attention to it, the day comes when it occupies, enthrals, dominates us, and the more we give ourselves to it, the more it possesses us and becomes a living and powerful force in our lives.

True as this is of those things which are perceptible to and knowable by human reason, it is all the more true of things which lie outside and beyond the perception of the senses. ' The things of God require study,' says Faber. Now in the Catholic religion we have a revelation of Eternal Reality, of a distinct world of Persons, Truths, Things and Operations, a world of which we are all – consciously or unconsciously – a part. Note I say a revelation, for the Catholic religion is a revelation, not a discovery; it comes from God, is not the product of man's search after God, but the answer to that search. It is a revelation, too, of what is – and always has been – *there*, eternally existent, outside and beyond and independent of time and creatures, for it is a revelation of God Himself. It is *there*, and, in one way or another, suddenly or gradually, we become aware of it, are awakened to our need of realising and entering it for ourselves.

It is Faith which enables us to take the first step. In the oldest, most widely and continuously used Baptismal Service of the Church, the first question addressed to him who seeks eternal life is ' What desirest thou ? ' ' Faith.' It is necessarily so, for ' without faith it is impossible to please God : for he that cometh to God must believe that He is, and that He is the rewarder of

Dp

them that diligently seek Him' (Heb. xi. 6). Faith
is a gift of God which enables us to accept that which
God reveals, 'a supernatural virtue by which, stimulated
and aided by the grace of God, we believe as true that
which He has revealed, not because of the intrinsic
truth of things, known by the natural light of the
reason, but because of the authority of God Himself,
who cannot deceive or be deceived.' That is, our reason,
aided by grace and moved by the will, accepts and
believes what the Church teaches, not because it is
convinced by arguments or proofs, not because it sees
or understands, much less ' feels ' that it is true, but
simply on the authority of God Himself. (It would
be absurd, of course, to think that the Church could
teach anything as *de fide* – that is, as necessary to belief –
which was false, since this would mean a total un-
certainty about the whole Christian religion, which we
only know of through the Church, which gave us the
Bible in precisely the same way that she has given us
the Faith and the Sacraments.)

The next step on the path of knowledge is that we are
taught about this new world of realities, this true
patria of ours, of which we are made free in Holy
Baptism, by our parents, priests, teachers, etc. If we
have the happiness of being brought up in a Catholic
atmosphere – and this counts more than anything
else – we learn early to pray, we gain a supernatural
spirit from living in contact with holy persons and
things which become as real and familiar to us as are
our parents, our home, our cats and dogs – an in-
estimable grace which he who lacks it finds difficult to
gain in later life. Yet for all, although especially for
the latter, a further step is needed – that is, to enter into
a personal, intimate experience of that world for themselves. And this can only be done by some form of
mental prayer, in which we pay attention to, concentrate and think upon, the Persons, Truths, Things,

Works and Ways of that eternal, supernatural world of
Reality to which we belong. 'Man arrives at the
knowledge of truth in two ways,' says St. Thomas :
' first, by that which he receives from another ; second,
by applying his own efforts : and the latter is meditation.' ' Faith,' says Faber, ' has a sort of vision of its
own : but there is no light in which it can distinguish
objects except the light of prayer.' In mental prayer
we are like the shepherds who, having heard the
Divine revelation, said, ' Let us now go and see ' for
ourselves, and thus going by faith they found Jesus and
' returned glorifying and praising God.'

We have seen already that union with God consists
in an act of Divine charity by which our wills are conformed to His will, that this is the main object of prayer[1]
in which we seek to know God in order that we may love
Him and do His will, for, says St. Teresa, ' in this consists the highest perfection, he who most excels in this
practice will receive the greatest gifts from God and
make most progress in the interior life ' ; and St.
Alphonsus, ' We ought to pray in order to be perfectly
united to God : and that which unites us to God is not
so much our good thoughts as the good movements of
our will.'

Now union with God is union with a Person, for God
is *someone*, not something, and this implies that the
knowledge of Him which is necessary is, in degree, the
same kind of knowledge, sought for in the same way,
as we have of persons in this world. Such knowledge is
twofold. We may know a person – as, for instance, we
know the King or the Prime Minister – by hearing of
them, reading about them, seeing their portrait or even
by catching a glimpse of them at a distance, the latter of
which transfers our knowledge from one of faith in the

---

[1] " Prayer tends to God through being moved by the will of charity,
as it were, and this in two ways. First, on the part of the object of our
petition, because when we pray *we ought principally to ask to be united to
God*." (Summa Theol. II. ii. lxxxiii. 1, 2).

word of others to personal sight and experience. So we hear and read about God, we see, or we may see, His portrait in Jesus Christ, in the Church, in the Bible, and in the Saints. But such knowledge is incomplete ; it lacks that personal, intimate verification which constitutes true knowledge of a person, the knowledge of friendship. There is an immeasurable difference between the knowledge I have of King George and the knowledge I have of my intimate friend. The latter has been gained, not imparted through others, by personal companionship, by frequent intercourse, by a mutual sympathy and regard, by an intimacy in which we have unveiled ourselves to each other so that no longer language, as is so often the case, ' conceals thought,' although it so often fails to express it. But we do not need words, my friend and I, for mind and will are at one, and silence is no barren refuge, but a home in which one rests in surest confidence.

This is that knowledge of God which is eternal life, a knowledge of friendship, of union of mind and heart and will, a knowledge experienced in the depths of one's being, a knowledge which cannot adequately be told or conveyed, for all our words are too cold, too foolish, too small –

> The love of Jesus, what it is
> None but His lovers know.

And even the greatest of them but stutter and stammer and multiply word upon word, only to know they can never say that which is in their hearts. ' My secret is mine.' Yet for such knowledge were we poor creatures made. ' Our natural will is to have God, and the goodwill of God is to have us ' (Dame Julian), nor will any other or lesser knowledge satisfy us ; little as we are, our littleness was created that it might be filled by the infinite God. And nowise may we gain this knowledge save by mental prayer. ' I am the Way,' cries

our Lord, ' Come unto Me,' ' Learn of Me,' ' Follow
Me,' and in mental prayer we most completely come
unto Him, place ourselves as disciples in His school,
follow Him in surrendering our minds to His Mind,
our wills to His Will, our hearts to His Heart.

The fruits of mental prayer, then, are knowledge,
appreciation, liberation, leading to the possession and
enjoyment of God Himself – knowledge which comes
from being with God, ' in Thy light shall we see light ' ;
appreciation born of a loving attention to Him, a discovery of the value and beauty of Divine things arising
from an absorption in them ; liberation from the
tyranny of the senses and of material and passing
things, the growth within us of the ' glorious liberty of
the children of God ' ; the possession of God Who responds to the desiring love shed abroad in our hearts
and dwells within us ; the enjoyment of the experienced presence of Him for Whom we were created,
the finding delight in God Himself Who alone is the
delectation, fulfilment and beatitude of human life.
' I have found Him Whom my soul loveth, I will hold
Him and not let Him go.'

There is yet another reason which gives point to the
unanimous conclusion of the Saints, that without
mental prayer it is morally impossible to arrive at even
a low degree of sanctity. For it is mental prayer
which makes the grace of the Sacraments and the
gifts of the Holy Spirit operative in our lives. It is
perfectly true that the Sacraments convey grace *ex
opere operato* – that is, in virtue of the sacramental rite
duly performed in accordance with the mind of the
Church, *not* in view of the faith or merits of those who
receive them. For the Sacraments are the acts of our
Lord Himself, the channels He has chosen through
which to bestow His grace. But this does not mean, as
say the ignorant, and indeed, as it sometimes appears
that some Christians imagine, that they act as charms

or magic are supposed to act – i.e. independently of any moral co-operation of the will with the grace given. One is constantly being astonished at the number of people who, although they frequent the Sacraments regularly and even frequently, yet show so little of the effect of the grace they receive in their lives that they are so unspiritual, so unsupernatural, so lacking in the mind and heart of Jesus. The real, fundamental and quite sufficient reason is that they do not pray, or at least that they do not pray aright. For without prayer grace remains, as it were, a dead weight in the soul, unassimilated and without force and power ; for prayer ' is the force of the soul,' as St. John of the Cross says, which turns to use and directs into its rightful channels the grace we have received. So it is that grace, aided and reinforced by prayer, tends to the transformation of our whole life, a transformation which can only be effected when we open ourselves, expose ourselves to the action of God within us. ' Mental prayer is the complement of the most Holy Eucharist, our Saviour having given both to us as means of uniting us to Himself. In mental prayer (*oraison*) we receive the same gifts as in Holy Communion, although not in an equal degree : in mental prayer, as in the Eucharist, we adore Jesus Christ present, in such a way that it seems we have but to part a curtain to see Him openly : in mental prayer Jesus Christ nourishes and fortifies the soul, He unites Himself to it directly ; He abides in us and we in Him, making our soul like to Himself, giving us a distaste for earthly things, filling us with love for heavenly realities and fortifying us against the devil ' (*Esprit de M. Olier*, iii., p. 34). Thomas à Kempis had already said that there are ' two tables set on either side in the storehouse of Holy Church. One is the table of the holy altar, having the holy bread, that is, the precious Body of Christ ; the other is that of the Divine Law, containing holy doctrine ' (*Imitatio*, IV.

xi. 4). It may be worthy of note, in passing, that experience shows that a devout, meditative reading of Holy Scripture immediately after one's thanksgiving for Holy Communion is of great value.

Thus is it, too, that evil is overcome by good, and in no other way. To how many the Christian life seems but a dreary and well-nigh hopeless struggle against temptation, a struggle which, with all the goodwill in the world, but barely keeps them where they are, if indeed, they are not going back. It should not be so and it need not be so. Temptations there will always be, effort there must always be, but there is infinitely more to be gained in prayer than by effort. The common fault of those who desire and are trying to serve God is preoccupation with themselves. It is a fatal mistake and defeats its own purpose. How shall we ever escape from sin and self, which is our one need, whilst we are constantly occupied with sin and self? ' O Lord, all our ills come from not fixing our gaze on Thee : if we looked at nothing else but where we are going we should arrive, but we fall a thousand times and stumble and stray because we do not keep our eyes bent on Him Who is the way ' (St. Teresa). And that very wise director, Fr. Dignam, writes to a religious superior, ' Boldly take the thought, that since you have for so many years gone on grubbing and puling and pining about your poor little self, with small fruit, you will in future leave it quite to our Lord's care, while you take care of Him.'

Half an hour's mental prayer every day, or less if we really cannot give as much, will do more for us in a month than constant self-examinations and gazing at our poverty and misery will do in a lifetime. Not that we must expect to become Saints in a month, but that this is the way to become saintly, for sanctity cannot be taught, it can only be caught by contact with sanctity. Not by mere efforts of our own, even aided by a prayer of petition now and then, shall we overcome our temptations, subdue our passions, and get rid of our chief enemy – self, but by daily placing ourselves in the Divine Presence ' in Whose Light we shall see light,' by daily exposing our poverty and frailty before Jesus our life, by contemplating Him in His mysteries and giving ourselves to the powerful influence of His Spirit, that He may imprint upon our souls a living image of His own perfection. ' " I have prayed and striven long," said a penitent, " and yet I have failed. How shall I pray better ? " " Go home and pray for God's glory." In striving there is a pain of effort, anxiety, failure, grief, humiliation, sadness . . . in the thought of God there is peace. What is life but " to know Thee," elsewhere we are all astray ; at other times we are giving out ; but in contemplation and praise we are receiving, and so it moulds our character. . . . Now we see " as a mirror," yet while so beholding, there is perpetual transformation ' (Archbishop Temple, *Life*, vol. i., p. 446).

2. Mental prayer has always been necessary to the Christian life ; it has never been more necessary than it is to-day. Amongst the reasons which make it so, four may be noticed in particular : (1) the dangers involved in the growing popularity of pseudo-mystic literature and cults ; (2) the tendency in those who have some little knowledge of mysticism to ignore the ordinary ways of the Christian life ; (3) the widespread ignorance which exists of the fundamental truths and principles of the Faith ; (4) the heretical temper of mind which so infects the atmosphere we live in. The avoidance or the cure of these evils lies, to a very large extent, in the practice of mental prayer.

For indeed it was the existence of similar reasons that caused the appearance of definite methods of mental prayer in the sixteenth century, and has rooted them so deeply in the normal Catholic life. Methodical mental prayer may have been, as Dom Chapman has written, ' an entire reversal of tradition,' though it would seem much nearer to the facts to call it a ' development ' rather than a reversal. But if we consider the actual conditions which the Counter-Reformers had to face, the prevailing ignorance of and neglect of prayer, even in the religious orders ; the high wave of heresy which struck at the very foundations of Christianity ; the substitution of a religiosity of feeling and sentiment in the place of the ancient Faith and worship ; the loosening of moral standards, witnessed to by the Protestant reformers themselves ; may we not say that a ' reversal ' was both necessary and justifiable ? As a matter of fact, the Counter-Reformers founded their work on and accomplished what they did by lives of prayer and the preaching of the necessity of mental prayer for all – a fact which some of the would-be counter-reformers of to-day might take notice of.

(1) Catholic mysticism has lately attracted a motley band of camp-followers who are a distinct peril to the unwary, who from their ignorance of the subject and of the dangers which are inherent in amateurs meddling with any science, are easily led astray by some facile presentation labelling itself mystic. From the eclectic adventures and modernist tendencies of one popular writer on mysticism to the latest ' esoteric ' cult, every phase of pseudo-mysticism flourishes in our day. Amongst the ranks of regular communicants may be found those who have ' taken up ' some variety of ' New Thought,' usually the product of an uneducated American from somewhere west of Chicago, or the astute mind of an Anglicised ' babu.' I have known the son of a Malayan head-hunter, educated in a Christian mission, quite successfully propagate in a small but profitable way a ' mystic ' cult which found adherents amongst men and women by no means fools except in this. I have met a Buddhist monk – one of

six who were about to embark on a mission to convert
England to ' esoteric Buddhism.' Not that the blessed
word ' esoteric ' had even entered their minds before
they found it in an English dictionary, for the gospel
they will preach in suburbania – they are not likely to
concern themselves with Poplar – will bear as little resemblance to the Buddhism of Thibet as the Moham-
medanism of Woking does to that of Bengal.

But the dangers are nearer and more difficult to distinguish. Many who would find no temptation in such
travesties fall easy victims to the errors contained in
such works – now easily procurable – as Madame
Guyon's *Short and Easy Method of Prayer* or the *Spiritual
Guide* of Molinos, together with more modern works of
a pseudo-mystical character. The uninitiated should
always consult an experienced director ; there is no
more to be ashamed about in not having a knowledge
of mysticism than there is of not having a knowledge
of any particular natural science. Anyone who is attracted to the subject would do well to begin by a
careful reading of the first seven chapters of the *Dark
Night of the Soul* by St. John of the Cross, and by a good
use of the *Spiritual Exercises* of St. Ignatius.

(2) Bunyan has drawn a vivid picture of those who
seek to escape the early and necessary steps in the
spiritual life, to miss the first rungs of the ladder, but
who, as Christian warns them, having come in without
the Master's direction, ' shall go out by yourselves
without His mercy.' Such is the way of that pseudo-
mysticism which aims at enjoying the fruits without
paying the price, at attaining the heights by a cable-
railway rather than by a steep and arduous climb, the
way of the tourist, not of the mountaineer. Catholics
are sometimes disturbed by finding the devotees of
some modern cult apparently enjoying a peace and
satisfaction that they are far from possessing. They
need not be alarmed, for the phenomenon is not new,

nor would any master of the spiritual life look upon it as anything but a dangerous symptom.

St. Ignatius, St. Teresa and St. John of the Cross were all familiar with such cases, and have some exceedingly plain words to say about them.[1] The various and ascending degrees of prayer may not so exactly correspond with the three stages of the spiritual life, the purgative, illuminative and unitive ways, as some writers would have us believe, but there is no doubt that beginners must begin at the beginning, as also that there are cases where the more advanced need at least an occasional return to mental prayer.

(3) The existence of a widespread ignorance of the fundamental verities of the Christian religion will hardly be questioned by anyone, but there is a great need of realising how very far that ignorance extends to our 'churchgoing' population, and even to professing Catholics. I have come into intimate contact, during several years abroad, with men and women who represented a very fair 'cross-section' of English life, and a large majority of whom were church-people. They were, with very few exceptions, almost completely ignorant of elementary Christian truths[2] and duties ; above all, they had not the slightest conception of what Christian prayer means, nor of its necessity. And the tragedy of it is that they go out to places and surroundings devoid of any spiritual and moral atmosphere, denied, too, the ordinary services and Sacraments of the Church, except at infrequent intervals, and have not got the one thing which would enable them to persevere – a habit of regular, desiring, loving prayer. This argues, it is obvious, a lack of proper teaching, and gives one to wonder what the clergy at home are

[1] St. Teresa, *Minor Works : Conceptions of the Love of God*, ii. 1, 2, 17, 30 ; for St. Ignatius *vide* Bremond, *Histoire littéraire*, ii. 138.

[2] For instance, such truths as are contained in the ' Foundation and Principle ' of the Ignatian *Exercises*.

occupied about when they do not even teach their
people how to pray. For whatever else they may be
taught will afford little of results unless they are shown
how to reflect upon, to grasp the meaning and consequences of, and seriously apply the truths which, it
may be presumed, they were told were necessary to
their eternal salvation. If one may always presume
even that ! The fact is that they do not realise either
the meaning or the value of what they have been taught
because they have never been instructed as to the
means of gaining such a realisation, they have not been
taught to handle and verify and use the truths of religion as they have the truths and principles of the science
or profession they have taken up. That bears some
relation to life ; their religion, none.

Hence arises that lack of *conviction* so characteristic
of modern Christian life. Men acquiesce, they in a
sense more or less believe, but there is little of vitality,
of force, of conviction about their religion. It is not
due, as is sometimes assumed, to a national characteristic of reticence, though some of it is undoubtedly due
to the feeling that God must not be mentioned in
polite society. But touch one of these ' reticent '
people upon a matter in which he is interested, which
he deems of importance – politics, sport, business –
and note the difference. If the average Christian of
to-day is reticent about his religion it is not because it
is so deep and so intimately dear a thing to him, but
because it is so shallow and so cheap. And it is so
largely because he has never meditated upon it, however much he may have argued about it, a thing he is
curiously fond of doing ; he has never seen it as one
reality, never been convinced that it is the one thing
that matters, never in a word, come face to face with
his God. As Lui of Granada wrote in his *Libro de la
Oration y Meditation,* ' On all sides we find large numbers of people who are irreproachable in faith but dis-

orderly in life . . . their faith is like money in a cash-box, or a sword in its sheath, or medicine on a chemist's shelf – that is to say, it is not used for the purpose for which it was intended . . . they believe quite unreflectingly.' There lies the fundamental weakness of English Christianity, that ' complacent vagueness,'[1] as Dr. Selwyn has termed it, which of itself sufficiently explains our feeble position and lack of spiritual influence, the paucity of true vocations to the priesthood and religious life, and the lack of missionary zeal. How shall we desire to become apostles of and propagate a religion in which we have so little conviction ?

(4) Lastly, there is that heretical atmosphere, legacy of almost forgotten men and days, which hangs, a numbing, chilling cloud, all about us : that temper of thought and attitude which had reduced faith to feelings, religion to morality and philanthropy, worship to subjective musings upon self, and which is almost totally devoid of any sense of the supernatural, a religiosity as remote from Christianity of the New Testament and of the ages as it would be possible to conceive. Not only has it infected the very air we breathe, but it has debased and cheapened the terms in which the Christian Faith has been enshrined from the beginning so that they no longer mean to us what they were intended to mean. We hear them – such terms as ' faith,' ' grace,' ' sanctification,' ' salvation,' ' worship ' – and almost instinctively conceive something other than the words actually mean. Even God has been relegated to a place outside the universe and sufficiently far off as not to trouble us, whilst Jesus Christ is little more than one who, as a popular preacher said the other day, ' was undoubtedly sincere but might, of course, have been deceived ' !

For all these evils, the evil of pseudo-mysticism, of attempting to build a spiritual house without sure

[1] *Church Times*, February 3rd, 1929.

foundations, of ignorance of and lack of conviction about the eternal truths, of the malaria of heresy, not less but more dangerous because less clearly defined than in earlier days, there is but one remedy – the practice of mental prayer. We have no longer to try to preserve a Faith held and believed, but to restore a Faith which has been lost, lost because men did not meditate upon it so that it became the very stuff and fibre of their lives. The Counter-Reformation, with its insistence on prayer, which brought back half Europe to the Church, did not reach England – nor yet has reached her. Signs and whispers of that living presence which once filled our land have we heard, and there was a moment when the spirit of it seemed about to dawn upon us. But we have well-nigh quenched it by our preoccupation with external things and by that futile activity which has become more and more characteristic of an apostolate which had been better devoted ' to prayer and the ministry of the word ' of God. A Bishop has been reported as saying recently, in referring to the ' World Call ' and its failure to produce any results commensurate with the energy expended on organisation and the like, ' Our very failures have driven us to prayer.' Would to God it were true, much more that we had begun with the knowledge that prayer must come first, that spiritual ends can only be attained by spiritual means, that the devils to-day will be driven out by no lesser force than ' prayer and fasting.'

We have, I say, to restore a lost Faith, and this is only possible when the teaching of that Faith is re-inforced by the prayer of meditation upon the mysteries we are called not merely to believe but to adore, to desire, to become possessed by. We have to scatter a fog of vague, pious sentimentality by the appre-hension of Realities, God, Jesus, Mary, and all they represent, seen, praised and loved. We have to banish ignorance by making men sit down and meditate upon eternal truths. There is little need to exercise ourselves about mysticism whilst the major part of our congregations have not grasped and entered into the meaning of the fact of God, of the end of man's creation, the Incarnation and Passion of the Lord, and the mysteries of the Gospel. We have to combat heresy ; and with what weapon shall we go forth if not with that of prayer and the convictions and burning love born of prayer ?

For cleric and laic alike that knowledge which is eternal life, that force which alone preserves from sin, that light which illumines the darkest path, that power which makes an apostolate alone fruitful, that salt which preserves the soul from the corrupting influence of worldliness, which makes Saints, is to be found in mental prayer. For, as says St. Teresa : ' Herein is nothing to be afraid of but everything to hope for. Granted that one does not advance, nor make an effort to become perfect, so as to merit the joys and consolations which the perfect receive from God, yet little by little he will obtain a knowledge of the road to heaven . . . no one ever took God for his friend without being amply rewarded . . . prayer is the door to those great graces which God has bestowed . . . if this door be shut I do not see how He can give them . . . to him who has not begun to pray I implore him by the love of our Lord not to deprive himself of so great a good ' (*Life*, c. viii.).

And in our own time the saintly Benedictine Bishop Hedley writes of daily mental prayer, ' It is the hour in which the soul lives : that is, lives its true life and rehearses for that life of eternity, in which prayer in its highest sense will be its rapture. It is the hour of its intensest discipline, when acts are produced which vibrate long afterwards through the hours of the day, through the spaces of life. It is the hour of calm when the thronging elements of man's personal life are ranged in order and marshalled in obedience, so that the will may aim at one thing and one thing only. It is the hour of the kindling of that precious fire – the fire of Divine Love – which must burn through every pulsation of life, or else life's deeds can never be borne to the heavens, but must drop like leaves to wither on the earth. It is the hour when the continual presence of the awful Sovereign of the creature is, in a certain sense, made actual and real, when the heart speaks to God, and – what is of infinitely greater moment – when God speaks to the heart.'

PART II
THE METHODS

CHAPTER I

Ignatian

THERE are certain preliminary considerations which should be borne in mind by those who use, or teach others to use, the *Spiritual Exercises* of St. Ignatius Loyola.

First, as to the book itself, it was not meant to be put into the hands of retreatants or others, nor were the exercises to be given indiscriminately to all. The book stands in a class by itself ; it is not to be compared with, or used as, such books on the spiritual life as Scupoli's *Spiritual Combat*, à Kempis's *Imitation of Christ*, St. François de Sales's *Introduction to the Devout Life*, etc. It is a text-book to be used by the Fathers of the Society of Jesus, themselves steeped in both the letter and spirit of it, in giving public or private retreats to all classes but mainly to those who were seeking to know and follow their vocation. This last constitutes and determines the essence of the book. The Saint himself writes to Fathers Laynez and Salmeron whom Paul III had appointed to be his theologians at the Council of Trent, ' When giving the exercises . . . I should take care to give to all in general the meditations on the first week, and no more, unless it be to a few persons who wish to arrange their lives by the methods of the elections ' (Letter xx. 177, *Letters of St. Ignatius Loyola*, selected and edited by the Rev. A. Goodier, S.J., 1914). The Directory, drawn up for the guidance of those giving the exercises, gives the same advice, and adds that copies of the book may only be given ' with much discrimination,' and with the permission of the

Provincial, to those 'who desire it, and seem likely to make good use of it' (*Spiritual Exercises*, edited by Fr. Longridge, Directory I. vii., p. 278 ; IX. vii., p. 293). As P. Bernard writes, ' The exercises are not a manual of perfection but a manual of election,' and Fr. Rickaby, ' The end of the *Spiritual Exercises* is such amount and quality of self-denial as shall bring you to do the work given to you by obedience or by Providence, wholly, steadily, intelligently, courageously, cheerfully. We make retreats either to find out our vocation or to enable us better to do the work of our vocation' (*Waters that Go Softly*, chap. xi. 90). ' The exercises,' writes P. Pottier, ' were composed above all for souls who, already keeping the Commandments, desire to advance in the way of perfection' (*Le P. Louis Lallemant et les grands spirituels de son temps*, ii. 141). And P. Léonce de Grandmaison, ' The *Spiritual Exercises* see before all a concrete case : their end is to place a man, who is free to dispose of his life and who is well endowed for the apostolate, in a state in which he may discern clearly and follow generously the appeal of God' (Art. in *Recherches de Science Religieuse*, December 7th, 1920).

The fact that the *Exercises* can now be obtained by anyone does not lessen the need there is of warning against a general, indiscriminate use, but rather increases it. It is not a book to be recommended to everyone, or in fact to anyone who has not the necessary knowledge required for a profitable use of it. Every priest should read it, study it as he would a scientific treatise, and, above all, meditate it, for he will not only find abundant fruit for his own soul, but invaluable aid in dealing with the souls of others. Novice masters and mistresses ought to know it by heart, and, adapting it to the spirit of their own institute, impart their knowledge individually with the care upon which St. Ignatius insists.

A second point concerns the methods of prayer given

in the *Exercises*. So many, even amongst those who write or give direction upon the subject, seem to be unaware that what is known as the ' Ignatian method of mental prayer ' is but one of several which the Saint gives (A. Brou, in *St. Ignace, Maître d'Oraison*, enumerates seven), and, further, that this particular method was not intended for general use, and is, indeed, unsuitable for ordinary folk. This fact requires some emphasis, since the majority of people may roughly be divided into two classes, those who know nothing of mental prayer and those who are vainly struggling with a method which was not meant for them.

The essentially Ignatian method was intended primarily for those who might be thought to have a vocation to the Society or for deepening the realisation of what their vocation meant, as in the case of those in the third year of the novitiate. But the Saint's mind with regard to meditation in general is clearly expressed in such letters as those to Sister Rejadella in 1536 and to Fr. Brandon. To the former he writes, ' All meditation, where the understanding works, fatigues the body. There are other meditations, equally in the order of God, which are restful, full of peace for the understanding, without labour for the interior faculties of the soul, and which are performed without either physical or interior effort.' Replying to Fr. Brandon's questions about the prayer of scholastics of the Society, he says that they must not be overburdened with meditations, but that two very simple, short, but frequently repeated exercises are to be required of them : one of loving attention to God and the other of offering all their works to our Lord (*Letters of St. Ignatius*, vol. ii., Madrid, 1875, Appendix, p. 560). Such became naturally the tradition of the Society, so that Fr. Gagliardi could write, ' It is characteristic of our prayer that it does not depend upon a rule determined and invariable, for that is proper to

beginners' (Gagliardi, *De plena cognitione Instituti S.J.,
de oratione*, i. 7), and St. Francis Borgia, writing to the
Provincial of Aragon, speaks of the *Exercises* as a good
guide for beginners, but adds that ' others may use
other methods of prayer . . . for the leadings of the
Holy Spirit are diverse, as are also the talents and the
minds of men ' (*Archives Romaines*, S.J.).

In view of these facts it is not so surprising to find
that neither the book itself nor the particular ' Ignatian '
method seems to have been much used in the earliest
days of the Society. M. H. Bernard, in his *Essai his-
torique sur les Exercises spirituels de S. Ignace*, writes that
St. R. Bellarmine ' does not seem to have been
distinguished by a scrupulous fidelity to the prescrip-
tions of the *Exercises*,' and in the *Libro de la Oracion
mental* of Padre Melchior de Villanueva, published in
1608, they are not mentioned, the author being entirely
dependent upon older writers. Alphonsus Rodriguez,
having spent four years in the Society, relates that he
had once made the exercises of the first week (A. de
Yussal : *Un maître de la vie spirituelle*, le Père Alphonse
Rodriguez in *Études*, February 3rd, 1917, p. 199). P.
Gil Gonzales, in the course of an official visit in An-
dalusia about 1583, says that ' The use of giving the
exercises is very rare ; where it is conserved, the results
are mediocre.' (For a brilliant review of the whole
subject see H. Brémond, *Histoire littéraire du Sentiment
Religieux en France*, vol. viii., pt. iv., c. l., to which I am
much indebted.)

I have no intention of belittling the ' Ignatian '
method, the suggestion would be absurd, but merely
of pointing out why it should not occupy a place for
which it was not intended, and as it has done, largely
through ignorance of the freedom in prayer which
St. Ignatius himself advocated and of the many other
methods which are more suitable for the average man
or woman. ' Just in proportion as the *book* of the

exercises is intended for use in a *Retreat*, and has its value largely from the *sequence* of subjects that it offers, it is less likely that St. Ignatius would have insisted on one method of meditation during " daily " meditation had he foreseen that custom coming to hold the position which it does ' (Fr. Martindale, S.J., in *The Month*, July 1930).

A further point may be noted, that is, the Saint's peculiar use of the terms ' meditation ' and ' contemplation,' in which he does not follow the usual definition and distinction made by St. Thomas, who says that meditation is a process of reasoning, a discursive deduction from the principles of truth, whilst contemplation is a simple, instinctive vision of truth. Père Lallemant puts the distinction very forcibly in the words, ' To meditate upon Hell is to see a painted representation of a lion ; whilst by contemplation upon Hell, the living lion stands before you.' St. Ignatius, at times, seems to use both terms indiscriminately, but considering both his nature and the end which he has in view, it would seem likely that his own idea of what ' meditation ' meant would be well expressed in Père Libermann's definition, ' The prayer of meditation is a sensible application of the mind to a supernatural truth in order to convince ourselves of it and to be brought to love it by the help of Divine grace.' For much as St. Ignatius wills the use of the intellect, yet he reminds us of the dangers of overstraining the mind, and would have us reflect only that we may be led to affective prayer, for, as he says in the second Annotation, ' it is not abundance of knowledge that fills and satisfies the soul, but the inward sense and taste of things.'

We may say, then, that he uses the term ' meditation ' in the ordinary sense, ' to think about,' ' to reflect upon,' whilst by ' contemplation ' he does not mean, as most ascetical and mystical writers do, either 'acquired' or 'infused' contemplation, which belongs to the higher stages of prayer, but usually 'to look at,' 'to look on,' 'to be a spectator of' some Mystery of our Lord's life which the memory and imagination vividly reconstruct, as in the directions for the first Contemplation upon the Nativity, in which we are to see, consider, hear and reflect upon all that, in this Mystery, concerns our Lord 'so recently become Incarnate.'

But when, in the middle of the Second Week, we come to the decisive and peculiarly Ignatian meditations on the Two Standards and the Three Classes designed to prepare the soul for the election of a state of life, we find the word 'Consideration' in the 'Preamble to the consideration of states of life.' The use of this term is made clear in the preamble, in which we are told that now that we have considered our Lord's example in some of the Mysteries of the Infancy 'we will begin, while going on with the study of His life, at the same time to investigate and beg grace to know in what life or state His Divine Majesty is pleased to make use of us. And therefore, by way of some introduction to this business . . . we will see the intention of Christ our Lord and contrariwise that of the enemy of human nature, and how we ought to dispose ourselves to come to perfection in that state of life, whatever it may be, which God our Lord shall grant us to choose.' The Meditations, then, upon the Two Standards and the Three Classes are actually a consideration of the two facts, God and myself; everything that has been done so far has now come to a decisive point in which I have to consider what I must do since God wills it, and how.

St. Ignatius gives no less than seven methods of mental prayer, including the examen, and so far from being, as the uninformed have said, insistent upon wooden methods and inflexible rules to which he would bind all, he goes further, as we have seen, and allows, even to Jesuits, the widest possible latitude in their prayer. One thing alone does he insist upon, and that rightly – that men need to be taught how to pray, a lesson no less needed to-day than in his time. But even so, the teaching given is to depend upon the varying characteristics, etc., of the individual soul, and for this reason he gives these seven methods so that the ignorant may find a way in which they may walk safely, and that others may find refreshment at times by turning from one method to another (Directory, xxxvii. 13, Longridge, p. 343).

The First Method of Prayer

Upon the Commandments (*sobre Mandamientos*)

' Suitable for those who are poorly educated or illiterate : each Commandment should be explained to them, and so to each of the mortal sins, the Commandments of the Church, the five senses and the works of mercy ' (Annotation 18), ' the which method of prayer is to give form, manner and exercises, how the soul should prepare herself and advance in them, and that the prayer may be acceptable, rather than to give any form and manner of praying ' (Three methods of Prayer).

The double reference to ' form and manner ' seems at first ambiguous, but what is meant is that this is a particular method of mental prayer, with its special exercises, rather than a form of vocal prayer. Further, this method is designed to a particular end, i.e. a clearer knowledge of self and of one's sins, a deeper penitence and a seeking of grace to amend one's life, to the greater glory of God, all of which is asked for in the preparatory prayer.

Assuming, then, that a person has been instructed in such manner as is contemplated in the Eighteenth

Annotation, this method of prayer consists of three parts : I. The Preparation.   II. The Body of the Prayer.   III. The Colloquy.

I. The Preparation, which is to be the same before all the methods. This consists of two Preludes :

(1) To consider what I am going to do. ' To let the mind repose a little, either sitting or walking, as shall seem best, considering meanwhile whither I am going and for what purpose.'

(2) A preparatory prayer, ' as in this manner, to ask grace of God our Lord that I may know wherein I have failed regarding the Ten Commandments ; and likewise to ask grace and aid to amend myself in future, begging for a perfect understanding of them, the better to keep them, to the greater glory and praise of His Divine Majesty.'

II. The Body of the Prayer consists in a consideration of the subject chosen, e.g. the Ten Commandments, the Commandments of the Church, the seven Deadly Sins and their contrary Virtues, the powers of the soul, the five senses, the works of mercy, etc.

In the first case, where the subject chosen is the Ten Commandments, each one is to be considered separately for the space of three Our Fathers and three Ave Marias, with the object of discovering how it has been kept or broken, pardon being sought for each failure. The time spent on each Commandment will vary, as when a man ' finds he has no habit of sinning, it is not necessary to stay on it so long.' On concluding the reflection, accusation and begging for grace, an end should be made by

III. The Colloquy with God our Lord according to the subject matter. A colloquy is a familiar, intimate, loving conversation, as of a child with its father, summing up in the freest acts of prayer what has gone before.

The same order is to be observed whatever the

subject of the meditation may be, the only difference being in the treatment of the subject. These may be noted :

1. On the seven Deadly Sins, 'the matter here is of sins, which are to be avoided, whereas before it was of Commandments, which are to be kept. . . . The better to know the faults committed on the seven Deadly Sins, let their contraries be considered, and so, the better to avoid them, let the person propose and take care with holy exercises to acquire and keep the seven Virtues contrary to them.'

2. On the powers of the soul, Memory, Understanding and Will. The Saint gives no directions here ; what is evidently intended is the consideration of how the three great powers of the soul have been used or abused, the endeavour to understand and appreciate their functions that we may use them aright.

3. The meditation on the five senses will be made in the same manner, but St. Ignatius adds the following direction : 'Whoever wishes in the use of his senses to imitate Christ our Lord, let him commend himself in the preparatory prayer to His Divine Majesty : and after the consideration of each sense let him say one Our Father and one Hail Mary. And whoever wishes in the use of his senses to imitate our Lady, let him commend himself to her in the preparatory prayer, that she may obtain him grace of her Son and Lord to this purpose ; and after the consideration of each sense let him say one Hail Mary.'

It will be obvious that this method is something more than an examen of conscience, although it is more like one than other methods of mental prayer. But it will be noted that St. Ignatius centres attention on the positive side of the subject : 'the Commandments which are to be kept,' 'the Virtues contrary to the seven Deadly Sins,' the use of the senses by our Lord

and His Mother. The meditations are to be upon
what God wills and loves and on what Christ does, so
that ' in His light ' we may see our sins and ever turn
to Him for pardon and grace.

What indeed could be made of such subjects may
be seen in Raymund Lull, *Art of Contemplation*, where
Blanquerna, meditating on the Commandments and
Vices by the exercise of the Memory, Understanding
and Will, rises to sublime heights of prayer.

' Blanquerna remembered in the Gospels the answer
that Jesus Christ had given concerning the Commandments and he was fain to contemplate these with the
Divine Virtues of God. And he said these words to
his Will, " Thou shalt love the Lord thy God, for thou
art commanded thereto by the Goodness, Greatness
and Eternity of God." . . . When Understanding had
comprehended the argument which Memory recalled
and related to him, he was conscious of the many times
that he had failed to comprehend the Virtue, Truth
and Glory of God, that the Will through Faith should
have greater merit. And since to the Understanding
in its totality has been given as great a commandment
as to the Will, therefore the Understanding exalted
itself in all its power to comprehend the Virtue, Truth
and Glory of God, and besought forgiveness because
through ignorance it had gone astray' (Professor Peers's
translation, chap. ix. ; *vide* also chap. xiii.).

This method would be of great value if used in
teaching the Faith to ignorant people, which, indeed,
is the idea St. Ignatius had in mind, for teaching alone
bears little fruit ; it is by prayer that conviction comes
and the will is moved to action. Fr. Polanco says that
this method is particularly appropriate for those who
wish to put their resolutions into practice, and we are
told that St. Francis Xavier so taught his converts to
use it that they might persevere, and that at times the
matter of the examen might form the subject of their

meditation. In the case of instructing illiterate people,
very largely ignorant of Christian verities, the Commandments might well be taken as a basis on which
practically the whole Faith could be made to rest.
Beginning with ' I am the Lord thy God,' a clear and
simple instruction would be given on the Oneness, the
Supremacy and Majesty of God, the contrast of man's
nothingness, and the Absolute claim of God upon his
love and service. The person would then be shown the
method of considering this for himself, a pattern
meditation might be made, and then he would be told
to make a similar prayer for a certain time every day
until the next instruction. If necessary, brief points of
such meditations might be given him, and at the next
meeting he should be questioned as to how he had made
his prayer. Such a plan, carefully worked out and
designed to the capacities of the individual, would be
actually the giving of the exercises in the way St.
Ignatius intended, and would be worth infinitely more
than the pious talks which are often all that is done in
this way during pastoral visitation, or the mere instruction on Catholic doctrine, culled from a text-
book, which often forms almost the whole preparation
for Confirmation, without giving the persons concerned
anything to do themselves which will influence their
hearts and wills.

The Second Method of Prayer

is by studying the meaning of each word of the prayer.
This method is a great advance upon the first, and,
indeed, if all the methods were placed in order of
degrees of prayer, would come after the elaborate
method designed mainly for the exercises themselves,
as that may be more strictly termed meditation, whilst
this leads directly to affective prayer. The prayer
begins in the same way as the first method, the

preparatory prayer being made to the Person to whom the prayer is addressed.

Then ' kneeling or sitting, as he may find himself more disposed and as greater devotion accompanies him, keeping his eyes shut or fixed on one place, without moving them hither and thither, he says " Father," and rests on the consideration of this word for so long a time as he finds meanings, comparisons, relish and consolation in considerations belonging to such a word.' So for the allotted time of prayer the Our Father, Hail Mary or any other prayer, psalm, portion of Holy Scripture is to be gone through, care being taken that ' if the person who is studying the Our Father finds in one word or two very good matter for thought and relish and consolation, let him not trouble to go further on ' – advice given by all spiritual guides. It reflects, indeed, the older tradition of prayer, as taught by the earliest monks, who founded their prayer on the psalms, responses, lessons, etc., of the Divine Office.

The prayer ends with the recitation of the Hail Mary, Creed, Anima Christi, and Salve Regina, ' vocally or mentally, in the customary manner,' and a colloquy with the Person ' to whom he has prayed in a few words, asking for the virtues or graces of which he feels himself to have greater need.' What could be simpler ? Many a soul who from lack of proper instruction has wearied herself to no purpose struggling with elaborate methods, and overwhelmed with the cumbrous meditations so often recommended, might begin to pray well at once if she were simply told, ' Just kneel or sit down and think of God and of what you intend to do. Ask our Lord and Mary to help you to pray well for His glory. Then very slowly say the Lord's Prayer, thinking quietly and simply of each word, drawing out the meaning of it, tasting its sweetness, dwelling on it or on a phrase such as " Thy Kingdom," " Thy Kingdom come," " Thy will," " Thy will be done," for as long as you can with profit, and then passing on. Let your whole self pray, i.e. be lifted up to the thought of God. Father, our Father – my Father – O Father infinite – eternal, loving – bountiful – I love Thee, I adore Thee, look on me, Thy child – *Thy* child – God's child – what love of Thine for me . . . etc.' To whom is not such most real prayer possible ? Of such prayer the Abbot Isaac says, ' This prayer of the " Our Father " contains all the fulness of perfection . . . it raises those who familiarise themselves with it to that prayer of fire which passes all human language ' (Cassian, *Conferences*, I. ix. 25), and St. Teresa tells us of certain persons well known to her who, being unable to meditate, were yet raised in contemplation whilst reciting the Paternoster. In Cassian, too, may be read that wonderful eulogy of the use of the versicle ' O God, make speed to save me,' of which the Abbot Isaac declares that the soul which repeats and meditates upon it continually will arrive at the beatitude of the poor in spirit whose is the Kingdom of Heaven (cf. *loc. cit.*, chap. xi.).

A Third Method of Prayer

will be by rhythmical beats, *oracion por compas*, or as in the first version of the *Exercises*, *per intervalla*.

This is less a method of mental prayer than one of reciting vocal prayers with care and devotion. It will be found particularly useful in times of aridity, when all prayer seems distasteful and it is practically impossible to meditate. I shall have more to say on this state in a later chapter ; here it will be sufficient to note that almost the only remedy is to say vocal prayers for a time.

As given by St. Ignatius, the method begins as before, the body of the prayer consisting of a mental recitation of the Our Father, Hail Mary, or other vocal prayers, ' one word only being said between one breath and another,' whilst one dwells on

(*a*) The meaning of the word,

(*b*) The Person to Whom one is speaking,

(*c*) Or to one's own lowly estate,

(*d*) Or to the contrast between such high estate and such lowliness of our own.

We have here, as elsewhere in the *Exercises*, the recognition of the fact, of greater importance than is often realised, of the interdependence of soul and body and the consequent need of using both in our devotion. It is with our whole being that we are to pray, ' in order to obtain from God,' says Pascal, ' the exterior must be joined to the interior . . . kneeling, etc. . . . To expect aid from the exterior (that is, the prevenient grace of the dispositions of prayer) is to be superstitious ; not to unite it to the interior is to be proud ' (*Pensées*, éd. Havet, xi. 3 *bis*).

Another method of prayer, not Ignatian, but suggested by his rhythmical method and by that English devotion, the Jesus Psalter, composed by Richard Whitford, which was so popular in the six-teenth century, and which is very useful as a form of ejaculatory prayer which may be said at any time, is to use the Holy Name as a sort of melodic refrain, linking up acts of praise, prayer and petition. Thus :

' Jesus, Jesus, Jesus, I adore Thee. Jesus, Jesus, Jesus, I love Thee : Jesus, Jesus, Jesus, have mercy upon sinners : Jesus, Jesus, Jesus, Thy Kingdom come,' etc. The prayers should be recited melodically as it were, the acts of adoration, etc., being uttered as they come into one's mind. There is hardly any situation in which it could not be used, and invalids, those suffering from sleeplessness, those who have to walk much in busy streets, etc., would find it invaluable for preserving the sense of the Presence of God and that atmosphere of the supernatural world which is so great a shield against temptations and distractions.

The Fourth Method

The Application of the Senses

According to St. Ignatius, this method is to be used as a means of going over and renewing meditations, especially the ' Contemplations on the Life of our Lord which have been made in the accustomed way, except in one case, the exercise on Hell, to which the application of the senses is alone given. Probably the most profitable use of it outside the exercises would be for those who are very familiar with the Mysteries of our Lord's life and who are tending toward affective prayer. Less instructed folk, too, who cannot make much use of the three powers of the soul, might well profit by making it before the Crib, the Rood or some picture. The exact manner of this application will depend upon the subject chosen for meditation. The Saint gives two examples which are sufficiently explicit. The exercise on Hell is made as follows :

After the usual preparatory prayer, which is ' to ask grace of God our Lord that all my intentions, actions and operations may be directed purely to the service and praise of His Divine Majesty,' we have the

First Prelude, which is to see with the eyes of the imagination the length, breadth and depth of Hell.

Second Prelude, to ask for what I desire . . . an intimate sense of the pain that the damned suffer, so that, if through my faults I become forgetful of the love of the Eternal Lord, at least the fear of pains and penalties may be an aid to me not to give way to sin.

First Point : to see with the eyes of the imagination those great fires, and those souls as it were in bodies of fire.

Fp

Second Point : to hear with the ears lamentations, howlings, cries, blasphemies, against Christ our Lord and against all His Saints.

Third Point : with the sense of smell to smell smoke, brimstone, refuse and rottenness.

Fourth Point : to taste bitter things, as tears, sadness and the worm of conscience.

Fifth Point : to feel with the sense of touch how those fires do touch and burn souls.

The meditation ends with the Colloquy with Christ our Lord, in which we bring to memory the souls that are in Hell : give thanks that we are not with them, and recall God's mercy and kindness towards us in having patiently allowed us to live so long in order that we might repent ; ending with an Our Father. The use of this method in the *Exercises* does not occur again until the Second Week, in which begin the Contemplations on the Mysteries of our Lord's Life, where it is to be used in the evening hour of mental prayer. St. Ignatius entitles it, ' The Fifth Contemplation will be to carry the five senses over the first and second contemplation,' which have been upon the Incarnation and Nativity. The usual preparation being made,

' The first point is to see the persons with the sight of the imagination, meditating and studying in particular their circumstances, and gathering some fruit from the sight.

' The second, to hear with the hearing the things that they say, or may say, and reflecting within oneself to gather thence some profit.

' The third, to smell and taste with the sense of smell and taste the infinite fragrance and sweetness of the Godhead, of the soul and its virtues, and of everything, according to the Person one is contemplating, reflecting inwardly and gathering profit from thence.

' The fourth, to touch with the touch, as for instance to embrace and kiss the place where such persons tread and sit, always contriving to gather fruit from thence.'

A colloquy is then made with the Holy Trinity, our Lord or our Lady.

The first and second points need no comment, but on the third it may be well to add a word. As I walk in my garden I see with sentiments of pleasure and interest the vari-coloured flowers, I rejoice in the lights and shadows among the trees, I hear the song of birds and the hum of bees, all this culminating in something higher, more subtle than mere sense appreciation. My mind, imagination, my inner self is, say on a spring day, exalted, filled with an æsthetic joy of life, or on a calm summer evening with a repose, a sweetness which refreshes both soul and body. I taste, as it were, that something which is spring or evening summertide. Or the same sense use of the imagination is kindled whilst reading a book ; I follow, say, the traveller pushing his way through dark forests or over mountain ridges ; every sense responds to his hardships, endeavours, dangers ; or again, in memory of bygone travels, I hear the far-off thunder of the sea upon a coral reef, recall the indescribable but subtly tasted atmosphere of the mangrove-guarded banks of a tropical river, or live again evenings spent by a camp fire, listening to a native chanting some old legend of his tribe.

Now all this is nothing else but an application of the senses of the imagination and is as rightfully employed, and with profit, in mental prayer. An example may best serve to make this method clear.

Subject : The Crucifixion.

First Point : see Jesus crucified – loving me – dying for me. See His Five Wounds from which flow the price of my salvation. His Sacred Heart opened to receive me – burning with Divine love, offered to the Eternal Father.

See and gather in my mind and heart the virtues of this Mystery – infinite love, patience, tenderness, generosity, etc.

See the Compassionate Mother – learn with her a tender compassion for Jesus suffering. See Mary Magdalene – intense, adoring love of the Queen of Penitents.

See St. John, wrapped in the Divine Mystery, adoring, uniting himself in love with his Lord. Gather fruit from this Tree of Life and those who are beneath it.

Second Point : Hear the Seven Words from the Cross. The prayerful silence of Jesus.

The loud cry with which He commends His soul to the Eternal Father.

His inward words to me.

Third Point : ' O taste and see ' the Hidden Godhead, the sweet virtues of the human soul of Jesus. The Sacred Humanity, so dear to God, to itself, to us. The Saviour's choices, poverty, suffering, contempt, thirst, dereliction, the Cross.

' Blessed are they who hunger and thirst after righteousness.'

' So longeth my soul after Thee, O God.'

Fourth Point : Touch the wood of the Cross, the sacred ground upon which falls the Precious Blood, the hem of Mary's garment. Feel and desire as Jesus and Mary felt and desired.

Colloquy : Pouring out my heart to Jesus – offering Him to the Eternal Father – compassionating with Mary.

Any of the Mysteries of our Lord's life may be treated in the same way, some quite easily, others perhaps only after some practice of the method.

The Fifth Method

Commonly known as the Ignatian Method

It would be impossible, within the limits of so elementary a volume as this, to treat with the fulness it deserves this, the most elaborate method of mental prayer which has ever been constructed. Moreover, so much more attention has been given to it than to other methods that it is unnecessary to give more than a sufficient outline of it, and to indicate its characteristic features.

The Method

I. *Preliminary Preparation*, to be made overnight. Choose and read over the subject. Re-read it and select one or two points for meditation, choosing those which contain the grace you are most in need of. The following questions addressed to the subject-matter will suggest answers which will serve as a guide on the morrow. *Who? What? Where? By what aids? Why? How? When? For whom? With what love? With what fruit?* Not more than three of these should be used, the main object being to concentrate on the particular fruit we desire to gain from our prayer.

A glance should also be taken at the Composition of Place, easily seen by asking, *Who speaks or acts? Where and with whom?*

Before going to sleep the mind should be fixed for a moment on (1) the hour we intend to rise (this will soon make an alarm clock unnecessary!) : (2) the points of our meditation. This must be brief; any prolonged attention is to be avoided as likely to over-excite the intellect or imagination and so prevent sleep. If we wake during the night we should quietly recur to our subject, 'not giving place to other thoughts' (2nd Addition of First Week). Fr. John Morris, S.J., in dealing with this preparation for mental prayer, answers an objection which often exists in the mind. ' It is quite a mistake to suppose that a meditation goes better when the subject is new and untouched. It is just the reverse. A repetition is often far more fruitful than the meditation when first made. Old and familiar subjects are better than new ones ; and the more thorough the preparation has been, the better the meditation will be ' (*Instructions to Novices*, p. 16).

II. *Introduction to the Act of Prayer.*

To rise at once, to lift the mind and heart in an act of adoration of God, to dress quietly but briskly, avoiding all slothfulness and fixing the mind on the Composition of Place, Him Whom we shall meet there and the grace we desire, are practices which will go far to ensuring a good prayer. Haste, solicitude, dissipation of mind, are always dangerous, and never more so than during those early moments of the day in which its whole tone is set.

III. *The Meditation Proper.*

' Standing a pace or two before the place where I am to make my contemplation or meditation ' (3rd Addition of First Week), for the duration of a Paternoster the mind is raised to God, before Whom we ' make a reverence or gesture of self-abasement,' Fr. Roothan advising the making of five short, fervent and generous acts here, of faith in the presence of God, of adoration, of contrition, an offering of our memory, understanding and will, and a petition for help, that ' all my intentions, actions and operations may be ordered purely to the service and praise of Thy Divine Majesty.'

(*a*) *The First Prelude*, which consists in briefly recalling to mind the subject and points chosen.

(*b*) *The Second Prelude*, the Composition of Place. ' Seeing the place ' (St. Ignatius), ' to go there ourselves ' (Fr. Roothan), ' to picture to oneself, and, as it were, to see with the eyes of the imagination the place' (The Directory).

Several authors, of whom St. Teresa (*Way*, chap. xxviii. 4) is one, give the advice that it is better to make the composition of place interiorly, i.e. as taking place within ourselves, rather than transporting, as it were, the mind to some distant scene, which requires more effort and may lead to overstraining the imagination. This, in some cases, is undoubtedly true, but it is clear that St. Ignatius would have the composition of place as clearly ' localised ' as possible, although, at the same time, as may be seen by his reference to our Lord ' so lately made Man ' (First Contemplation on the Incarnation), it is to no mere historical past he would have us recur, but to the living present, the ' state ' no less than the ' act,' as Bérulle would say (*vide* Part II., chap. vi.).

The composition of place, write Mons. Howley in his valuable study *Psychology and Mystical Experience*, is ' the pedagogic process of " picturing out " applied to spiritual things . . . the *conversio ad phantasmata* of the schoolmen used as a spiritually educative process. Until we strive to picture out our conceptions, they remain vague, shadowy, indistinct, notional, with but feeble energising force to affect our volitions ' (*op. cit.*, p. 467). With this may be compared St. Thomas's ' We cannot know God directly, but we can argue to His existence and nature from creatures by abstraction and negation. But intellectual ideas thus formed in the mind are not really understood by the intellect unless it represents them to the imagination; it " turns to images," *convertit se ad phantasmata*, so that it may behold the universal in the particular, wherein alone it has real existence' (*Summa Theol.* I. lxxxiv. 7).

(*c*) *The Third Prelude*, asking for (1) an interior, i.e. supernatural knowledge of our Lord ; (2) that we may love Him more dearly ; (3) and follow Him more nearly. The time given to this part of our prayer should not be more than five minutes.

IV. *The Body of the Meditation.*

This consists of the application of the memory, understanding and will to the subject before us.

The memory brings forward the subject and, as it were, hands it over to the understanding which reflects upon it, enters into it, regards it from this side and that, seeking, above all, the meaning which it has for oneself, the especial lesson contained, the particular demand it makes. As the practical conclusion becomes apparent, we may ask :

What, in respect of this, have I done hitherto ?

What shall I do from to-day ?

What obstacles shall I encounter ?

What means must I take ?

So we come to the exercise of the will which, moved by the understanding, turns to God in acts of various virtues suggested by the consideration, the particular resolution, and the colloquies. In placing the work of the three powers of the soul in this logical order it must not be thought that they are kept distinct from one another, no acts of the will, for instance, being made until the meditation proper is concluded. On the contrary, any thought which moves the will should at once be put into prayer, for the whole object of the reflection is to produce this. ' The more acts of the will there are interspersed amid the work of the understanding, and the longer and more fervent they are, the better the meditation is being made' (Morris, *op. cit.*, p. 37).

' When we meditate, we do not pray ; when we pray, we do not meditate ; to reason explicitly and to pray explicitly are two things irreconcilable at the same moment.' But ' of the meditation is born the desire, and of this springs the prayer . . . the effort of the will, in mental prayer, gathers up all those sentiments (faith, hope, charity, confidence, humility, etc.) in order to concentrate itself in a simple unity, in the act of desire and petition ; act double in appearance, but in reality as truly one as the flight of a bird by the double action of its wings in one single balanced movement ; an act which may be repeated a hundred or a thousand times ' (Paulot, *L'Esprit de Sagesse*, pp. 276, 284).

The resolution is of the utmost importance, for, as Fr. Morris says, ' the object of our meditation is not simply to spend an hour devoutly and meritoriously ; our prayer is made that we may purify our souls, that we may clothe them with virtues, that we may amend our lives, that we may strengthen ourselves in our vocation, that we may guard ourselves against temptations, that we may do all our actions perfectly, that we may correspond with the grace of God, and please Him in all things.'

It must be practical, particular, adapted to our present state, something to be done the same day and be rooted in distrust of ourselves together with a great confidence in God.

The colloquies are the fervent outpourings of the heart to God, our Lord and His Mother, the Saints and Angels ' after the fashion of St. Augustine's *Soliloquies* and many parts of his *Confessions* ' (Rickaby, *Spiritual Exercises*, p. 176). ' A colloquy is properly made by speaking, as a friend speaks to his friend, or as a servant speaks to his master, at one time asking some favour, at another time accusing oneself of some wrong done, at another communicating all one's affairs and asking counsel in them ' (St. Ignatius, *Exercises*). In making them, the desire of the heart is more important than words, and in them we should always beg for grace to keep our resolutions, and may add petitions and general intercessions as we will.

Following the meditation, St. Ignatius would have a quarter of an hour spent on the reflection, which may be made sitting or walking about. The object of the reflection is ' to look and see what success I have had in my contemplation or meditation ; and if it has gone badly, I will look into the cause whence the failure proceeds, and so having looked into it I will be sorry, purposing amendment for the future ; and if it has gone well, I will return thanks to God ' (*Exercises*, Fifth Addition of the First Week).

Fr. Roothan insists strongly on the necessity of the reflection, both that we may learn how to meditate and also profit by meditation. It is largely due to a neglect of this practice, he thinks, that so many go on making daily meditation without any serious amendment of life, and adds that often when a meditation has been a failure, or apparently so, the reflection supplies the loss.

Now even if we admit, as is the case, that a great deal of the difficulty of this method would soon be over-come by anyone of goodwill and courage, that the various divisions and acts would soon become automatic, the fact remains that it is only practically possible for those who have a certain aptitude, time and freedom from worldly affairs. And as I have already said, it was not intended for all, but only for those who are able to make the exercises in full, a very different thing even from what we call a ' long retreat.' Valuable as it is, especially when aided by the Additions and Annotations provided in the *Exercises*, to be especially studied by priests, there is no doubt that the average cleric, much more the layman or woman, will do better to choose a simpler method, Ignatian or otherwise.

CHAPTER II

Franciscan

ALTHOUGH Franciscan spirituality is distinctly affective in character, more deeply rooted in the older tradition, and more akin to St. François de Sales and the Oratorian School than to St. Ignatius, it has yet produced some very striking and beautiful methods of mental prayer which deserve to be much better known than they are.

St. Bonaventura, the Seraphic doctor, whose voluminous writings form the theological and devotional basis of Franciscan piety, defines mental prayer in the words, ' Pure mental prayer is made when the lips move not but the heart speaks to God ' (*Sentences*, Bk. IV., Dist. XV., Pt. ii., Art. ii., Q. 3). In his *De Progressu Rel.* (Bk. II., chap. lx.) he writes more fully : ' In mental prayer the mind alone unfolds its desires before God, pouring forth to Him the affections of the heart, interiorly clinging to Him by love and reverently adoring Him. Words, because of their inadequacy, are not used, for the more completely the soul empties itself into God the deeper go the affections and the less ability one has of expressing them.'

References to the practice of mental prayer in early Franciscan literature can hardly be called ' methods ' in the modern sense, but there is a certain methodicity in some of them. Spiritual reading is made much of as the ' seed and material of meditation ' (David of Augsburg, *d. circa* 1272, *De Exterioris et Interioris Hominis compositione*, a widely read book which greatly influenced Gerald of Zutphen, *De Reformatione*

Memoriæ), reflection upon what is read leading to prayer. St. Bonaventura has an interesting comment on such reflections : ' We may consider our meditations on our Bridegroom, the Word of God, His beauty, His power, His majesty, as His conversations with us.' In the *De Progressu Rel.* (Bk. II., chap. lxi.) he shows how in our prayer we may assume ' the rôle of different persons according to the different needs and dispositions of the heart,' i.e. as a criminal before his judge, a servant before his master, a soul in temptation and difficulty before its Saviour, a child before its father, etc. The author of the *Speculum Disciplinæ*, probably Bernard de Besse, recommends the pausing for reflection and prayer whilst reading Holy Scripture or spiritual books.

The *Stimulus Amoris*, which was commonly thought to be the work of St. Bonaventura but is more probably from the pen of James of Milan, a Friar Minor who was a lector in that city towards the end of the thirteenth century, gives a method of meditating on the Passion which may be noted. The Passion of our Saviour, he says, may be considered in six ways, for our imitation, compassion, admiration, exultation, transformation, and repose. ' Consider what things He suffered for you, and how He conducted Himself in all His sufferings ; and as far as you are able, conform yourself to Him your Model . . . we shall find great cause for admiring the Passion of Christ if we consider who, what, for whom, and from whom He suffered.' Contemplating the Sacred Wounds, we shall be moved not alone to compassion and admiration, but the exultation in the threefold revelation that man is redeemed thereby, the choirs of angels restored and God's infinite mercy made known. So too by continual contemplation of the Crucifix are we transformed into Christ crucified, and find in Him our one repose. ' If you meditate well on His Passion, you shall thereby enter into His side and quickly come to His Heart.'

But it is with St. Pedro of Alcantara (1499–1562) whom St. Teresa praises – ' Y qué bueno nos le elevó Dios ahora en el bendito fray Pedro de Alcántara. No esta ya el mundo para sufrir tanta perfeccion ' (*Life*, chaps. xxvii. and xxxix.) – that we come first to a definite method of mental prayer comparable with those of St. Ignatius, and which entirely deserves the encomium of Gregory XV, who declared that ' A most efficacious light for leading souls to God is poured forth from its pages. Its teaching is heavenly. Indeed, the marks of His presence throughout make it evident that the Holy Ghost guided the pen of the Saint.'

The *De Oratione et Meditatione*, commonly known under the title of *A Golden Treatise of Mental Prayer*, has been translated into Eastern as well as nearly all European languages ; indeed, though it may be by accident, I have seen more copies of it in the Far East than at home. An excellent unabridged edition (would that the example were more faithfully followed !), translated from the Spanish edition of Don Pablo La Fuente in 1882, itself carefully conformed to Medina's edition of 1587, was published in 1905 by Mowbray, the translation being by the Rev. G. F. Bullock, M.A., and the editing by Fr. Hollings, S.S.J.E. A new edition has lately been published in the ' Orchard Books ' series, the translating and editing being the work of Fr. Dominic Devas, O.F.M.

St. Pedro does not merely give a method of prayer or certain meditations, but a concise though very complete treatise on prayer, based mainly on the *Libro de la Oracion y Meditacion* of the Dominican, Luis of Granada (1505–1588), St. Thomas, St. Augustine, St. Bernard and St. Bonaventura. There is one characteristically

' Ignatian ' touch in the chapter on how to meditate on
the Passion, in which he says : ' We should have our
Lord present before our eyes . . . as actually suffering,
and with all the circumstances of that suffering ;
especially in these four points, viz.

> ' Who is it that suffers ?
> ' For whom does He suffer ?
> ' How does He suffer ?
> ' For what cause does He suffer ? '

He refers once to à Kempis, who, with the Brethren
of the Common Life, was greatly influenced by earlier
Franciscans and, in turn, influenced St. Ignatius and
the Spanish School through translations into Castilian
of their works.

The Alcantarine Method is given in chapter v., the
preceding chapters being devoted to two sets of meditations for each day of the week, the first set being on
' The Memory of thy Sins,' the vanity of the world,
death, judgment, Hell, the glory of the blessed in
Heaven and the Divine Blessings, the Saint beginning his week, in the Spanish way, on Monday. The
second set deal with the Passion. The method has
six divisions :

I. *The Preparation*

An Act of Recollection. Kneeling, standing, ' prostrate
on the ground, or, if need be, sitting, having made the
Sign of the Cross, let us gather up our thoughts, and
put away from us all the things of this life ; then let us
lift up our mind to our Lord, as knowing that He is
looking for us.'

An Act of Contrition. If the meditation be made
in the morning, the Confiteor should be said ;
if in the evening, we should examine our consciences, grieve over our shortcomings, and humble
ourselves before God. The words of Abraham (Gen.

xviii. 27) and of the Psalmist (xxiii. 1–3) may be used.

A Petition for the Divine Assistance. The ' Veni Creator,' with its versicle and collect, and a petition for the grace of attention, devotion, interior recollectedness, fear and reverence, ' that we may so use this time of prayer that we may come from it with new fervour and strength for all the needs of His service. Prayer which does not produce this fruit immediately is very imperfect and almost valueless.'

II. *The Reading*

' of what we have to meditate upon in prayer.' This must be ' attentive and serious,' not merely that we may understand with our minds, ' but still more we should give to it our whole will that we may taste the sweetness of what we read.' The reading should not be long, for its object is to lead to meditation and prayer.

III. *The Meditation*

This may be of two kinds, intellectual or imaginative. The former will be used with such subjects as the Perfections of God, His blessings, etc., the latter with more concrete ones, such as the last things, the Mysteries of the Life and Passion of our Lord. In the latter ' we should try to represent to our minds each item of our subject as it really is, or would become, and as though the action were being performed in our presence in the very place in which we are.' This actual representation of our subject is much better than letting our minds travel into the past as to an historical act taking place afar off. We must not use too much violence in this exercise of the imagination, ' lest it weaken its capacity ' and we exhaust ourselves so that we are unable to pray well.

In a later chapter, St. Pedro gives certain counsels as to this part of mental prayer, in which he lays stress

upon the fact that his aim is ' love and the affections of
the will rather than the speculations of the understanding,' so that ' as soon as one should feel himself
fired by the love of God he should forthwith put aside
all these considerations and thoughts . . . and leave
meditation for the love of contemplation.' The whole
of this section deserves careful study.

IV. *The Thanksgiving*

First, for the subject upon which we have meditated,
then for the blessings of creation, redemption, vocation, etc. ; for God's goodness in having created us in
His own Image and Likeness, for having endowed us
with the powers of Memory, Intellect and Will that
we might remember, know and love Him, for our
Guardian Angel, the Incarnation and Redemption,
for our birth of Christian parents, our Baptism and the
other Sacraments, and for all the particular inspirations
and blessings He has bestowed upon us, saying, if we
will, the *Benedicite omnia opera* or Ps. ciii.

V. *The Oblation of Ourselves*

Aroused by the thought of what God has done for us,
we cry, ' What reward shall I give unto the Lord for
all the benefits which He hath done unto me ? ' and
go on to make a twofold offering to Him ; first, to be
His servants for ever, submitting ourselves wholly and
entirely to the Divine Will ; and second, ' We should
offer to God the Father, all the merits and labours of
His dear Son, all the travails of His soul which, in His
obedience, in this world He endured, from the Manger-
crib to Calvary ; for all these are our health and the
inheritance which He hath bequeathed to us in that
New Covenant by which He hath made us heirs of so
great a treasure. For as that is no less our own which
He has bestowed upon us of His grace than that which
we have obtained by our own efforts, so those merits and
gifts which He hath bestowed upon us are as much our

own as if we had toiled and laboured for them ourselves . . . this is the best and most precious offering we
can make.' I have transcribed this passage more fully,
not only from its importance, but also because it
anticipates the teaching of the French Oratorian
School, and especially of St. John Eudes.

VI. *The Petition*

This is to be of the most confident and comprehensive order. We begin ' with all the fulness of love and
zeal for the honour of our Blessed Lord,' with the
prayer that all men may come to know, praise and
adore Him ; going on to pray for the Pope and all the
prelates of the Church ; for rulers ; for all the members
of Christ's Mystical Body ; for the righteous ; for
sinners ; for the holy souls ; for all the sick and poor,
prisoners and captives. Then we beg for ourselves the
remission of our sins and grace to overcome our
temptations, for the virtues in which consists all
Christian perfection, Faith, Hope, Charity, Holy Fear,
Humility, Patience, Obedience, Fortitude, Poverty of
Spirit, Contempt for Worldly Things, true Discretion,
Purity of Intention and other like virtues ; and lastly,
for such lesser virtues ' which will yet help us to keep
the greater ones,' as temperance, control of the tongue,
guardianship of the senses, the gravity and recollectedness of the exterior, sweetness of manner, good example,
strictness with ourselves, and so on ; concluding with
a prayer of most earnest longing and desire for the love
of God, of which the Saint gives one of the most beautiful to be found in spiritual literature.

The most striking thing about this method is its
completeness. It is not merely a meditation as is
commonly understood, distinct from our other prayers
and devotional exercises ; it embraces them all in one
act, which St. Pedro thinks should occupy not less than
an hour and a half to two hours, half an hour of which

GP

he would have devoted to the preparation ' to tune
the viol and calm the imagination.' This, in our
restless and nerve-ridden days, may seem excessive,
though it is largely what we need, and would save
many the fortunes they spend on rest cures and the like,
but it was by no means thought so in St. Pedro's day.
St. Teresa advises that sinners should spend at least
two hours daily in mental prayer (*Life*, viii. 9), although
she admits that she herself ' for some years . . . was
more occupied with the wish to see the end of the time
appointed . . . and in watching the hourglass, than
with other thoughts that were good ' (*ibid*. viii. 10).
And if we take our mental prayer, as St. Pedro clearly
intends, as the prayer of the day, including in it our
morning or evening prayers, examen of conscience,
spiritual reading, thanksgiving, intercession, etc., we
can hardly call the time devoted to it over-long, though
most people nowadays would probably have to divide
it up in separate times during the day. Even then, it
would be a distinct advantage to link all our spiritual
exercises each day to one main, predominant thought
arising out of our mental prayer.

Fra Mattia Bellintani da Salo (*b.* 1534) entered the
new Capuchin Reform some ten years before the death
of St. Pedro of Alcantara, and began to preach throughout Italy in 1561. His whole life was that of a ' true
Apostle,' as St. Charles Borromeo called him ; a cease-
less activity founded on prayer (vide *The Capuchins*,
Fr. Cuthbert, O.S.F.C., vol. i., p. 204). Amongst his
many writings is the *pratica dell' orazione mentale, o
vero contemplativa*, in which, having given an explanation
of the Paternoster, he goes on to speak of vocal and
mental prayer, and gives a method for the latter which
he divides into the usual three parts, preparation,
meditation and acts of the will.

I. *Preparation in General* (remote) consists in avoiding

sin and in cultivating the desire for prayer. A noteworthy characteristic of his teaching is his emphasis on
the necessity for this desire which brings us to prayer,
makes it fruitful, and preserves us from worldly thoughts
and that frittering away of time in unnecessary things
which hinder and disturb so much of our life.

The Immediate Preparation is made by two profound
acts.

(1) Of Humility of Heart.

(2) Of Contrition for our Sins.

II. *Meditation.* The subject should be divided into
points, so that the mind, proceeding logically and
easily by degrees, may better take in the whole. This
part of the method is most important for beginners,
since they need matter to kindle the fire of desires and
affections of the will.

III. *Acts of the Will*, in which the soul is drawn
to Him upon Whom she has meditated, and pours
herself out in acts of fear, of contrition, of desire,
hope and of love. From these are derived the resolutions and prayers with which our prayer should
conclude.

(1) The definite purpose of amendment and of a
deeper love for God.

(2) The oblation of one's whole self to Him.

(3) Acts of praise, thanksgiving and love.

M. Bremond describes the method of Père Joseph du
Tremblay as ' one of the most stimulating, most attrac-
tive and simplest that I know of,' and remarks on the
little success attained, either in his own or in later times,
of the author's *Introduction à la Vie spirituelle par une facile
méthode d'oraison*, ' one of the most beautiful works of our
religious literature ' (*Histoire littéraire du Sentiment
Religieux en France*, vol. ii., chap. iii., sect. 5).

The method consists of three parts :

I. *The Preparation*, in which are four acts :
(1) Of making a right intention.
(2) Of profound humiliation.
(3) Of recalling to mind the subject chosen.
(4) Of withdrawal from distractions.

II. *The Meditation.* The application of the memory, imagination and intellect to the subject in four acts, by which we seek a knowledge
(1) Of God, the prototype of the particular perfection manifested in the mystery we are considering.
(2) Of oneself.
(3) Of what our Lord does or suffers in this mystery.
(4) Of the end for which He works or suffers.

In an hour's prayer, about twenty minutes are to be spent on this part.

III. *Affections of the Will.*
(1) Of Oblation.
(2) Of Petition.
(3) Of Imitation.
(4) Of Union.

It will be seen that this method, whilst reminiscent of the Ignatian plan, is infused with the Franciscan spirit, and intended primarily, as it was, for Capuchin novices, is designed to lead them to the higher degrees of prayer. The first act of the meditation proper, too, emphasises that note, which was to become so prominent in Bérulle and the Oratorian School, of the pre-eminence of God Whose perfections and ways should ever be the first object of our worship and our prayer. We shall see this conception developed to its fullest extent by St. John Eudes.

CHAPTER III

Carmelite

WHILST the Carmelite School of spirituality tends towards contemplation, as the Prologue to the Constitutions of the Discalced Carmelites states – ' By a disposition of the Divine Will . . . our principal end is contemplation and the love of Divine things ' – and so is largely affective even in the earlier stages of prayer, it does not neglect discursive prayer, a fact to be remembered by those who are tempted to tread the mystic path without it. St. Teresa herself, like St. Jane Frances de Chantal, though she desires her daughters to practise the simplest forms of affective prayer, and insists always that prayer consists ' not in thinking much but in loving much ' (*Foundations*, Bk. III., chap. v.), yet has no doubt that mental prayer is necessary in the early ways of the spiritual life (*Way of Perfection*, Bk. V., chap. xix.). Indeed, in speaking of the highest degrees of prayer, she frequently insists on the need there may be of returning to meditation, which would hardly be possible if it had never been learnt and practised diligently.

St. John of the Cross says plainly, ' I do not want anyone to be mistaken as to what I think about the state of beginners ; meditation, the acts and discursive exercises in which the imagination plays its part are indispensable. This necessity arises from the fact that the soul requires matter upon which to exercise herself interiorly, of that which allows her to find a sensible taste of spiritual things' (*The Dark Night of the Soul*, Bk. II., p. 3, Spanish ed., 1912). Joseph of the Holy Spirit

(*d.* 1736), the last of the great Spanish mystics, says :
' Contemplation, unless preceded by meditation, is
dangerous for the soul ' (*Theol. Myst.*, Scol. I., Disp.
xxvii. 11).

In the nineteenth chapter of the *Way of Perfection*
St. Teresa speaks of the 'many suitable books written
by good authors . . . containing meditations for every
day of the week . . . these books contain excellent
teaching and a good method for the beginning and
conclusion of mental prayer.'   She had in mind such
works as the *Vita Christi* of Ludolph the Carthusian, the
Treatise on Prayer of Luis of Granada, the *Art of Serving
God* of Alonzo of Madrid, and the *Treatise on Prayer and
Meditation* of St. Pedro of Alcantara, all of which she
was familiar with.   She defines mental prayer as
' using the understanding much ' (*Inter. Castle*, M. VI.,
chap. vii. 12) ; it consists ' in thinking over and realising
what and with Whom we speak, and who we are that
presume to address this great Sovereign.   To consider
this and other matters, such as how little we serve Him,
and how greatly we should do so, is mental prayer '
(*Way*, xxv. 2).   The gate by which we enter the interior
castle of the soul, and so gain that innermost mansion
wherein God dwells, ' is prayer and meditation ' –
' I advise everyone to practise it, even though they do
not possess the virtues, for this is the first step to obtain
them all ; it is most essential for all Christians to begin
this practice ' (*Way*, xvi. 2).   Before vocal prayer, since
this, to be good, must also be mental, ' a considerable
time should be spent first in meditation . . . that you
may realise Whose presence you are approaching, and
to Whom you are about to speak, keeping in mind
Whom you are addressing ' (*Way*, xxii. 3, 5).   ' To
understand these truths is to practise mental prayer '
(*ibid.* 6).   In several places she mentions suitable
subjects for this kind of prayer.   ' The life and death of
our Lord, and all we owe Him . . . let us begin by

considering the mercy God showed us by giving us His only Son ; let us not stop here, but go on to reflect upon all the mysteries of His glorious life . . . some part of the Passion, such as Christ's apprehension, dwelling on this mystery, and considering the points in detail to be pondered and thought over. . . . This is an admirable and very beautiful kind of prayer' (*Inter. Castle*, M. VI., chap. vii. 12, 13 ; cf. *Life*, xiii. 19, 20). Even those who have attained to contemplation, 'when the fire in our hearts does not burn and we do not feel the presence of God, must search for Him as He would have us do' (*ibid*. ii.), meditating upon the mysteries of the Incarnate Life, 'especially when these events are celebrated by the Catholic Church,' so that 'we shall not stand like blockheads, wasting our time in the hope of again receiving what we before enjoyed' (*ibid*. ii. 14). 'Meditation on the creature, and on His power in creating them, may be at times as pleasing unto Him as meditation on Himself, the Creator' (*Foundations*, vi. 7).

Of her own prayer she writes : 'At first, meditation on Thy grandeurs was an aid to me, and showed me more clearly my own immeasurable baseness' (*Exclamation* i.), and, 'This was my method of prayer ; as I could not make reflections with my understanding, I contrived to picture Christ within me ; and I used to find myself the better for thinking of those mysteries of His life during which He was most lonely. . . . I did many simple things of this kind ; and in particular I used to find myself most at home in the prayer of the Garden, whither I went in His company. I wished, if it had been possible, to wipe away that painful sweat from His face. . . . I believe my soul gained very much in this way, because I began to practise prayer [*oracion*] without knowing what it was' (*Life*, ix. 4 ; cf. iv. 10). Later, in speaking of the difficulties and rewards of fidelity to meditation she adds, 'These labours have their reward, I know it ; for I am one who underwent them for many years ' (*Life*, xi.).

For those who, like herself, as she frequently tells us, ' cannot pursue a train of thought nor restrain the freaks of imagination,' she suggests the reading of a book of devotion so as to learn how to collect the thoughts (her own early practice for many years), to meditate on the words those Divine lips uttered ' ; and, more especially, ' first of all, you must make your examen of conscience, say the Confiteor and make the Sign of the Cross – then, as you are alone, seek for some companion – and where could you find a better one than the Master ? . . . Picture this same Lord close beside you. See how lovingly, how humbly He is teaching you . . . practise it, practise it ? . . . I am not now asking you to meditate upon Him, nor to produce great thoughts, nor to feel deep devotion : I only ask you to look at Him ' (*Way*, xxvi.).

Even those who can make use of their understanding she advises not ' to spend the whole of their time in that way ; for though it be most meritorious, yet they must not, when prayer is sweet, suppose that there will never be a Sunday or a time when no work ought to be done. They think it lost time to do otherwise ; but I think that loss is their greatest gain. Let them rather place themselves in the presence of Christ and, without fatiguing the understanding, converse with Him, and in Him rejoice without wearying themselves in search-ing out reasons ' (*Life*, xiii. 17). She outlines a medita-tion on the scourging of our Lord, in which ' it is well that we should make reflections for a time . . . but a person should not always fatigue himself in making these reflections, but rather let him remain there with Christ, in the silence of his understanding. If he is able, let him employ himself in looking upon Christ, Who is looking upon him ; let him accompany Him and make his petitions to Him ; let him humble himself and delight himself in Christ, and keep in mind that he never deserved to be there ' (*Life*, xiii. 31, 32).

St. Teresa's teaching as to the conditions of mental prayer is so valuable and so imbued with her own spirit that it must be considered in any attempt to understand the Carmelite ideal. *The Way of Perfection*, specially written for her nuns, naturally begins by referring to the Rule and Constitutions and her own previous teaching upon them, but she deals especially with three matters, taken from the Constitutions, of which, she says, ' it is essential for us to understand how much they help us to preserve that peace, both interior and exterior, which our Lord so strongly enjoined ' (*Way*, iv. 3). They are love of one another, detachment from all created things, and true humility. The latter, fruit of self-knowledge, she continually insists upon as the one and only foundation of the life of prayer. ' Your foundation must not consist of prayer and contemplation alone ; for if you do not acquire the virtues and practise them, you will always be dwarfs, and please God no worse may befall you ' (*Inter. Castle*, M. VII., chap. iv. 12, 13). Humility ' is the principal aid to prayer ' (*Way*, xvii. 1) ; ' it is not only a *good* way, but the best of all ways, to try and enter first by the rooms where humility is practised,' but in order to gain self-knowledge ' the soul should sometimes cease thinking of itself to rise in meditation on the greatness and majesty of its God. . . . It is a great grace of God to practise self-examination, but too much is as bad as too little, as they say, believe me, by God's help, we shall advance more by contemplating the Divinity than by keeping our eyes fixed on ourselves. . . . I think we shall never learn to know ourselves, except by endeavouring to know God, for beholding His greatness we are struck by our own baseness. His Purity shows our foulness, and by meditating on His Humility we find how very far we are from being humble' (*Inter. Castle*, M. I., chap. i. 9, 10).

'We must walk in great humility; it is failure in this, I believe, which is the fault of those who make no progress' (*Inter. Castle*, M. III., chap. ii.). 'Where there is true humility, although God should never grant supernatural gifts [*regalos*] He will give a peace and resignation which will satisfy the soul even more' (*Inter. Castle*, M. III., chap. i.).

On this foundation 'always begin and finish your prayer with the thought of your own nothingness'; continually looked to and renewed, we must build up the house of our prayer life, beginning with a 'great and most resolute determination never to halt until we reach our journey's end, happen what may, whatever the consequences are, cost what it will' (*Way*, xxi. 1). Especially she warns us against those who tell us that we may injure our health or may fall into illusions. 'Take no notice of the warnings people give you or the dangers they suggest. It is absurd to suppose that one could travel along a road full of bandits to reach a costly treasure without running any risks. . . . A want of humility, of the virtues, may endanger you, but prayer – prayer! Never would God permit this!' (*Way*, xxi. 4).

An entire generosity is another requisite; we must give ourselves wholly 'not as one who gives a thing, meaning to take it back again.' Another reason why our resolution should be firm is that it 'lessens the Devil's power of tempting us. He is very frightened of determined souls, knowing by experience how they hurt him – if the enemies of our souls find us fickle, irresolute and wanting in perseverance in the right path, they will never leave it alone, day or night, and will suggest to it endless fears and difficulties. We must act courageously, then, knowing that all depends upon our gaining the victory, and without any doubt that unless we allow ourselves to be defeated, we are sure to succeed' (*Way*, xxiii.; cf. *Life*, xi. 20, xiii. 3, 4).

'His Majesty loves and seeks courageous souls ; but they must be humble in their ways and have no confidence in themselves ' (*Life*, xiii. 3).

Nothing is more important in the early stages of the spiritual life than to resist that ' temptation of beginners,' the reformation of others. ' Let us look at our own faults, and not at other people's. . . . We ought not to insist on everyone following in our footsteps, nor to take upon ourselves to give instructions in spirituality when, perhaps, we do not even know what it is. Zeal for the good of souls, though given us by God, may often lead us astray ' (*Inter. Castle*, M. III., chap ii. 19).

' There is another temptation, which is very common ; when people begin to have pleasure in the rest and the fruit of prayer, they will have everyone else be very spiritual also. To desire this is not wrong, but to try to bring it about may not be right, except with great discretion and great reserve, without any appearance of teaching.' She gives an illustration from her own experience, for she had made others endeavour to pray, only to find that they contrasted what she said of the blessedness of prayer with her lack of the virtues, in spite of her prayer. ' And thus, during many years, only three persons were the better for what I said to them ; but now that our Lord has made me stronger in virtue, in the course of two or three years, many persons have profited ' (*Life*, xiii. 11, 12).

The soul that would enter the second mansion must seek to ' withdraw itself from all unnecessary cares and business, as far as compatible with one's state of life. This is so essential, that unless done at first, I think it impossible ever to reach the principal room [i.e. Divine union], or even to remain where he is, without great risk of losing what is already gained ' (*Inter. Castle*, M. I., chap. ii. 16). ' You know that His Majesty taught us (Matt. vi. 6) that the first point is that prayer should be made in solitude ' (*Way*, xxiv. 3).

We must gain the habit of retiring within ourselves, and this means both detachment and mortification. ' Prayer and self-indulgence do not go together ' (*Way*, iv. 2).

No advice is more necessary than that no one ' must expect to reap the reward at the beginning ; . . . what a farce it is ! Here we are, with a thousand obstacles, drawbacks and imperfections within ourselves, our virtues so newly-born that they have scarcely the strength to act (and God grant that they exist at all !), yet we are not ashamed to expect sweetness in prayer and to complain of feeling dryness in prayer.' If our Lord gives us consolations, let us thank Him for them, but ' His Majesty knows what is good for us, it is not for us to advise Him how to treat us . . . the sole aim of one beginning to practise prayer should be to endure trials, and to resolve to the utmost of her power to conform her own will to the will of God ' (*Inter. Castle*, M. II., chap. i. 14, 15).

We must learn, too, how to treat our faults aright. God allows us to fall in order ' to teach us to be more on our guard in future, and to see whether we grieve much at offending Him. Therefore if you lapse into sin some-times, do not lose heart and give up trying to advance, for God will draw good even out of our falls ' (*Inter. Castle*, M. II., chap. i. 16).

Much that the Saint says about the treatment of distractions and aridity will be found in the chapter on difficulties. The last thing to be noted here is her insistence that the true test of prayer is the practice of the virtues and good works – ' not sweetness in prayer, ecstasies, visions and other divine favours of the same kind ' (*Way*, xviii. 5). ' When I see people very anxious to know what sort of prayer they practise, covering their faces and afraid to move or think, lest they should lose what tenderness and devotion they feel, I know how little they understand how to attain union with

God, since they think it consists in such things as this. No, my sisters, no ; our Lord expects *works* from us ! ' (*Inter. Castle*, M. V., chap. iii. 11).

The first Carmelite to give a distinct method of mental prayer is John of Jesus-Mary (1564–1615), who was mainly instrumental in spreading the reform beyond the borders of Spain, notably in Italy. His *Instruccion de los novicies* became the text-book of the Carmelite novitiate, and it is in the second chapter of Part III. of this work that we find his Method of Mental Prayer. He follows the divisions given by Luis of Granada and St. Pedro of Alcantara, preparation, reading, meditation, thanksgiving, oblation and petition.

I. *Preparation.*

Remote

(*a*) The avoidance of occasions of distraction.

(*b*) The renouncement of superfluous occupations.

Immediate

(1) Consideration of the Divine Majesty, leading to reverential awe inspired by His transcendence and to love evoked by the thought of His condescension.

(2) Consideration of our own nothingness and sinfulness in order to gain humility and penitence, basis of true prayer.

II. *The Reading*, which may precede or follow the preparation. We must not seek for knowledge in itself, as in study, but for such knowledge as shall lead us to love God more. Any point which especially strikes us should be dwelt upon, for it is such thoughts which move the affections and the will.

III. *The Meditation* ' is nothing else than a discourse addressed by the intellect to the will,' with the end that we may assimilate and be penetrated by a particular truth, and so led to prayer, ' which nourishes and fortifies the will and impels it to action.' Thus, the shorter and more condensed the meditation is, the better the prayer will be.

IV. *The Thanksgiving* for the blessings of God, particularly those which our meditation has brought before our mind. In this act we should unite ourselves with the whole family of God in heaven and earth, especially with the heart of Jesus and of the Blessed Virgin Mary, in order to offer to so good a God all that immense sum of thanksgiving as from a single heart.

V. *The Oblation.* A fourfold act, springing from a heart full of gratitude.

(1) As a sacrifice of thanksgiving and praise in union with the merits of our Lord and His Holy Mother.

(2) As a sacrifice of expiation for our sins.

(3) As a peace-offering, in order to obtain all that we need in order to arrive at the possession of God Himself.

(4) As an affirmation of our faith in God and of the homage we desire to render to Him, and of closer union with Him.

VI. *The Petition* – ' for have we not the right to claim that for which we have offered the price in advance ? '

With confidence, then, in the goodness of God, the Passion of His Son and the Divine promise, ' Whatsoever ye ask, believe that you shall have it and it shall be given you,' we beg the pardon of our sins, and for all things of which we have need ; above all, for that sovereign good, the joy of the Vision of God. And that we may attain to that blessed end we ask for humility and all other virtues, for victory over our temptations, especially over our ruling passion. Nor shall we forget the needs of others, excluding no one and especially interceding for Holy Church.

The Ven. John adds several notes of explanation which, he says, require serious attention. Answering the question as to whether it is necessary always to adhere strictly to the method, he replies that whilst it will be found useful to do so unless God gives the soul some particular *attrait*, yet it is not absolutely necessary. For to pray by affective motions of the will is the whole purpose of the method, and whatever part most aids to this should be centred upon and remained in.

In the meditation proper we should picture the persons and things of the particular subject we have chosen as near to us, or even within us, as a help to avoid distractions. Yet this exercise of the imagination must not be too vivid, for it is possible ' to mistake our representations for the reality itself' and so fall into illusion. The warning is, of course, as old as Cassian, and is constantly repeated by spiritual writers, nor is it unneeded to-day, as priests who have to do with the devout are well aware.

It is necessary to guard ourselves against too much reliance in images formed in our minds by our thoughts, for, as a matter of fact, the same image – that of our Lord, for instance – may be the work of God, of the Devil or of our own imagination, and in all cases we must not trust our own judgment on such matters, but that of an experienced director.

Reflections should be used with moderation, more insistence being laid on the affections of the will. In all things the will should govern ; care must be taken not to strain the mind by violent efforts ; we shall only come to taste God by habituating ourselves in peace. We must not rest in every emotion (*tout goût spirituel*) which we may experience, for some are but on the surface and easily dissipate themselves without bearing any real fruit.

' The spirit bloweth where it listeth ' ; it is as the whistling of the shepherd calling his sheep to pasture, so that if in our prayer we are drawn towards some thought which is not in the subject we have prepared, we must not hesitate to follow its call, since it will lead us to true prayer.

Those who are experienced, by long use, in meditation need but spend a short time in reflections, for their will, strongly convinced, will be habitually well disposed to prayer, and this is a sign of virtue or force of soul ; there are others who also need to reflect little, being of a sensitive and impressionable nature : great attention is necessary to distinguish between these two quite different classes.

In the case of distractions, he recommends great care in coming to our prayer – guard of the eyes and against idle gossiping ; if at the time of prayer distractions persist in spite of our efforts to drive them away, we should recite some vocal prayers slowly and meditatively, or even read some book in the same way.

No fixed rule can be given as to subjects of prayer for each individual, ' the best is that out of which each one draws most profit ' ; but as this depends both on the individual mentally and the Divine attraction, nothing should be decided without advice.

It will be seen that the Ven. Carmelite holds the balance very wisely between the action of grace upon the soul and the need of human efforts under the influence of a responding to grace. He knows that prayer is an art, and so needs a sound and strong discipline as its foundation. He will have his disciples follow a method, not, however, for the sake of the method, but that, as in all art, they may rise to that perfect execution which is only possible to those who have submitted themselves to the guidance of a master and the rules he imposes. But he never loses sight of the fact – and it is a characteristic of all the true teachers of the spiritual life – that the Holy Spirit is the one

Conductor in the path of prayer, and that no method
or director is meant to do more than aid the soul to
follow the *attrait* of the Divine Spirit the more easily
and freely.

A brief reference may be made to two other Carmelites
of the Reform who speak of mental prayer.

The first, the Ven. Thomas de Jésus (1568–1627),
was the founder of the Carmel Reform in Belgium and
the author of treatises *De Oratione Divina* and *La Meil-
leure Part*, in which he defines meditation as ' not a dry
research into Divine things, but an investigation accompanied by prayers, affections and compunction of
heart.' A later writer, Joseph of the Holy Spirit
(*d.* 1736), makes the common six divisions of mental
prayer and says that meditation ' is an act of the intellect passing from one consideration to another . . . its
occupation above all is the search for that devotion
which determines the will to love, so that love is really
the final end of the act of the intellect ' (*Mystica
Isagoge*, Lib. IV., ix. 2, Tom. I., edit. 1720). Meditation proper contains three acts, the representation, the
reflection and the calm attention. ' The first is an act
of the memory, representing to the intelligence, after
the reading and preparation, the subject to be meditated. Much time need not be spent on this. Then
follows the reflection, more prolonged : then the
tranquil attention, by means of which, without effort,
the intellect perceives quietly, for example, all the
ingratitude of the sinner and the goodness of his
Saviour, the Christ suffering. The soul will dwell more
upon this act than upon the preceding in order to pass
to the rest of the classical parts of mental prayer.'

CHAPTER IV

Salesian

IT is not too much to say that with St. François de
Sales the practice of mental prayer passes from the
cloister into the world. He does not merely repeat
what had always been said – that the Christian living
in the world is bound to seek perfection no less than
the priest or religious – but dots the i's and crosses the
t's, emphasises the fact that such perfection obviously
cannot be sought for by all in exactly the same way (*Vie
Dévote*, chap. iii.), at the same time telling how those
' who live in towns, in households, at the Court, who
by reason of their circumstances are obliged to live an
ordinary life in outward show . . . can live in the world
without receiving any worldly taint, can find springs of
sweet piety in the midst of the briny waters of the
world, and can fly among the flames of earthly con-
cupiscences without burning the wings of the holy
desires of the devout life' (*Introduction to the Devout Life*,
Preface, p. xxiii. ; new translation by Fr. Allan Ross).

Few men have been more fitted for such a work. Of
good family, destined by his father for the law, educated in Paris and Padua, having travelled extensively
in France and Italy, nourished on both the Italian and
Spanish spirituality, knowing intimately the spiritual
leaders of his day, spending the early years of his
priesthood in apostolic labours among the Chablais,
later becoming the director of numerous souls living in
the world, as well as of religious, as familiar with the
common ways of life as with those of Courts, with
merchants and their wives no less than religious and
clergy, it is little wonder that his *Vie Dévote* and the

Traite de l'Amour de Dieu have become classics of Catholic literature and devotion, and indeed of a large world outside the Church, for, like his namesake of Assisi, he is revered by Protestants, although they usually only know him by his writings, and that in abridged, mutilated or misleading translations.

St. François teaching on prayer in general, in the *Introduction*, the *Love of God* and his letters, is most valuable, and I shall have occasion to use much of it in the third part of this book. His method of mental prayer for those living in the world is found in the second part of the *Introduction to the Devout Life*, and consists of four parts.

I. *The Preparation*, in two acts.
    (*a*) Placing oneself in the presence of God.
    (*b*) Invoking His assistance.

(*a*) There are four principal ways of making the first act.

(1) ' Consists in a lively and attentive apprehension of the omnipresence of God, which means that God is in everything and everywhere . . . say with all your heart and to your heart : O my heart, my heart, God is truly here.'

(2) By reflecting on the presence of God within the soul residing ' in a special manner in the heart.'

(3) By considering ' our Saviour Who in His humanity looks from Heaven upon all persons in the world.'

(4) By an act of the imagination alone ' representing to ourselves the Saviour in His sacred humanity, as though He were near to us.' If the prayer is made before the Blessed Sacrament, ' then this presence will be real and not imaginary ; for the species and appearances of bread are as it were a tapestry, behind which our Lord really sees and observes us.' Only one of these acts must be used at a time, and that briefly and simply.

(*b*) The invocation is an act of deep humility by which the soul, realising the presence of God, ' prostrates herself with profound reverence, acknowledging her unworthiness to appear before so sovereign a Majesty, yet, knowing that His goodness desires it, she asks of Him the grace to serve Him well, and to adore Him in this meditation.' Short and fervent words may be used if desired, and we should invoke our Guardian Angel and the holy persons concerned in the particular mystery we are to meditate upon ' in order that the interior sentiments and movements which they received may be communicated to us.'

(*c*) A third, but not invariable point, is the composition of place, as given by St. Ignatius, which is ' to represent to the imagination the scene of the mystery . . . as though it were actually taking place in our presence.'

II. *The Considerations*, ' the action of the understanding, which we call meditation, no other thing than one or many considerations made in order to stir up our affections towards God and Divine things.' If one thought gives sufficient ' relish, light and fruit,' we must dwell upon it ; if, however, we ' find nothing to our liking ' in one, we may pass on to another, but always 'quite gently and simply, without undue haste.'

III. *The Affections and Resolutions.* The object of the meditation is to produce ' good movements in the will or affective part of our soul, such as the love of God and of our neighbour, the desire of Heaven, zeal for the salvation of souls, imitation of the life of our Lord, compassion, admiration, joy, fear of God's displeasure, of judgment and of Hell, hatred of sin, confidence in the goodness and mercy of God, confusion for our bad lives in the past ; and in these affections our spirit should expand and extend itself as much as possible.'

But we must not stop at these affectionate acts of the will, but convert them into special and particular resolutions. For example, if we have meditated upon the first word on the Cross we should be moved to imitate the example of our Saviour, not in a vague, general way, but in particular, saying, 'Well, then, I will not hereafter be offended by such and such annoying words, which such and such a person, a neighbour of mine, perhaps, or a servant, may say of me, nor by such and such an affront which may be put upon me by this person or that.'

IV. *The Conclusion*, in three acts :

(*a*) *Of Thanksgiving* for the affections and resolutions we have been led to make and for the goodness and mercy of God revealed in the mystery we have meditated on.

(*b*) *Of Oblation*, offering to God this same goodness and mercy of His, the death, the blood and the virtues of His Son, and, together with these, our own affections and resolutions.

(*c*) *Of Petition*, that God may give us the graces and virtues of His Son, may bless our affections and resolutions and give us grace to put them into practice ; for the Church, our pastors, relations and friends, for all beseeching the aid of our Lady and of the Angels and Saints, and concluding with a Paternoster and Ave.

Spiritual Nosegay. As when we walk about a beautiful garden we desire to carry away a few flowers and enjoy their perfume, so we should gather one or two points from our meditation ' in which we have found most relish and which are most proper for our advancement,' so as to recall and act upon them during the day.

St. François adds ' some very profitable counsels ' on meditation. We must bear in mind the resolutions and intentions we have made in order to practise them during the day, for this is the great fruit of our prayer. To meditate upon virtues without putting them into practice is vain and dangerous, leading us to think we are other than we actually are. We should take care not to dissipate the effect of our prayer, keeping, so far as is possible, silent and recollected, accustoming ourselves to pass from prayer to the duties of our state of life ' with so much gentleness and tranquillity that the spirit be not disturbed thereby,' for since prayer and active work are both according to the will of God, ' we must make the passage from the one to the other in a spirit of humility and devotion.'

If, after we have made the preparation, our hearts are drawn by some special *attrait* towards God, we must ignore the method, for ' it is a general rule that one must never restrain the affections, but always allow them free play when they present themselves.' This was the Saint's constant teaching ; in a letter to a lady he says, ' If it please God to give us affections without reasonings and considerations, it is for us a great grace. The secret of secrets in prayer is to follow attractions in simplicity of heart ' (*Letters to Persons in Religion*, p. 290).

But resolutions should always be made at the end, since they are concerned with particular and familiar objects, and if made earlier in the prayer would be a cause of distraction to us.

It is good to make use of colloquies, speaking to our Lord, to the Angels and Saints, to one's own heart, to sinners and even to inanimate creatures, as the Church does in the Benedicite.

We must not be in the least troubled when we experience dryness or lack of any sensible taste or consolation in our prayer, for we ' should come to holy prayer purely and simply to pay our respects and give proof of our fidelity,' as a courtier goes into the presence chamber of his prince a hundred times a year

45823

only to be seen by him and pay his respects.' We must
not doubt that this is good prayer; indeed, often
of more real value than when we are filled with
consolations; yet we may, in such case, make use of vocal
prayers, ask our Lord to visit us in our unworthiness,
stir up our devotion by outward acts, if we are alone,
as kissing the crucifix, prostrating ourself, etc. Or we
may have recourse to a book, reading it with attention
until moved to devotion.

Such is St. François's method and instructions on
mental prayer for beginners. For his further teaching,
always as sane as it is entirely supernatural, his letters
should be consulted. We must not, however, overlook
what he says at the end of the *Introduction*, replying to the
criticism he anticipates that his book presupposes that
everyone has the gift of mental prayer. It is true, he
says, that the book implies this, and also true that
everyone has not the gift, 'but it is also true that almost
everyone is able to have it, even the most dull-witted,
provided that they have good directors, and that they
be willing to strive to acquire it as much as it deserves'
(*Introd.*, Pt. V., chap. xvii.).

It is true, people do not meditate, think they cannot
meditate, simply because they have not been taught,
or have been taught by an unskilled director, who
knows little, either of the diversity of souls or the
rich abundance of methods which exists. If he does
not succeed with his favourite method – usually the
Ignatian – he abandons them as hopeless instead of
seeking to follow the attraction of the Holy Ghost. At
least he could, as St. François says, get them to pay
attention to reading or hearing read the subjects upon
which mental prayer should be made. But the truth
is that the large majority of our people have never had
a word said to them on the subject, and are amazed to
hear of its necessity and at the immense good they
derive from it.

CHAPTER V

Liguorian

TO those who only know St. Alphonsus di Liguori – and their number is legion – by what they have heard from those with scarcely more knowledge than themselves, of his reputed laxity in moral theology and his 'extreme' mariology, a study of the life, labours and writings of this great and saintly religious and Bishop, with his burning love for Jesus Christ and his consuming zeal for souls, would be a revelation. Few men have crowded even into a long lifetime the work which St. Alphonsus accomplished in the face of incredible difficulties, or left a more striking witness to the spiritual solidity of their life and teaching than such an order as that of the Redemptorists. Unfortunately, a good life of the Saint has yet to be written, but a true estimate of his spirit may be gained from his works and from those of Père Desurmont, mention of which will be found in the bibliography. St. Alphonsus does not give, as St. Ignatius, St. François and others, a detailed method of mental prayer. But it is quite easy to construct one from his teaching, and long use of such a method has proved its peculiar and practical value. I give it first as entirely drawn from the Saint's works and then in a slightly modified form which has been found useful.

I

I. *The Preparation.*

Remote

The brief consideration overnight of the questions,

With Whom do I pray ? Upon what subject ? What particular act ?

I go to pray with God, with our Lord, with our Lady or with the Saints – upon this particular subject – specially seeking this virtue which I shall make central in my acts of prayer.

Proximate

(1) An act of Faith.

(2) An act of humble penitence.

(3) A petition for grace to pray well.

II. *The Body of the Prayer.*

(1) *The Consideration.* Taking the subject chosen, and keeping in mind the particular act of virtue I desire to make, I recall, by reading or memory, that upon which I wish to dwell. Then, exercising my intellect, I reflect or reason upon it, that I may see it more clearly, become more convinced of its truth. As I do so I must make energetic acts of faith, accompanied with prayer for a firmer faith. ' Lord, I believe ; help Thou mine unbelief.' (This is a characteristic Liguorian touch.) I go on to apply this to myself – what is it to me ?

(2) *The Act of Virtue.* This consists of acts of prayer founded on the different virtues necessary to the Christian life, especially penitence, humility, detachment, confidence, love of God. St. Alphonsus attaches great importance to this part of our prayer, for it is here that the will is moved to love and desire the virtues, and until one does so there will be little exterior practice of them. In this he, in common with other saints, has anticipated what our modern psychologists so often vaunt as new discoveries. The constant repetition of a desire tends to its accomplishment. As Pascal says, ' By talking of love we fall in love ; it is the easiest thing in the world.'

(3) *The Prayer of Petition.* No writer on mental prayer

insists so strongly on the prayer of petition as St.
Alphonsus. To him it is almost, if not certainly, the
centre of all, since not only are we in absolute need of
grace, but God has made His gifts conditional on our
desire and search for them. So, in this third part of
our prayer, all the energies of the soul must be bent on
bringing our necessities before God, in beseeching Him
to grant us all graces necessary for our salvation and
sanctification. Above all, we must continually ask for
love and perseverance.

III. *The Resolution*, which is to be both general and
particular. (See Modified Method.)

II

1. *The Preparation.* Kneel quietly for a few moments,
letting your whole self sink into a state of rest, that you
may realise the presence of God. Then make the
following acts slowly :

Act of Faith. O my God, I believe that Thou art here
present, and I adore Thee from the depths of my own
nothingness.

Act of Humility. O my God, I acknowledge that for
my sins I deserve to be in Hell. I am sorry that I have
offended Thee, because Thou art so good, and I beg, by
Thy grace, that I may never sin again.

Petition for Light. O Eternal Father, for the sake of
Jesus and Mary, give me light in this prayer that I may
make it to Thy glory and the good of my soul.

Paternoster. Ave Maria. Gloria.

Invoke the aid of your guardian angel and patrons.

2. *The Meditation.* Fix your attention on the subject
you have chosen. Make a mental picture of it as
clearly as you can, though without effort or strain. As
you reflect quietly upon what you see, what it means,
and especially to you, you will be moved to make acts
of prayer, adoration, praise, thanksgiving, humility,
penitence, love, etc. – any acts of prayer, in any words,

in any order. Petitions for spiritual gifts may be added.
Go on until your time is up, constantly recurring to
your picture and renewing your fervour.

3. *The Conclusion.* Which should be short, intense
and business-like. It consists of three acts of resolution
and three of prayer.

(1) A general resolution to avoid all sin, mortal and
venial, to-day.

(2) To give yourself entirely to God in all things
to-day.

(3) A particular resolution to avoid or to do something for our Lord to-day.

Three Acts of Prayer

(1) An act of thanksgiving for the grace received in
your prayer.

(2) A fervent petition for grace to keep your resolution.

(3) A Pater and Ave for the Church, for sinners and
for the holy souls.

Conclude by kneeling at our Lady's feet, saying the
Memorare, and asking her blessing.

The main points of St. Alphonsus's teaching on
prayer will throw light on the method here given, and
may be summarised as follows :

The principal ends of mental prayer are, first, to
unite ourselves to God, ' and that which unites us to
God is not so much the good thoughts of our spirit as the
good movements of our will or holy affections. Now
the affections which are produced in meditation are
acts of humility, of confidence, resignation, renouncement, but above all of love and of contrition. . . . But
the perfection of love consists in the conformity of our
will with the will of God ; . . . thus St. Teresa says
(*Inter. Castle*, M. II., chap. i.), " All that it is necessary
to seek in prayer is to conform our will to God's will :

be well persuaded that in this consists the highest
perfection – he who most excels in this practice will
receive the greatest gifts from God and make most
progress in the interior life"' (*Œuvres Ascétiques*, Tome
III., p. 265, edit. D. P. Dujardin, Paris, 1881). The
Saint goes on to say that many seek only themselves
in their prayer, their hearts being full of earthly things,
and thus they do not find God. Again he quotes St.
Teresa (all his writings are a catena of quotations from
Holy Scripture, the Fathers and the Saints) : ' Detach
your heart from all things and seek God ; you will find
Him.' Our prayer can only unite us to God when it is
a search for God by a constant detachment and solitude
of heart.

Second, to obtain the graces of God necessary to
advance us in the way of salvation, St. Alphonsus
constantly insists that the principal fruit of meditation
is prayer. It is this insistence, indeed, which especially
distinguishes his method from others. We do not
reflect in meditation in order to reflect or to gain
knowledge, but in order to pray. ' Meditation is like
a needle after which comes a thread of gold, composed
of affections, prayers and resolutions' (*Véritable Épouse
de J. C.*, chap. xv. 11). Meditation is necessary, for
unless we think about God we shall have nothing to say
to God. It is not a study of God, but a looking at Him,
which draws our hearts and wills to Him. ' So when
you have meditated a point, and feel yourself moved by
some good thought, raise your heart to God and offer to
Him fervent acts of humility, of confidence, of thanksgiving, but above all frequently repeat, in your prayer,
acts of contrition and love . . . chains of gold which
attach our soul to God.'

Third, to seek, not spiritual sweetnesses in prayer,
but to learn what God desires of us. Mental prayer is
nothing else but a conversation of the soul with God ;
we express our sentiments, desires, fears, petitions :

and God speaks in our heart, making known His goodness, His love, and that which we ought to do in order
to please Him.

But we shall not always find consolations in our
prayer ; more often, the saintly soul suffers from
aridity. . . . ' It is in this state that we profit most.
Humiliate yourself, then, and resign yourself, seeing
yourself without fervour, without desires, and as incapable of making any act of virtue . . . content yourself
with saying, " Help me, O Lord ! have pity on me,
abandon me not." Have recourse to Mary our
Mother and Consolatrix. Happy are those who in
desolations remain faithful to their prayer ! God will
fill them with His graces.'

Yet we are not to reject consolations. ' Far from
rejecting Divine consolations, as some false mystics
maintain we ought to do, let us receive them with
gratitude, without, however, stopping to enjoy them, or
take complacence in them. . . . These spiritual consolations are gifts far more precious than all the riches and
honours of the world ' (*The Love of Jesus Christ*, xv.).

St. Alphonsus thought that most people needed a
book of meditations to guide them in the choice of
subjects and the arrangement of points, and composed
many such books himself, which will be found especially valuable for beginners. At the same time he
would not have anything formal in prayer, for ' it is a
familiar conversation and an intimate union with
God ' (*Vérit. Épouse de J. C.*, chap. xv.). ' It is wrong
to imagine that to speak to God with a great confidence
and familiarity is a lack of respect to His infinite
Majesty . . . not only is He not indignant with us when
we do so, but He loves us to go to Him with the liberty
and tender affection which children show to their
mother ' (*Manière de converser familièrement avec Dieu*,
chap. i.).

He insists strongly that the preparation to our prayer

is most important and that it is very necessary that the
act of the presence of God should be one of a living
faith (*Vérit. Épouse de J. C.*, chap. xvi. 11). That is, it is
not an act of intellectual consideration or, still less, of
feeling, but a firm and implicit Credo. God *is* present;
all we have to do is to acknowledge His Presence,
placing ourselves deliberately in that Presence by an
act of pure faith. The heart of prayer consists in the
affections and resolutions awakened in the will by
reflection upon Divine truths or mysteries. These may
be as diverse as possible, covering the whole of our
Godward desires and our needs, but St. Alphonsus
especially indicates four acts which should find their
place in all our prayer , of confident humility, of
contrition, of love and of perseverance. ' I implore the
reader not to grow weary of my constant demand that
he should ask for love and perseverance. For those
two gifts contain all the rest : to obtain them is to
obtain all ' (*Préparation à la Mort*, Préface).

Mental prayer without resolutions would be not only
useless but dangerous ; they are the true end toward
which all our prayer should converge. We ought
daily, and for that day alone – since it is easy to do for
one day what might seem a hopeless task for a long
period, and since our Lord only bids us consider the
task and ask for the grace for each day as it comes – to
make a fervent general resolution of giving ourselves
entirely to God and of avoiding sin : and a particular
resolution concerned with the immediate needs of our
spiritual life.

Mental prayer is, morally speaking, necessary for
all the faithful ; it is, then, much more necessary for
priests. ' Ah, gentlemen,' cries St. Alphonsus, preaching to priests and ordinands, ' do not think that mental
prayer is an exercise only to be practised by solitaries
and not by those occupied in the active life. Tertullian
calls all priests *Genus deditum orationi et contemplationi.* . . .

I repeat it, we must not be content with a quarter or half-hour's prayer, but more, more. Find me an apostolic worker who has been sanctified without much prayer ; I have never heard of one.' He will have no excuses. I, says one, cannot meditate ; I find nothing in it but desolation, distraction and temptation. The saint replies, You do not go to prayer to find pleasure for yourself, but to seek and to please God. Our Lord is pleased with your good intentions, your perseverance in spite of difficulties, and will abundantly recompense your efforts. To abandon prayer because of lack of consolation, distractions and so on, is to give pleasure to the Devil ; it is the one thing he desires. Without mental prayer one can hardly have the priestly spirit.

My time, says another, is devoted to study ; I cannot afford to spend it on prayer. But St. Paul writes to St. Timothy, ' Attend to thyself and to doctrine,' that is, apply yourself first to prayer for your own sanctification and then to study for the salvation of your neighbour. Unless we are saintly, how shall we sanctify others ? And the science of the Saints, which consists in loving God, is to be found, not in books, but in prayer. I do not deny that study is useful and necessary for priests ; but the most necessary study is the Crucifix.

A third says, I should like to pray, but my sermons, the confessional and other activities occupy all my time. St. Alphonsus replies, You are a priest, and I praise you for your work for souls but not for that you forget your own soul. The truth is your work of apostolic activity is useless without prayer ; you deceive yourself in so acting, for, noble as such a work is, it is no less dangerous for him who embarks upon it without prayer. If you would draw others to God you must draw near to God yourself. ' One priest of mediocre knowledge but animated by a great zeal will gain more souls for God than any number of learned but luke-warm ones' (*Selva ou Dignité et devoirs des prêtres*, Instruct. v.).

Man of prayer himself, St. Alphonsus made it the basis of all his reform of the clergy and of a priestly education. Skilled in every branch of theology, and using every care that his clergy should be well in-structed, his greatest wish was that their lives should be rooted in that practice of prayer from which alone apostolic labours derive force and fruitfulness. And we, who sometimes dare to criticise him, might better sit at his feet and humbly learn from one who did more for souls in a single week than most of us accomplish in a lifetime.

The consideration of mental prayer according to the Liguorian method would hardly be complete without some reference to the explanations of it given by Père Desurmont, one of the ablest and most faithful modern exponents of the Redemptorist tradition.

He defines mental prayer as ' an application of the faculties of the soul to the things concerning the end of man, under the form of a conversation with heaven ' (*La Charité sacerdotale*, Tome I., p. 402), or as ' nothing else but an interior work of the soul occupied with itself and with God ' (*Le Retour continuel à Dieu*, p. 139). It is founded solely on faith ; all prayer should be rooted in a firm belief that ' the person with Whom I would speak is truly present with me, and that my conversation with Him is not a vain imagination but an absolute reality.' Such an act of faith does not seek for vision or feeling of the Divine presence ; it is a simple and energetic ' I believe.' The essential conditions of all prayer are that it should be real, a conviction that one is not speaking ' into the air ' but to a Person ; simple, ' natural as to tone without any desire of emotion, familiar and ordinary ' ; and appropriate to one's actual state. It is the actual self which must pray ;

' the greatest of sinners can pray provided only that he prays as a sinner ; the man of evil will can and ought to pray ; but as a man of evil will . . . the lukewarm as lukewarm, the just as a just man ' ; the one essential is that each comes as he is in reality. Two other things facilitate our prayer ; first, the liberty of using vocal prayer during the meditation ; and second, freedom on repeating the same thing over and over again, as does the Church in the liturgy, litanies and the like.

The act of mental prayer has four divisions :

(1) *The Meditation or Consideration.* ' For we pray in order to gain good thoughts.'

(2) *The Act of Virtue*, tending toward the renewal of a good will.

(3) *The Prayer*, in which we seek the grace and blessing of God.

(4) *The Resolution*, since we pray in order to do more firmly what is right.

The act of meditation, which should not occupy more than a third of the whole time given to prayer, should not consist of long reflections or reasonings, but of a simple and attentive consideration of the subject chosen. The essentials of good meditation are this simple looking at a truth or fact, acts of faith in it, accompanied by prayer for the increase of faith. ' Lord, I believe ; increase my faith.'

The act of virtue which follows is founded in the fact that it is in and by prayer that we become virtuous, for in our prayer we are most capable of good thoughts and desires, receive clearer light upon them, and that we are most in possession of ourselves. Here, then, we should specially make acts of penitence, humility, detachment and love of God, since it is these virtues we most need to regulate our exterior. We should endeavour to make these acts as perfectly as we can, not in intensity, but in quality, as, for instance, that our acts of penitence should be inspired by love rather

Ip

than by fear. Yet we must realise that we cannot gain
virtue by our own effort, but only by the gift of grace,
and, as Père Libermann so constantly insists, we must
not try to precede grace or want to do things too
perfectly, but simply and desiringly place ourselves in
our Lord's hands and be led in all things as He wills.
And when we perceive the poverty of our acts, how
very far they are from being perfect, let us make known
to God our sorrow for this, and our desire of making
them more perfect according to His will.

The prayer of petition, in which we bring all our
needs before God, should also be as perfect as we can
make it, and that both as regards the dispositions which
accompany it and the things it asks.   Humility and
confidence, born of a deep sense of our nothingness
and unworthiness, and of the mercy of God, fount of
all that He does outside Himself, are the two essential
dispositions to all prayer.   St. Alphonsus, as has been
said, attaches the greatest importance to this part of our
prayer, in which he would have us beg from God all
that we desire for His glory and our own salvation.
' The true prayer [*prière*] in our meditation (*l'oraison*),'
says Père Desurmont, ' is the continual *élan* of the soul
towards the two principal goods which our Lord has
prepared for us and desires us to ask from Him. It is a
supernatural and generous sign of the heart towards
paradise and towards God.' Nor must we forget the
common and particular needs of the Church and of our
neighbour.

The resolution is both general and particular ; the
first is that of continuing and applying our prayer all
through the day to the double end of loving God and
saving our souls. The second is that of combating our
ruling passion, enemy of our perseverance and love for
God.

Père Desurmont adds that in preparing for our prayer
we should ask and answer three questions : ' With

Whom ? With God . . . our Lord . . . Mary . . . the
Saints. Upon what subject ? What act ? Choose
ordinarily from amongst those which are fundamental,
humility, confidence, knowledge of God and self-
penitence, love of God, the will of God, renouncement,
imitation of Jesus Christ, etc.'

In times of aridity, multiply vocal prayers, putting
into them all the energy possible at the moment.
Believe that prayer is always of value, but do not look
for sensible results ; the best prayers are those which
apparently produce nothing. Make much of good
desires even if you cannot fulfil them. The Ven. Paul
Libermann has a striking note on this subject. ' Divine
grace,' he says, ' sometimes directly inspires the soul
with a desire without enabling us to carry it out ; for
at times God gives a desire which he does not will us to
execute . . . but simply that we should profit solely by
the desire itself, which produces more good to the soul
than if, by grace, we should have been able to realise
it. . . . We may sometimes ask our Lord to enable us to
accomplish that which He has made us desire, but we
must be on our guard against endeavouring to do it of
ourselves, by force, as it were. It is necessary to feel
moved to accomplish a desire in addition to possessing
that desire. Desires which are sterile in themselves, in
so far that they are not fulfilled, sometimes grow in
strength, or at least persevere in intensity, and then they
produce great fruit, although they do not develop in
act (not by our fault, but because God does not will
them to do so). They produce great humility, a great
abasement before God, a very great fervour of heart, a
perfect abandonment to the Divine will ; and in souls
in whom God works by love, they operate that languor
of love which leads to a great perfection. An evil which
often arises is that souls, feeling that impression of desire
which grace excites in them, act of themselves in a
violent endeavour to accomplish the desire experienced.

They want to go further than our Lord wills ; and what is worse, even whilst the Master does not enable them, they will to go on. Ordinarily, the results of this are bad. It arouses self-love, spiritual ambition, presumption, etc. ; presently it leads to discouragement, and by and by to contention, trouble, disquietude and and even to scrupulosity. In all cases, such conduct causes the soul to enter a wrong path, exposes it to illusions, and places it under the empire of the imagination and of its own action ' (*Lettres*, Tome III., cclxi.).

Mental prayer, then, according to Père Desurmont, is ' the direction of the soul towards its end,' and by its four primary operations leads to the renewal of the spirit by the consideration of the faith in meditation, the renewal of the heart by the acts of the virtues, the renewal of grace by the prayer of petition, and the renewal of a good will by the resolution. Without ever neglecting the essentials, there must be nothing mathematical, rigid in prayer, but all must be done simply and with ease, more attention being given to this or that act according to the needs and *attraits* of each soul.

' The glorious liberty of the children of God,' this is the characteristic of the Liguorian prayer. ' Liberty to mingle vocal prayers with meditation ; liberty to repeat time upon time what we wish to say to God ; liberty of adapting the acts of mental prayer to any method, liberty to follow with discretion the inspiration of the moment or, on the contrary, of keeping to a method once for all determined, as in the words and ceremonies of the Mass ; liberty to descend at times, in case of need, to a lower state of prayer, or, with permission, to mount a step higher ; liberty to make use of pious books and to appropriate their language ; liberty of meditating in an easy position, provided it be reverent and helpful; in one word, liberty to make the work of prayer as easy as may be, provided it be done, and done well ' (*La Charité sacerdotale*, Tome I., p. 421).

CHAPTER VI

Oratorian

THE methods of mental prayer, according to M. Olier and his disciples, commonly known as the Sulpician method, and of St. John Eudes, who left the Oratory in order to found the Congregation of Jesus and Mary, generally called the ' Pères Eudistes,' are so thoroughly dependent upon and impregnated with the teaching of Cardinal Bérulle and his disciples that it will be necessary to give an outline of the spirituality of these great masters, so little known in England, except as it is found diffused in the works of Fr. Faber, and in the third volume of P. Pourrat's *Christian Spirituality*, a work every priest should possess and study.

Two powerfully dominant thoughts form the background of Bérullian and Oratorian spirituality – the absolute supremacy of God and the utter nothingness of man, altogether dependent on God. These two conclusions Bérulle arrives at, not directly or by philosophical premises, but by the fact and implications of the Incarnation. He sees Jesus Christ, not only as the full revelation of the Father, but the perfect attitude toward the Father, the true Adorer, Religion incarnate – He who, by virtue of the fact that He is God and man in one person, is alone capable of rendering to God that adoration, love and service of which He is worthy. ' Apostle of the Word Incarnate,' as he was styled by Urban VIII, Bérulle thinks primarily of our Lord in His relation to the Father and as He is in Himself rather than as what He is to us. As it is only in and through

Jesus that we can know and approach and adore the Divine Trinity, so the principal occupation of the Christian is ' to know, to love, to adore Jesus in Himself.' The central act of religion is adoration ; our first thought and care is not self-improvement – *culture du moi*,[1] as M. Bremond calls it – but an attitude of worship, a constant recognition and expression of the fact that we were created for God, a truth taught from one end of Holy Scripture to the other, but strangely neglected in our day.

This attitude is only possible when we realise and enter into the truth that Jesus is our Life, and so our Model.

Bérulle is immensely struck with the self-annihilation of the Son of God in the Incarnation, and from this is led to the thought of man's nothingness. ' There is more of nothingness in our being than being.' That which we call life is but a capacity, an emptiness created that it might be filled by Him Who alone is Life. ' Jesus is the accomplishment of our being, which subsists not save in Him, and is only perfect in Him . . . we ought to regard our being as an emptiness . . . and Jesus as our fulness . . . His spirit our spirit, His life our life, the plenitude of our capacity ' (*Œuvres*, p. 1180,

---

[1] In using this phrase of M. Bremond's I must not be taken as accepting his attribution of it to the Ignatian spirituality. On the contrary, I think his criticisms of St. Ignatius and the *Exercises*, both in his brilliant study *Histoire littéraire du Sentiment Religieux en France*, and in his article on ' St. Ignace et les Exercises ' which began in the April 1929 number of *La Vie Spirituelle* grossly unfair to both the Saint and his teaching. The French school of spirituality which M. Bremond so enthusiastically and lyrically admires needs no such comparison with that of St. Ignatius to commend it, and in so emphasising his personal and largely literary predilections he but affords another sad example of the constant temptation to set one religious order or school of spirituality against another. M. Bremond has missed an opportunity : he might have accomplished a synthesis : he has preferred to widen a gap. Apart from this, there is no other modern work which can compare in value with this monumental *Histoire* of M. Bremond, and it may be hoped that every priest will at least read it in the English translation by K. L. Montgomery, which is as perfect a piece of literary work as is the original. But with Bremond one must read P. Pottier and F. Cavallera (see Bibliography), who show how untrue to fact is the former's attempt to make Bérulle the master and source of the teaching of Lallemant and his disciples.

1181). ' Take life in that mystery of life [the Incarna-
tion] : take life immutable and eternal in that mystery
of life eternal and immutable ' (*Œuvres*, p. 952).

' Our first knowledge ought to be of our empty and
imperfect condition ; and our first movement ought to
be to Jesus as to our accomplishment. In this search for
Jesus, in this adherence to Jesus, in this continual and
profound dependence upon Jesus, is our life, our rest, our
strength and all our power to operate ' (*Œuvres*, p. 1181).

There must, then, be a twofold act of our whole
being, a continual and complete self-renunciation and
a continual and entire adherence to Jesus. All our
religion is summed up in the two words of our Lord :
' Deny thyself,' ' Follow Me.'

Nor is this following a mere external imitation, as
of an artist copying a model. ' Be ye imitators of God,'
says St. Paul, ' as dear children.' It is only by the
possession of the life of Jesus within us that we can
imitate Him. ' Christian virtue,' writes P. Quarre, ' is
not the imitation of the life and virtues of a perfect
man . . . but a living image of the virtue of Jesus,
God-Man : or, more truly, it is the very life and virtue
of Jesus in man ' (*Thrésor spirituel*, p. 181).

' Give yourself wholly to the spirit of Jesus, and to
this spirit of Jesus as operating in and imprinting itself
in souls a living image and a perfect resemblance of
His states and conditions upon earth ' (Bérulle,
Œuvres, p. 1054). This reference to the states of our
Lord's life on earth brings us to a central doctrine of
Bérulle and the French Oratorians, one which influences and animates their teaching on prayer. In our
Lord's life there are ' states ' and ' actions,' the latter of
which are passing, of the moment, the former permanent, abiding, possessed of an eternal character. The
birth of our Lord, for instance, is an act taking place at
a certain moment and in a particular place, in itself
passing and unrepeatable. But the Incarnation is a

state, permanent and abiding in time as in eternity ;
the Son of God is eternally begotten of the Father,
eternally is given to men. Calvary, again, is an act, so
far as all its outward manifestation is concerned,
taking place ' there,' not ' here ' ; ' then,' not ' now.'
But how much more is it a state, having a permanent,
eternal character, since the Crucified is the ' Lamb
slain from the foundation of the world,' ' the Lamb
standing as it had been slain.' So Bérulle would have us
contemplate, enter into and gain the spirit and virtue of
not only these mysteries of the Incarnate Life, but of all
those of which the Gospels tell us, which ' pass in certain circumstances, endure, are present and perpetu-
ated, in certain other ways. They are past as to their
execution but present as to their virtue, which never
passes, as the love with which they were accomplished
will never pass . . . for the spirit of God, by which that
mystery has been accomplished, the interior state of the
exterior mystery, the efficacy and virtue which make
that mystery living and operative in us, the state and
disposition by which Jesus has acquired us to His
Father . . . even the actual taste, the living disposition
by which Jesus accomplished that mystery, is always
living, actual and present in Jesus. . . . For as God in
His glory is Himself our heritage and portion, Jesus
also in His states and mysteries is Himself our portion.
. . . He wills that we have a singular part in His various
states, according to the diversity of His election for us
and of our devotion to Him. Thus He apportions
Himself to His children, making them participate of the
spirit and grace of His mysteries, appropriating to one
His life, to another His death, etc.' (Œuvres, pp. 940, 941). [1]

---

[1] This conception, whilst largely developed by Bérulle, was not
original in him. St. Ignatius had already spoken in his directions for
the first contemplation on the Incarnation of our Lord, ' ansi nueva-
mente encarnado,' and Fra Thomé de Jesu, the Augustinian (1529–
1582), in the instructions on prayer which preface his Trabalhos de Jesu
has a typically Bérullien passage : ' Think of and call to mind those
mysteries which form the subject of your exercise, not as things passed

In our prayer, then, we adore Jesus in Himself, all that He is, and in all that He does, 'for all His days and moments are adorable by the dignity of His Person'; the least actions of Jesus are to be considered. 'Who can treat anything as little where all is so great, where each thing, however small it may seem, so nearly touches the Divinity?' We seek to penetrate into His mind 'to put on the mind of Christ,' to know His desires and sentiments and will; we read between the lines of the Gospel that we may enter into that unknown life 'the many things not written' of which St. John speaks. The virtues of the Christian life – humility, patience, love, etc. – must not be meditated on as abstract principles, but contemplated in the humble, patient, loving Jesus, and this very act of 'looking unto Jesus' serves to conform us to Him, transform our souls into His likeness.

All this is, of course, to be found in the New Testament; it is the Johannine and Pauline Gospel developed with a fulness which had hardly been achieved so completely before Bérulle. No commentary, ancient or modern, has ever so illuminated the 'mystery of the Gospel' as taught by St. Paul as does the teaching of the Oratorian school.

Père Condren and Père Olier develop the sacrificial aspect of our Lord's life. Jesus is not merely 'a priest for ever' outside of us, as it were, but He is in us all that which He was and is to God; He is our sacrifice, our adoration, our prayer. 'What grace does the mystery of the Incarnation work in us?' asks Père

and gone, but as though they were actually present before you and you were there at the moment, gazing on them. For although they are passed in fact, yet their virtue remains. Nor is that love, wherewith our Lord did them, passed away, but lives to-day, as infinite, as unchangeable, and as completely the same as when He dwelt on earth and for love of us suffered and died. Thus, seeing that He is present and actually burning with that same love . . . we ought, also, on our part, to regard His acts, not as things passed away, but as still present; for we seek from them profit and advantage to ourselves, not as things already finished and done, but from things living and eternal.'

Olier in his *Catéchisme Chrétien*. 'It works in us a putting off and entire renunciation of ourselves ; more, it accomplishes a putting on of our Lord by a total consecration to God.' Entire self-abnegation, that we may be filled with the life, virtue, power, priesthood of Jesus, this is to be a Christian, according to the Oratorians, who yet, indeed, say now more than St. Paul, ' I live, yet not I, but Christ liveth in me.'

One concise and comprehensive phrase sums up all the teaching of St. John Eudes (1601–1680) : ' The Christian life is nothing else but a continuation and achievement of the life of Jesus in each one of us.' He is possessed by the Pauline doctrine expressed in the Apostle's constantly repeated phrase ' in Christ,' of which Bishop Westcott said, ' It is in itself a full Gospel . . . sufficient to illuminate our whole conception of the Christian Faith . . . the central truth of Christianity,' for which ' I would gladly have given the ten years of my life spent on the Revised Version to bring it to the heart of Englishmen.' In chapter ii. of his *Règles Latines* the Saint groups all the texts containing this doctrine under seven heads : (1) The Christian ought to adhere to Christ ; (2) to put on Christ ; (3) to abide in Christ ; (4) to live with Christ ; (5) to live the life of Christ risen from the dead ; (6) to go by the spirit of Christ and to do all things in His Name and Spirit ; (7) to put on the character and virtues of Christ living in Heaven.

The Christian ' baptised into Christ ' is in a real sense one with Christ, not only sharing in all that Christ is and does, but called to continue and reproduce the life of Christ given to him in that Sacrament ; he is *alter Christus*. ' The Eternal Father having done you the honour of receiving you into companionship with Him in Holy Baptism, as one of His children and one of the members of His Son, He has obliged Himself to look upon you with the same eye, to love you with the same heart, and to treat you with the same love with which He regards, treats and loves His Son' (*Œuvres Complètes*, ii., p. 212).

'As St. Paul says that he fills up what is lacking of the sufferings of Christ for His Body's sake, which is the Church,' so it may be said of the true Christian, who is a member of Jesus Christ, one with Him by His grace, that he continues and accomplishes, by all that he does in the Spirit of Jesus Christ, the actions which the same Jesus Christ performed whilst He was on earth. So that, when a Christian meditates, he continues and completes the meditation which Jesus made on earth ; when he labours, he continues and completes the laborious life of Jesus on earth ; when he converses with his neighbour in the spirit of charity, he continues and completes the life of Jesus talking with men ; when he takes food or rest, he continues and completes the subjection in which Jesus Christ willed to be in these necessities. . . . So should we be as Jesus on earth, continuing His life and works, doing and suffering all, holily and divinely, in the spirit of Jesus, that is to say, in His dispositions and intentions' (*Œuvres Complètes* i., p. 164).

Thus ' the practice of practices, the secret of secrets, the devotion of devotions, is not to be attached to any practice or particular exercise of devotion ; but to have a great care in all your exercises, of giving yourself to the holy spirit of Jesus . . . that He may have full power and freedom to work in you according to His desires, to fill you with such dispositions and sentiments of devotion as He wills, and to lead you by such ways as He pleases ' (*Royaume de Jésus*, p. 452).

This short *résumé*, altogether unworthy of the subject, may yet be sufficient to enable us to enter into the methods of mental prayer composed by M. Olier, and used by the Sulpicians, and that of St. John Eudes, both of which are as singularly beautiful as they are distinct from any which preceded them. The fundamental ideas which underlie the Sulpician method are to be found in M. Olier's *Introduction à la Vie et aux Vertus Chrétiennes.* ' Christianity consists in three points . . . to regard Jesus, to be united to Jesus, to work in Jesus. . . . The first is called Adoration ; the second Communion ; the third Co-operation.'

There are several recensions and explanations of this method, from amongst which I choose that which M. Letourneau calls the traditional text and upon which the *Entretiens* of M. Tronson are based. It is made up of three parts – the preparation, the body of the prayer and the conclusion.

I. *The Preparation.* The remote preparation consists in (1) a great purity of heart ; (2) a perfect mortification of the passions ; (3) a great fidelity in the guard of the senses, interior and exterior, especially against vanity and curiosity.

The immediate preparation consists of three acts :

(1) Of placing oneself in the presence of God.

(2) Of humility, recognising one's unworthiness.

(3) Of recognising our inability of ourselves to render anything to God.

Each of these has two acts.

(1) (*a*) An act of faith in the presence of God in the place where we are and in our hearts.

(*b*) An act of adoration of the Divine Majesty.

(2) (*a*) Acts of penitence, humiliation, confusion and contrition occasioned by the thought of our sins.

(*b*) Of union with and abandonment to our Lord in order that we may appear before His Father in the Person of Jesus and pray in His Name.

(3) (*a*) A renouncing of our own spirit, which is incapable of guiding us in the way of salvation, and of our affections, which ordinarily turn toward evil.

(*b*) An invocation of the Holy Spirit that we may make our prayer in His light, by His movements and as conducted by Him.

II. *Body of the Prayer.*

A. *Adoration.* (1) The consideration of the subject.

(2) The rendering of our duty to God according to the subject, ordinarily consisting of seven acts, **adoration**, admiration, praise, thanksgiving, love, joy and compassion. It is not necessary always to follow this order ; we should abandon ourselves to the affections which God gives us and repeat those to which the Holy Spirit attracts us.

B. *Communion.* The consideration of the subject is designed to lead us to a fervent desire to participate in the perfection, virtue or mystery we have adored. To this end three acts are necessary :

(1) Of contrition, in which we see not merely the beauty of the virtue, etc., but the necessity of it for ourselves. For unless we are persuaded of our need we shall ask for it either coldly or not at all.

(2) Reflection upon ourselves, our lack of virtue, of the obligations we are under to practise the particular one we are meditating upon, of regret for the past neglect of this perfection, of confusion at the realisation of our present poverty and misery, of desire for the future that we may earnestly seek to escape from our lukewarmness into a real communion with our Lord. This reflection will lead us to

(3) Petition, humble, confident and persevering, that God will give us the grace we need. We should do so by humbly representing to Him that it is His will ; that it will be to His glory ; that one so imperfect and lacking in grace should not be suffered in His Church ; the merits of His Son ; the Divine promises in Holy Scripture, etc. Further, we must beg the favour and aid of the most Holy Virgin, our guardian angel, our patrons and other Saints. Nor must we forget the

needs of Holy Church and of those for whom we ought specially to pray.

III. *Co-operation or Resolutions.* The two words, says M. Olier, mean the same thing (*Catéchisme Chrétien pour la vie intérieure*, chap. viii.), but the first expresses more strongly the power of the Holy Spirit upon which we are more dependent than upon the good works of our own will : whilst the term *resolution* marks more expressly the determination of our will. Remembering, then, the need of our co-operation with grace, we make the resolution to live for the future in conformity with the light we have received in our prayer, and especially to practise, the same day, the perfection or virtue we have considered. Such resolutions should have six qualities ; they must be particular, present, efficacious, humble, full of confidence and often reiterated. They should be made with an entire distrust in ourselves and an entire confidence in Jesus Christ, without Whom we can do nothing.

IV. *Conclusion,* in which

(1) We thank God for having allowed us to come into His presence, and for the graces given to us in our prayer.

(2) We pray Him to pardon all our faults and negligences in this prayer ; to bless our resolutions this present day, our life and our death.

(3) We select some thought from our prayer to carry with us during the day, the spiritual nosegay of St. François de Sales ; and conclude with the *Sub tuum præsidium,* placing all we have done and hope to do in the hands of Mary.

M. Olier, in his *Introduction à la Vie et aux Vertus Chrétiennes,* gives a ' Manner of meditating upon the Virtues ' which is worthy of note. He founds it on the Divine command in the Old Law, ' These words shall be in thy heart . . . and thou shalt bind them for a sign

upon thy hand and they shall be between thine eyes '
(Deut. vi. 6, 8), and describes his method as having
Jesus before our eyes, in our hearts and in our hands. He
takes as a model an exercise upon the virtue of penitence.

First Point. Having our Lord before our eyes. Consider with reverence Jesus Christ, penitent for our sins.
Honour in Him the Holy Spirit of penitence, Who
animated Him throughout all His life and has filled the
hearts of all the penitents of the Church.

Hold yourself in reverence and respect towards so
holy and Divine a thing, and after that your heart has
poured itself out in love, praise and other duties,
remain some time in silence before Him, in those same
dispositions and religious sentiments rooted in the
depth of your soul.

Second Point. Having our Lord in our heart.

After having so reverenced Jesus Christ and His Holy
Spirit of penitence, we spend some time in seeking that
same Spirit for ourselves. We pray that Spirit, to whom
alone it belongs to make in us a new heart and to form a
spirit of penitence in the soul, to be pleased to descend
upon us. We implore Him, by all the inventions of love,
to come into our soul in order to conform us to Jesus
Christ penitent, continuing in us the penitence which
He began in Him and enabling us to bear part and
measure of the pain due to a body full of sin such as
ours.

We give ourselves to Him to be possessed by Him and
animated by His virtue : then remain in silence before
Him, that we may be interiorly filled with His Divine
unction, to the end that we may exercise, on all occasions, such mortification as pleases Him.

Third Point. Having our Lord in our hands.

That is, to will that His Divine will should be accomplished in us who are His members, who ought in all
things to be submissive to our Head, and not to have
any movement which Jesus Christ, our life and our all,

has not given us ; Who, filling our soul with His Spirit, His virtue and His power, ought to operate in us and by us all that He desires.

He is in pastors : Pastor ; in priests : Priest ; in religious : Religious ; in penitents : Penitent ; operating in each the work of their vocation ; He ought then to work in us the effects of penitence, and we ought always to be in this spirit, co-operating faithfully with all that He wills to do in and by us.

To pray thus, says M. Olier, is to pray according to our Lord's intention, for these three points correspond exactly with the first three petitions of the Paternoster.

The Eudist Method

I. *Preparation.*

A. Act of faith in the presence of God.

B. Act of intention to make our prayer solely for His glory and to please Him.

C. Act of humility, acknowledging our unworthiness to appear before Him and our inability to pray of ourselves.

D. Act of union with our Lord, Whose prayer we continue and Whose dispositions we desire to enter into.

E. Act of petition for the aid of the Holy Spirit, of our Lady, the Angels and Saints.

II. *Meditation.* In each mystery of the life of Jesus there are seven points to be considered.

A. Application of the mind or meditation proper.

(1) The body, or outward part of the mystery ; the scene, the persons, the actions, the words, etc.

(2) The spirit, or inward part of the mystery ; the dispositions and intentions of our Lord ; the mind of God the Father ; the interior thoughts of those concerned in the mystery, etc.

(3) The general and enduring effects : that which is permanent, living, active in the mystery.

(4) The particular effects ; the plan and designs which our Lord had in the mystery ; why He acts and speaks as He does.

(5) The relation of the mystery to Mary, for she had a special and extraordinary share in all the states and mysteries of Jesus her Son.

(6) The mystery in its relation to the Saints and Angels who had a particular share in it, as St. Gabriel, our Lady and St. Joseph in the Incarnation ; St. John Baptist, St. Elizabeth, the Holy Innocents, etc., in the Divine childhood ; the Apostles in the Public Life ; St. John, Magdalene, etc., in the Passion.

(7) The special and singular part we have in the mystery, for, as the Saint says, our Lord had always, in each of His mysteries, 'some thought or plan, some particular love in regard to each one of us.'

B. Application of the heart or affections.

(1) Adoration of Jesus in all the details of the mystery.

(2) Admiration, joy and love at seeing Jesus so great and God so glorified in this mystery.

(3) Thanksgiving for the glory given to God and the grace merited for mankind by Jesus.

(4) Humility and penitence for that we have so little honoured this mystery or profited by the graces which flow from it.

(5) Offering to Jesus of all the praise which He has received in Heaven and earth in this mystery.

(6) Offering of ourselves to Jesus to honour Him in this mystery and to gain profit from it.

(7) Prayer to Jesus that all men may come to honour this mystery and share in its fruits.

C. Application of the will or resolutions.

(1) Renewal of our resolution of renouncing self, of offering ourselves entirely to Jesus, of uniting ourselves

KP

to the dispositions of His Heart, in order that we may continue His life.

(2) A particular resolution, humble and fervent, derived from the mystery we have meditated on, and corresponding to the duties of the day and the opportunities which are likely to present themselves.

III. *Conclusion.*

(1) A thanksgiving for the lights and graces received in our prayer.

(2) A petition that God will pardon all our failures and negligences in it.

(3) The placing of our resolutions in our Lord's hands, who alone can ensure our keeping them.

(4) The spiritual nosegay.

(5) The begging of the Virgin, the Angels and Saints to continue our meditations for us and continually to aid us to profit by it.

St. John Eudes is not content with instructing us how to pray ; some of the most beautiful and helpful parts of his works are the *Elevations*, in which he treats the mysteries of the Gospel in the ways he has indicated and gives exquisite outpourings of his affections and devotion to the Holy Trinity, our Lord, His Blessed Mother, the Saints and Angels. In his desire that Christians should constantly contemplate, adore and reproduce the life of Jesus, he gives a series of meditations for each day of the week which will serve to indicate his thought.

Sunday : The Divine life of Jesus in the bosom of His Father from all eternity.

Monday : The first moment of the Life of Jesus on earth.

Tuesday : The life of Jesus during His childhood.

Wednesday : The hidden and laborious life of Jesus during the thirty years.

Thursday : The life of Jesus amongst men and in the Blessed Sacrament.

Friday : The suffering life of Jesus.

Saturday : The life of Jesus in Mary and of Mary in Jesus.

It is easy to see – and experience will abundantly prove it – that such a manner of meditating upon the Gospel as St. John Eudes gives must increase and deepen our knowledge of that Divine life which is our salvation in such a way as to lead to a more fervent love of our Lord and a more intense desire to imitate Him. Moreover, the Saint teaches, in common with the whole of the Oratorian school, that, as says P. Bourgoing, ' All the mysteries of Jesus Christ . . . His thoughts, words, desires, movements and all His holy operations, interior and exterior, are as rays of the sun . . . imprinting their virtue ' upon those who simply contemplate and adore them. For our Lord communicates His own perfections to His members who yield themselves to His influence, so that, drawing the water of eternal life from the ' wells of salvation,' they so participate in His merits and in the different states and mysteries of His life, so enter into the dispositions of His sacred Heart, that they ' put on Christ,' ' live in Christ ' according to His word, ' Abide in Me and I in you, so shall ye bring forth much fruit.'

The Ven. Paul Libermann, a convert from Judaism, unites in his teaching many characteristics of both the Oratorian and Sulpician spirit. Trained in the seminary of St. Sulpice, he received Minor Orders in December 1828, but on the eve of his ordination to the priesthood he was seized with epilepsy and for the next ten years he occupied the position of a kind of ' general help ' at Issy. As his health gradually improved he began to work among the sick, then among the students, and later became a guide in spiritual things to all in the house. The need of missionaries for Africa and the West Indies became a matter of engrossing interest to him, and in 1837 he joined the first novitiate of the Eudists. Two years later he went to Rome to reflect

upon what he now felt to be a vocation to establish a
new missionary congregation, and after a period of
much trial, founded the Congregation of the Immacu-
late Heart of Mary. In 1841 he resumed his theological
studies at Strasburg, and was ordained priest on
September 18th, 1841. A very large collection of his
letters of spiritual direction have been published in
three volumes by the Congregation. On the subject of
mental prayer he writes to a man of the world, ' I am
not astonished that you have difficulty in making your
meditation. There are several causes of this ; first, that
you have not yet had the courage to do that which,
above all, would enable you to overcome the greatest
difficulties, that is, to make a general confession . . .
you ought to open yourself to a man of God, telling him
of all that passes within you.' Defects in preparation
and in the method of prayer constitute two more
obstacles. Mental prayer is composed of four parts,
the preparation, the entry, the body of the prayer and
the conclusion.

The preparation is *proximate*, consisting of (1) A great
purity of heart – that is, freedom from mortal sin and
a firm will not to commit venial sin, and an entire
detachment from creatures. ' It is not necessary that
one should have all these dispositions in a very high
degree ; but the more one is pure, the more prayer is
made easy and grace drawn to the soul.' (2) A great
watchfulness of self, yet without disquietude and
agitation. (3) A sincere, firm and true desire of
advancing in the perfection of love for our Lord, by
means of self-renouncement and prayer. These dispositions are of the highest importance, but it is not
necessary to have them at the beginning ; it is enough
to see their necessity and to endeavour calmly to acquire
them, putting all our confidence in God.

The *immediate* preparation consists in the overnight
choice of the subject, ' for otherwise we shall not know

where to begin or what considerations to make,' and a little recollection before retiring that we may rest in peace before God. The prayer itself should be made as soon after rising as possible, and in solitude. Some vocal prayer may be used to dispose the spirit toward a more perfect recollection. Penetrated by a conviction of the presence of God, you will enter naturally into sentiments of adoration, love, humility, in presenting yourself before God, you 'so poor, so miserable, so covered with sins and deserving of punishments.'

The actual meditation follows. The *entry* is made by fixing the mind upon the subject, and in doing this it is always best to consider it in relation to our Lord. Thus we are led to acts of adoration, etc., toward Him, though it is not necessary to have many different acts ; one alone may be enough. So 'we pass unconsciously to the *body of the prayer*,' making use of such considerations as will tend to convince us of the truth of that upon which we are meditating.

The *conclusion* consists of (1) A return upon oneself in order to see what we need to do in relation to the truth we have meditated upon, how we can conform our lives more to it, or what are the sources of our previous neglect of it ; (2) The making of resolutions, practical not vague, firm, to be executed as soon as occasion offers ; (3) Petition for grace to be faithful, invocation of the help of Mary, our patron, etc. Père Libermann also recommends the 'spiritual nosegay' of St. François de Sales, 'a text of Holy Scripture . . . or some very simple, very loving and very practical thought' (*Lettre* xiii.). To a seminarist he writes, 'For your prayer, take a mystery of our Lord and endeavour to apply yourself to it. Represent to yourself this good Master in the state of that mystery, and let yourself go in the desires and feelings of your heart ; uniting yourself to Him, embracing His feet, prostrating yourself before God, attaching your soul to that divine Lord in

all sweetness, without agitation, without efforts. Go
on to consider His interior, His dispositions and sentiments, His desires, His relation to His Father. Unite
your interior to His and so copy His dispositions in
yourself' (*Lettre* clxxxviii.).

A most interesting letter as illustrating his *rapports*
with the Oratorian school is that to a seminarist written
in 1843 : ' I understand perfectly your difficulty in
your prayer. If you employ yourself in reasoning, it
becomes nothing but an amusement of spirit and a
labour. If you do not reason you grow weary and
" bored " and remain in vagueness. It is this vagueness
which weighs upon you and troubles you. You may be
able, perhaps, to fix beforehand the subject of your
prayer, without, however, taking it as something to
exercise your reason upon. Take for subject the
mysteries of our Lord or of the most Holy Virgin. See
the Divine Saviour in His mysteries or states of life.
Consider Him in the various actions which He accomplishes in these mysteries ; consider thus practically
these actions in Him and the perfection with which He
performs them ; consider, further, the interior principles of these actions, the movements of the holy soul of
Jesus in their accomplishment. Take, for each meditation, two or three of these practical considerations,
which, ordinarily, may be subdivided. Pause from
time to time in order to make affections, if you are so
moved ; if not, to adhere by your will and spirit to that
which you see in Jesus. It is not necessary to repeat in
words, over and over again, that you do so adhere ;
but do so really from the bottom of your heart ; and if
the sentiment does not flow easily of itself, remain in
silence and adhere by a certain disposition of faith and
of good desire ' (*Lettre* cclxxxix.).

PART III
EXPLANATIONS

CHAPTER I

Some Chief Difficulties of Mental Prayer

THREE truths in connection with mental prayer should be constantly kept in mind : (1) That the main object of our prayer is to get into personal contact with God Himself ; to gain such a knowledge of Divine realities as shall lead us to desire, love and seek them for their own sake. (2) That the means of our so getting in touch with God is through the Sacred Humanity of our Lord. ' No man cometh unto the Father but by Me.' (3) The true test of the value of our prayer is not the ease with which we make it or the consolations we may experience, but the deepened realisation of our own nothingness, the increase of our love and desire for God, and of our obedience to the Divine Will, and the closer conformity of our exterior conduct with our interior life. ' Right relation between prayer and conduct is not that conduct is supremely important and prayer may help it, but that prayer is supremely important and conduct tests it ' (Archbishop Temple, *Christus Veritas*, p. 45). We must not, writes Père Poulain, ' analyse our prayers incessantly, but watch our external conduct.' The pull of our lower nature constantly acts as a drag upon us, so that our exterior lags behind our interior life ; and while we must not allow this to discourage us, we must not acquiesce in it as if it were an inevitable thing. The reconciliation of the exterior with the interior life is the hardest, as it is the most necessary task we have to accomplish, and it can only be accomplished by the exercise of a great patience, an ever-growing sense of our inability to be or do anything save by the grace of

God, and the acceptance of our failures as means by which we learn that humility which is the foundation and touchstone of the spiritual life.

To speak, then, of the difficulties which beset the life of prayer is to speak largely of difficulties which really exist in the whole of our life – which is one – but which become more apparent and intense at the time of prayer. The reason of this will appear later. At the outset two facts need emphasising. First, that we need not and must not be surprised or discouraged to find that difficulties exist, for prayer is a supernatural work against which our fallen nature, the world and the Devil constantly array themselves. ' My son, if thou come to serve the Lord, prepare thy soul for temptation. Set thy heart aright and constantly endure, and make not haste in time of trouble ' (Ecclus. ii.). We must rid ourselves of the too widespread idea that religion is meant to comfort us, in the modern sense of the term, to make life easier and more pleasant, an idea totally alien to the Gospel and the experience of the Saints. On the contrary, it is a stern and uncompromising guide on a long and dangerous journey, conducting us, not as millionaire tourists in our own time and way, but by the way of Jesus : ' Ego sum via, sequere Me.' Difficulties, then, must be expected and looked for, and the wise man, knowing that he is no pioneer who must blaze his way through an unknown country, but a pilgrim following a well-trodden way, will seek for aid from those who have gone before, and have left word of the dangers to be met with and the means of combating them. Second, we must not always expect to conquer and get rid of our difficulties and temptations. There is a great deal more in Holy Scripture as to the need of enduring temptation than of conquering it. ' Blessed is the man that endureth temptation,' says St. James ; and the classic passage in the First Epistle to the Corinthians (x. 13) does not say that there is no temptation which our Lord will not enable us to escape, but none that He will not enable us to bear. Our Lord Himself prayed that, if it were possible, He might be spared the supreme trial of the Passion, but the Father's will was that He should endure it. St. Paul ' besought the Lord thrice ' for deliverance from a sore temptation, but received the reply : ' My grace is sufficient for thee.' ' All our peace in this miserable life must be placed rather in humble endurance than in the absence of contradictions,' à Kempis tells us ; and Baron von Hügel has truly said : ' The fact is, religion thrives, not by the absence of difficulties, but by the presence of helps and powers.' In every Christian life, whether in the cloister or in the world, there will be one thing or more for which there is no remedy but endurance, a cross which has to be carried, a position which has to be hung on to until it please our Lord to relieve His servant. It is indeed such things which make saints.

A further word about temptation in general. It is well-known that our capacity to resist disease depends more upon the general health and fitness of the body than upon any particular prophylactics. The fact that the various organs are functioning in such a way as to establish that unified balance of his physical nature which we term health enables one man to live immune in an unhealthy environment where another in weak or disordered health falls a ready victim to any disease with which he may come in contact. No less certain is it that the surest safeguard against temptation is a state of fervent, generous Christian practice, by which we are kept in a state of salvation, i.e. health of soul.

Why is temptation so grave a danger to us ? Because the unity of our nature has been destroyed, and is only in process of restoration, so that when temptation comes it finds some response from within, some answering desire from that lower nature not yet ' subdued to the spirit,' still incompletely dominated by reason and faith. It is, then, of primary importance that we should aim at the restoration of the unity of our nature, of the attainment of that health which is the result of a right correspondence with the source of our life, so that we may present a united front to the attacks of evil. And this means a more entire return to God, ' Whose unity is the mould of all things.' The more we give ourselves to Divine things, the more every side of our nature reaches out to and touches reality, the more that very contact, that correspondence with the Healer and Restorer of our race, establishes us in that unity which is the greatest defence we have against ' the fiery darts of the evil one.'

Distractions. – Distractions in prayer are nearly always thought and spoken of as if they were something peculiar to the practice of mental prayer, whereas the fact is that the cause of them usually lies in the rest of our life ; it is only when we come to pray that we notice and are hindered by what has been there unnoticed all the time. We have to remember that we are a unity – one person – persisting through innumerable forms of activity, so that when we come to pray we are just what we are outside our prayer. We cannot leave that self which we are outside the church door, nor will the holiest surroundings transform normally dis-tracted beings, as most of us are, into recollected ones. ' As the mind is all day long, so it will be in the Presence of God. As we think all day long, so shall we think as we kneel at the altar ... habits of undisciplined careless-ness and frivolity . . . can produce no fruit from the seed of God's grace. If our minds have become so dissipated that they have lost the power of thinking out properly the matters which concern our earthly life, it is no wonder that they cannot lay hold of the mysteries of faith ' (Maturin, *Practical Studies in the Parables*, p. 14). ' It sometimes happens that you go to your prayer after having spent the whole day dissipated and without recollection ; it is no wonder you are distracted, for you well deserve it. You follow your own inclinations, you are cross-grained and resentful in your obedience, lacking in sweetness and condescension towards your neighbour, and then you go boldly to prayer in order to unite yourself to God and to have consolation and sweetness. If you find the door shut, why should you be surprised ? ' (St. Jane Chantal, *Entretien*, xxxiv.).

' The time of prayer,' writes Faber, ' is God's punishment time. It is then that venial sins, little infidelities, inordinate friendships and worldly attachments rise up and complain of us, and we shall be chastised for them.' Distractions at prayer, then, are the fruit of seeds sown outside our prayer, and it is there that they must primarily be dealt with. But, before considering the remedies to be applied, we must see what are the main causes of distractions. They are threefold : (1) the Devil ; (2) an undisciplined life ; (3) the result of the necessary interaction of soul and body.

(1) ' The Devil,' says St. Nilus in his *Treatise on Prayer*, ' is very envious of the man who prays, and uses all possible means to defeat his purpose without ceasing, suggesting thoughts to his memory and endeavouring to excite his carnal passions, so that, if possible, he may prevent his ascent to God.' To pray is definitely to range ourselves on God's side, to take into our hands the one weapon before which Satan is powerless, so that it is at our prayer that we are especially subject to his attacks, as was our Lord in the wilderness and Gethsemane. And his main object is not so much to cause us to commit any particular sin as to cloud and distract our mind, to spoil our prayer and cause us to abandon it. ' He suggesteth many evil thoughts that he may weary thee and frighten thee,

that he may call thee away from prayer and holy reading' (*Imitation* III., vi. 4).

Now we are to remember that such temptations, however vile and persistent, are not sins, nor even imperfections. We cannot help them coming to us, and we can deal with them so as to make our prayer even more pleasing to God because of them. ' Resist the Devil and he will flee from you.' It is true ; but there is a right and a wrong way of doing so. Nothing in the spiritual life can be fruitfully accomplished by violence ; we must not endeavour to drive temptations away by violent efforts, nor by forcing ourselves to ignore them, for all such efforts only tend to rivet our attention on the very thing we are trying to avoid, and this defeats the end aimed at. The right method, all the saints tell us, is quietly, without any anger or impatience, to turn our eyes towards God and rest in that haven of His peace which no storm may disturb, 'anchored in the Will of God,' as says St. Catherine of Siena.

' When your heart is wandering and distracted, bring it back quietly to its point, restore it tenderly to its Master's side ; and if you did nothing else the whole of your hour but bring back your heart patiently and put it near our Lord again, and every time you put it back it turned away again, your hour would be well employed ' (St. François de Sales, *Instructions* vi.). ' The thing is inevitable, so do not let it distress or disturb you, but let the mill clack on while you grind the wheat : that is, let us continue to work with the will and intellect ' (St. Teresa, *Interior Castle*, IV. i. 9, 12).

' If distractions come, you must not disquiet yourself, nor search to repulse them with violence and impatience ; it is enough to turn yourself away peacefully and to bring back your attention to God. The Devil will neglect nothing in order to suggest distractions during prayer, hoping by this means to make us abandon it ; to give up our prayer because we are distracted is to do what he desires,' says St. Alphonsus Liguori.

The author of *The Cloud of Unknowing* bids us ' if any new thought or stirring of sin ' come between us and God, ' try to look as it were over their shoulders, seeking another thing, the which thing is God. . . . An this device be well and truly conceived, it is nought else but a longing desire after God, to feel Him and see Him as it may be here ; and such a desire is charity, and it obtaineth alway to be eased ' (*Cloud*, chap. xxxii.).

St. Pedro of Alcantara says, ' The remedy against evil and untimely thoughts is to fight manfully and perseveringly against them, but without any violence or anxiety of spirit. It is not so much a matter of strength and force as of grace and humility. We should turn to God without any scruple or anxiety (seeing there is here no fault, or but a slight one) and say, Thou seest, Lord, what I am, and what else indeed could be expected of such a one unless Thou cleanse me ? Then, one should take up again the thread of the meditation and with patience wait for the visitation of the Lord, Who will not fail to come to the lowly in spirit. If, however, these thoughts still disturb you and you still with perseverance resist them and do all you can, you may hold this for certain – that you gain much more ground by this resistance than if you had been finding joy in the Lord with all savour and without hindrance.' Both St. François de Sales and St. Jeanne Chantal say the same ; ' if we do nothing else but combat the distractions and temptations which assail us, our prayer will be well made,' writes the former, whilst St. Chantal teaches her nuns, ' The fact that we hold ourselves in the presence of His Spirit constitutes prayer . . . if we are humble in suffering the assaults of vain thoughts and distractions it is as acceptable to Him as the highest aspirations we have had at other times. The longing of a loving heart for God and its endurance of unwelcome difficulties is one of the most perfect prayers ' (*Œuvres*, vol. ii., p. 324).

There is scarcely anything in any teaching on the spiritual life which requires more emphasis than the truth that all our spiritual exercises are means toward seeking and knowing God, and not for our pleasure and comfort. The very first act, says M. Olier (*Caté-chisme Chrétien*, Leçon vii.), ' is to renounce ourselves and our own wills,' for all our natural desires lead only to the gratification of self, even in our good works. ' The aim and end of prayer,' says Père Bourgoing, ' is the reverence, recognition and adoration of the sovereign Majesty of God, of that which He is in Himself rather than of that which He is to us . . . our prayer is not made for our own spiritual profit and utility but for the sole glory of God ' (*Les Vérités et Excellences du J. C. Notre Seigneur*. Avis).

And St. Vincent de Paul, ' When you go to prayer you should do so purely to please God, saying, " I am not worthy to converse with God, but since obedience demands it and it is God's will, I shall go to honour our Lord " ' (*Conference on the End of the Company*, edit. published by Pierre Coste, c.m., Paris, 1923, vol. x., p. 131).

(2) An undisciplined life.   A slack, undisciplined, unmortified life necessarily leads to a distracted prayer, for not only are we the same persons in prayer as in every other action, but any real attempt at prayer is an endeavour to be more truly ourselves. All day long we go about disguised, to a very large extent hiding our real self that others may not see what we are, and this not seldom to such a degree that the disguise becomes more real to us than our actual self. But when we come to pray, our real self, torn by a myriad interests, our interior mental life, crowded with distractions, surges out into that silent sanctuary wherein we seek the peace of God. ' If we find the door shut, why should we be surprised ? '

The main remedy, then, which must be sought seriously and perseveringly, is to be found in a careful attention to the remote preparation for prayer, notably in

(a) The guard of the heart.

(b) The custody of the senses.

(c) The spirit of recollection.

(a) Fr. Roothan, S.J., in his *De la Manière de Méditer*, says there are three main obstacles which hinder our practice of prayer, pride and the vain esteem of self, dissimulation or the desire of appearing to be what we are not, and the sins to which the soul is attached and which it does not seriously endeavour to combat. Père Lallemant asks why so many religious and devout Christians who practise the duties of their religion, and in consequence ' in a high physical degree the gifts of the Holy Spirit,' yet manifest so little of the Spirit in their lives and actions, resenting being corrected, seeking the praise and esteem of the world and all that leads to their own self-love. He answers that it is due to the fact that they give way continually to venial sins which bind the gifts of the Spirit and prevent their operation, since these venial sins exclude the reception of the grace necessary to produce the action of the gifts (*La Doctrine Spirituelle*, Pt. IV., chap. iii. 3). St. John of the Cross, too, has some most illuminating chapters, of which I have ventured an analysis, in *The Dark Night of the Soul*, upon the sins and imperfections of beginners in the spiritual life. [1]

[1] On the distinction between venial sin and imperfections. A venial sin is a disordinate act which cannot be referred to the end of charity, in the order of means. It is a voluntary act at variance with the Divine law, and so is sinful, but it is not the deliberate choice of that which is contrary to the Divine law, as in the case of mortal sin, and so does not destroy or even diminish sanctifying grace in the soul. But it lessens the fervour and strength of the soul and leaves it more open to mortal sin. An imperfection is not sin at all, but is the lack, in an act morally good, of a certain perfection which ought to be there, a lack, as it were, of generosity and fulness in performing an action, or a choosing of a lesser good in a matter not sinful, being content with the mediocre when we might give the best, considering what duty requires rather than love.

LP

It is not enough that the soul who desires to pray well should deliberately abstain from mortal sin ; there must be a continual guard of the heart from venial sin and imperfections, from all which would hinder a free and joyous approach to God. ' We must keep our hearts free,' says St. Pedro de Alcantara, ' from all kinds of idle and vain thoughts, from all strange affections and inclinations, and from all virulent and passionate emotions' (*On Prayer & Meditation*, Pt. II., chap. ii.). Dom Chautard, in his invaluable *L'âme de tout Apostolat*, tells us that our Lord only admits souls into intimacy with Himself ' in the measure in which they apply themselves to destroy or to avoid ' all that would defile the soul, and goes on to give a list of such things.

' Spiritual sloth in not raising one's heart to God ; inordinate affection for creatures ; brusqueness and impatience ; rancour, caprices, softness and seeking for comfort ; a facility in speaking of the faults of others without good reason ; dissipation and curiosity about matters which do not concern the glory of God ; talkativeness and empty words, vain and temerarious judgments of our neighbour ; vain complaisance in oneself ; contempt for others and criticisms of their conduct ; the desire of esteem and praise for our actions ; display of that which is to our own advantage ; presumption, obstinacy, jealousy, lack of respect towards those in authority, murmuring ; lack of mortification in eating and drinking, etc. ; that swarm of venial sins or at least voluntary imperfections which take possession of us and deprive us of the abundant graces which from all eternity have been reserved for us ' (*L'âme de tout Apostolat*, Pt. V., chap. i., p. 273).

We must seek, then, for that purity of heart of which our Lord speaks, that detachment from creatures and from self above all which is necessary to those who seek God ; we must ' make ourselves indifferent,' as

says St. Ignatius, so that we do not desire or set our
hearts upon anything except as our Lord wills, that
'single eye' which, looking steadfastly toward God,
only sees creatures in relation to Him ; we must be
convinced that little things are often as dangerous in
hindering our walk in the path of perfection as are
great things ; indeed, for the devout Christian, even
more so, since whilst he would shrink from mortal sin,
he allows himself a licence towards venial sins and
imperfections which mars his efforts and spoils his
prayer. For what does it matter, asks St. John of the
Cross, whether a bird be tied to a stake by a rope or by
a slender thread, so long as it is tied and cannot fly ?

(b) The custody of the senses, those five avenues
through which temptation continually presents itself.
There is much of evil which those living in the world
in our days cannot help but see and hear, but much
more that they could avoid seeing and hearing had
they the will to do so. With few exceptions – and in
these necessary exceptions the grace of God is never
lacking – there is no occasion for us to hear and see,
still less to say, half the things which, if they do not
lead to sin, yet disturb the peace and calm of the soul.
'Keep thy tongue from evil' and from that idle speaking to which our Lord refers so sternly, for talkativeness
and all that it leads to are most harmful to the spiritual
life. It is too often the mark of a shallow spirit ; indeed,
it would seem that the less a man thinks – and thinking
is fast dying out – the more he talks. 'Talking,' said
Faber, 'is a loss of power,' and it certainly tends to
dissipate that sense of the presence of God which is the
greatest guard of the soul. Deliberately to choose to be
silent at times, to watch and weigh our words when we
speak, would accomplish more for many than the pious
practices they so much enjoy.

Another sphere in which custody of the senses is
necessary, especially in view of our prayer, is that of

concentration in the spirit of St. Catherine of Genoa's
'One thing only and one thing at a time.' To pray
well demands not merely concentration, but a concentration which has nothing forced or violent about it.
St. François de Sales never tires of insisting upon the
need of calmness and tranquillity in our approach to
God. But to have this at our prayer means that we
must strive for it outside of our prayer, and one of the
greatest aids to this is to learn to do each thing as it
comes, as if it were the only thing we had to do, and
having done it, or being compelled to leave it to go on
to another duty, to do so in the same spirit. So, occupied and fully and calmly concentrated on each duty
as it presents itself, repressing all impatience, excitement and the vain attempt to do or think of half a
dozen things at once, we shall come to our prayer in
the same spirit, and find ourselves free from a swarm of
distractions which are simply due to the lack of any
concentration in the rest of our life.

(c) The spirit of recollection. We ' live and move
and have our being in God,' and ' this is the work of a
perfect man, never to let the mind slacken from
attending to heavenly things, and amidst many cares to
pass on as it were without care ; not after the manner
of an indolent person, but by a certain privilege of a
detached mind, not cleaving with inordinate affection
to anything created ' (*Imitation* III. vi. 26).

Mediocre Christians who content themselves with a
bare performance of obligations frequently excuse
themselves from attempts at further progress on the
ground that their manner of life in the world, in itself
quite lawful, prevents any such recollection and
devotion as à Kempis and all spiritual writers insist on.
They should be taught to see, first, in what true devotion consists, for which the early chapters of the
Spiritual Combat of Scupoli, and of *The Introduction to a
Devout Life* of St. François de Sales, and the second part

of St. Pedro de Alcantara's *On Prayer & Meditation*, may
be consulted ; and second, in what exactly recollection
consists. The world of affairs is full of men who are
intensely recollected because they are intensely interested in some particular aim or project. They do a
thousand things a day, but behind all they do, domi-
nating and influencing all their life, is one supreme
thing. They are not always actually thinking of it ;
they may, indeed, and will at times, be thinking of
and doing the commonplace things, eating, drinking,
playing, that all men do. But always, even if not
consciously at the moment, one thing and one alone
is supreme and central ; for that thing they live ;
without it, life to them would lose all meaning. They
are men of recollection.

And recollection in the spiritual life means precisely
the same thing ; it is the spirit of the man who is
possessed with the reality of God as the true end of all
human life, who knows that he exists ' to praise,
reverence and serve God, and by this means to save his
soul.' He is not, any more than his neighbour,
possessed with the reality of money or fame, always
consciously thinking of God, but he does all for God,
sees all in relation to God, seeks God in and through
the commonplaces of daily life. For to him God is no
mere word, no vague shadow afar off, no mere abstract
principle, but the living, personal God Who is not only
in all things by His Presence, Essence and Power, but
in the depths of his own soul, God of his heart and life.

This is no more than elementary Christian truth, yet
for most it is but dimly adverted to, and even the
practising Christian needs definite means of recalling
and preserving the fact of it to himself. Such aids are
the practice of making the first act of the day an act of
profound adoration of God, in Whose Presence we
awake. To begin each day by kneeling in silence and
uniting ourselves to the unending adoration of Heaven

and earth is one of the most useful and influencing practices it is possible to perform.[1] It should be followed by the Morning Offering, another most valuable practice, in some such words as these : ' O my God, I offer to Thee, by the hands of Mary, all the thoughts, words, actions and sufferings of this day in union with the Sacred Heart of Jesus in the holy Mass.'

The intention manifested in these acts not only sets the tone of our life for the day, but endures in reality before God, even if we do not think of it. These two acts, in the case of those who have little time, with a Pater and Ave, might well suffice for morning prayers, for the prayer consists, not in many words, but in intensity of desire.

The practice of ejaculatory prayer, of raising our heart and mind to God in acts of adoration, praise and love as we go about the day ; the frequent offering of our actions to Him, remembering that the ordinary duties of our state of life are the chief means of our sanctification ; the taking of some thought in our mental prayer to recur to during the day, St. François's spiritual bouquet, are all efficacious means of keeping ourselves in that spirit of recollection which is one of the great secrets of the Christian life. But the illustration I used above of a similar spirit in men of the world reveals what is most necessary. They are recollected, I said, because they are interested, because something is seen by them as eminently lovable and desirable. There is our need, to see God as supremely lovable and desirable in Himself. The fundamental weakness of Christian life to-day is largely due to the fact that we

[1] 'The mystery of birth renews itself in every morning . . . this living being becomes a prayer . . . Do you see how much depends on this first hour of the day? It is its beginning. Man can start at it without any beginning, without thought, without an act of the will – merely slipping into it. Then it is not truly a *day*, but a time of rags and tatters, without mind or face. But a day is a way : it needs direction. A day is a work : it demands definite resolution. A day is your whole life : your whole life is as your day – but that needs a countenance ' (Romano Guardini, *Sacred Signs*, p. 82).

are more concerned with self than with God, with the question of saving our soul rather than adoring, praising and serving God, with fighting temptations rather than seeking God, a ' glory for me ' rather than a ' glory be to God ' religion. We do not think enough, contemplate enough, adore enough, God *in Himself* ; our minds are so filled with self that we habitually think of God in relation to ourselves, our needs and desires. But all religion is founded on what God is and ever was and would be had He never uttered the *fiat* of creation. God the Self-Existent, the Eternal, Abiding, Unchanging Reality ; Who is not the sum total of created perfection, but altogether ' other '. than creation, differing not in degree but in kind from all the works of His hands. ' What art Thou, then, my God ? What can I say, but the Lord God ? O most high, most good, most powerful, most Almighty, most merciful, yet most just ; most hidden, yet most near ; most beautiful, yet most strong ; stable, yet incomprehensible ; unchangeable, yet changing all things ; never new, and never old, renewing all things and " making old the proud and they know it not " ; ever in action, yet ever at rest ; still gathering, yet lacking nothing ; supporting, filling and overshadowing all things ; creating, nourishing and ripening ; seeking, yet knowing all things ' (St. Augustine, *Confessions* i. 4).

We need a conversion *to* God, not merely *from* sin ; a realisation that we were created ' to be for the praise of His glory ' (Eph. i. 12) ; that our first aim should be to ' seek first the Kingdom of God and His righteousness ' (Matt. vi. 33), the principle and foundation upon which our life is to be based, ' to praise, reverence and serve God, and *by this means* to save our souls ' (*Spiritual Exer. of St. Ignatius : Principle*).

To this end all our religious exercises should tend ; so long as we mainly seek our own good we shall rest in ourselves ; so long as we are occupied with self and our

sins shall we remain bound to self and sin. 'Flee from
the consideration of yourself and of your sins as from a
fire,' says Père Condren ; 'no one ought ever to think
of himself except to humiliate himself and to turn in
love to our Lord' (*Lettres*, p. 134). 'Seek the Lord
and your soul shall live,' 'for if ye truly seek Me with
all your heart ye shall surely find Me,' and to find
God is to have found that one absorbing interest before
which all else is as naught.

(3) The third cause of distractions in prayer, as of a
great many difficulties in the spiritual life, is the fact
of the close relation between body and soul, so that
whatever affects one must necessarily affect the other.
In fact, the less we differentiate between soul and body,
as if they were two separate entities linked together,
as it were, the better. In *A Catholic View of Holism*,
Mons. Kolbe quotes from a previous book of his, *The
Art of Life*, the following illuminating passage : 'This
body of ours is not a separate thing, different from the
soul. We deny that it has any organic life of its own
which a superadded soul comes in by some mysterious
influence to control and direct. Sensation is not a
gathering by the soul of impressions on particles united
to, but external to, itself. The body has not even a
being it can call its own ; whatever the body is, the
soul makes it. . . . I am one being, not two. My soul is
simple in its essence, as well as various in its powers ;
and it is one and the same thing which thinks beyond
the body's range, which in the body feels, which
organises the body itself, and which constitutes (or gives
being to) the very minutest particle of which that body
is composed ' (*op. cit.*, cxii., p. 47 ; cf. St. Thomas,
Summa Theol. 27, III. Q. lxxvi.).

We have to remember, then, and to reckon with the
fact that any mental or spiritual effort affects the body
as, on the other hand, bodily conditions affect the soul.
As Baron von Hügel says, ' Nothing we may feel, think,

will, imagine, however spiritual, however *real* spiritually, but has in this life to be paid for by the body.
True, the joy of it will even do our body good ; still, a
certain subtle, unintentional strain has been introduced
into our nervous system. The same in its degree and
way would be true if we took systematically to music or
mathematics. There is no necessary harm in this, and
no means of fully avoiding it. Yet it is important that
we should be aware of the fact. For such awareness
will help to give us a certain sobriety and moderation
in all this our emotional life – a sobriety and moderation which will, if wisely managed, greatly add to and
aid that fundamental Christian virtue, *creatureliness* '
(*Selected Letters*, p. 278).

Now this affects our prayer in two ways ; either (1)
we come to it bodily or mentally tired, or (2) the act of
prayer itself, especially if it is marked by more than
usual fervency or sensible consolation, tends to produce
a certain fatigue. In the first we suffer at the time ;
in the second, afterwards.

In the first case, where we come to prayer fatigued
in mind or spirit, we should make our prayer one of
quiet rest, in simple confidence, placing ourselves at
our Lord's feet, remembering the Psalmist's ' O rest
in the Lord,' and our Lord's ' Come unto Me, all ye
that are weary and heavy-laden, and I will give you
rest.' He knows that human tiredness, He Who, being
weary, sat by the well-side, knows that feeling of being
' at the end of the tether,' as we see in the Agony in the
Garden. For indeed ' I have no need to evade my
human weakness or to be other than I really am ; no
need to play any false rôle or assume any exterior
convention ; it is enough that as a man I resemble the
Son of man, and so long as I do not descend to sin, I
am one with Him Who, in Himself, has experienced all
our miseries. . . . Lord, I offer you, then, my infirmities,
my fatigue, my long wearinesses, this profound

drowsiness which periodically seizes me and from which
I am rarely free . . . it is enough that I accept it with
You and for You, without bitterness or wrath, content
to know that in this I resemble You ' (Pierre Charles,
S. J., *La Prière de toutes les Heures*, vol. I., vii.).

In cases of fatigue arising from physical conditions
we may act in the same way, but it is also necessary to
take physical remedies. ' Physical strength is necessary
in order to pray well,' says Faber, and St. François de
Sales, ' To eat little, work hard, have much worry of
mind, and refuse sleep to the body, is to try to get
much work out of a horse in poor condition without
feeding him up ' (*Letters to Persons in Religion*, xv.,
p. 303). Père Poulain says that we often read in the
lives of the Saints of long prayers and great mortifica-
tions, and think we ought to imitate them, but that this
' is an exaggeration if we do more than our strength
permits . . . this aptitude for prolonged prayer
is a highly desirable thing, but it is a special gift ; we
do not have it merely because we try to produce it '
(*Graces of Interior Prayer*, chap. x., p. 140). St. Teresa
treats this question in her usual commonsense way :
' This poor prisoner of a soul shares in the miseries of
the body. The changes of the seasons, and the alteration of the humours, very often compel it, without fault
of its own, not to do what it would, but rather to suffer
in every way.' She goes on to say that in such times
the soul must not be forced ; discretion must seek
whether ill-health be the cause ; ' the poor soul must
not be stifled ' ; a change should be made in the hour
of prayer ; the soul must not be tormented to do the
impossible ; exterior works of charity, spiritual reading,
going for a walk in the fields, holy recreations, may take
the place of mental prayer for a time. ' Take care, then,
of the body, for the love of God, because at many other
times the body must serve the soul ' (*Life*, chap. xi.).

On the other hand, we must be on our guard against

that temptation to become anxious about our bodily
health, for, as St. Teresa tells us, when the Devil sees us
a little anxious about our health, he wants nothing
more to convince us that our way of life must kill us.
'Being myself so sickly, I was always under constraint
and good for nothing, till I resolved to make no account
of my body nor of my health . . . my health has been
much better since I have ceased to look after my ease
and comforts' (*Life*, chap. xiii. 9, 10).

Discretion, then, but not slackness or unnecessary
thoughts about, and care of, the body, but a true,
steady and sane mortification such as the Church has
ever insisted upon, which, as Abbot Vonier has said,
'aims not to weaken but to make a man pure and
strong.' As a matter of fact, most of us need more
mortification, not less, for the main thing we suffer
from is not mental or physical weakness, but just
flabbiness. The remedy for half our ills is to 'pull
ourselves together,' and to ask ourselves, not 'What do
I want?' but 'What do I need?'

'We think that our nerves are out of order when we
are wanting in attention; that we are anæmic when we
are wanting in thoroughness; that we are broken down
when we are not yet broken in; that we require a
physician when what we really need is a schoolmaster
of the old type' (Münsterberg).

We shall often find that little bodily ailments, drowsiness, inattentiveness, and so on, will vanish if we offer
them to our Lord and practise a little extra mortification – e.g. kneeling upright at prayer. For a discreet
mortification brings power both to soul and body.

In the second case the act of prayer may, and often
does, cause fatigue, and this not infrequently results in
a reaction afterwards and a fall into sin. This may be
due to overstraining the mind in the reflective part of
prayer, to especial fervour and feelings of sensible
devotion, or to the lack of consolation.

All overstraining and forcing of the intellect in prayer is to be avoided. We come to prayer, not to gain new and great thoughts, but to perceive the reality of old ones, so as to be more moved by them – not, in St. Teresa's words, to think much, but to love much. ' Let the will quietly and wisely understand that it is not by dint of labour on our part that we can converse to any good purpose with God ' (*Life*, chap. xv. 9).

' The loftiest and most recondite speculations are not prayer ; sometimes they are rather the swellings of pride,' says St. Vincent de Paul, and again, ' Too much mental application heats the brain and brings on headache . . . we should be moderate in these matters ; excess is never praiseworthy in any respect, and especially is this true of prayer ' (*St. Vincent de Paul and Mental Prayer*, p. 280).

Nor, teaches the same saint, is moderation in the matter of fervour and sensible devotion less necessary. Truly we need fervour, and to the soul who is fired by the love of God all things seem possible and we may be tempted to do too much, and this sometimes comes from the Devil, who, ' when he cannot directly induce us to do evil, inclines us to take on more good than we can accomplish, and so overloads us that we are crushed under a weight that is too heavy and a burden we cannot bear.' The result of this is that ' after all these useless efforts (to make virtue felt and, as it were, natural) there must be some relaxation, the grip must be let go,' and there often follows ' a distaste for all sorts of devotion, a distaste for virtue, a distaste for the holiest things, to which one only returns with the greatest difficulty and trouble ' (*op. cit.*, pp. 189–193). St. Ignatius says the same (*Letters* : ' To the fathers and brothers at Coimbra ').

Aridity or Desolation.

By these terms is meant that state of the soul

bereft, to a greater or less degree, of any pleasure or
consolation in prayer; when there is no 'feeling' of the
presence of God or of the action of Divine grace;
when the mind is devoid of thought, the heart cold and
unmoved by spiritual things, and the will without any
desire or energy; when we do not want to pray, and,
if we force ourselves to do so, find it almost impossible.
St. Ignatius defines desolation as ' a darkening of the
soul, trouble of mind, movement to base and earthly
things, restlessness of various agitations and temptations moving to distrust, loss of hope, loss of love;
when the soul feels herself thoroughly apathetic, tepid,
sad and as it were separated from her Creator and
Lord' (*Spiritual Exercises, Fourth Rule for the Discernment of
Spirits*). 'My heart is dried up, and my soul like a land
without water. I cannot shed tears. I find no savour
in the Psalms. I have no pleasure in reading good books.
Prayer does not recreate me. The door is not open to
meditation. I am lazy in my work, sleepy in my
watchings, prone to anger, obstinate in my dislikes, free
in my tongue, and unrestrained in my appetite.' Thus
St. Bernard describes a state which every Christian
knows in some form or another, a state which may be
either a friend or an enemy according to the cause from
which it springs, and the way it is received and treated.

Before we come to the causes and remedies of aridity
one very necessary lesson has to be learnt – that is, that
we shall make little or no progress in the spiritual life
until we are convinced that it is a supernatural life of
faith, not a merely superior natural life of sense-
impressions, feelings and emotions. ' Luther, and still
more Calvin, have ruined this spirit of faith, unloosing
in the Christian world the passion of feeling, of experi-
encing the new life of the converted and regenerated
man,'[1] so that to-day large numbers of professing
Christians practise a religion which is centred in self

[1] Bremond. *Histoire Litt.*, vol. iii., p. 380.

and is dependent upon the emotions of the moment. It is entirely pragmatic ; worship, prayer, Sacraments, truths, all are judged by the feelings they do or do not evoke in the individual. Sensible devotion and comfort, ' uplift,' the stirring of surface emotions, are made the test of the truth of a doctrine, the value of a practice or the good of prayer.

All this is as demoralising as it is un-Christian and untrue. ' The just shall live by faith,' and faith is a habit of the soul which holds on to God in sunshine and dark alike, which puts no trust in feelings, which, whilst it will welcome and use consolation when it is given by God, does not depend on it, nor is to be drawn aside from its upward path when the way grows hard and lonely. For the man of faith seeks not himself or his own satisfaction, nor even the gifts of God, but God Himself for His own sake. He worships as the Church commands, not because or when he likes to do so, but because worship is his primary duty as a creature ; he receives the Sacraments not because or when he experiences some sensible feeling of good, but because they are the means of his union – felt or not – with God : he prays with the same regularity and constancy as he breathes, knowing that no felt emotion is required to convince him that his spiritual life depends upon the first as his physical does upon the second.

It will be well, then, to devote some attention, first, to considering in what true devotion consists, and, second, to a very necessary distinction between ' sensible devotion ' and those spiritual consolations with which God is wont at times to visit the soul.

Those who are familiar with the *Spiritual Combat* generally attributed to Lorenzo Scupoli (1530–1610), and with the *Devout Life* of St. François de Sales, will remember that both writers begin by defining the nature of true devotion. ' True and living devotion,' says the latter, ' is no other thing than a true love of

God ; yet not any kind of love ; for in so far as Divine love beautifies our souls, and makes us pleasing to His Divine Majesty, it is called grace ; in so far as it gives us strength to do good, it is called charity ; but when it reaches such a degree of perfection that it makes us not only do good, but do so carefully, frequently and readily, then it is called devotion ' (*Devout Life*, Pt. I., chap. i.). So also St. Pedro of Alcantara, quoting St. Thomas : ' Devotion is nothing else than a certain promptitude and facility in well-doing ' (*On Prayer and Meditation*, Pt. I., chap. i.), which, he goes on to say, is gained ' by means of meditation and contemplation on Divine things.'

Devotion lies in the will, not in the affections and feelings ; it is directed toward God, not toward His gifts. ' Love, in order to be pure, ought not to be occupied with any sensible impression or sentiment. It loves because God is infinitely lovable in Himself, not because of His gifts, nor for any consolation in His service.'

Thus ' it is most important that those who would love God should see that the sanctity and fidelity of love do not consist in visits and sensible impressions of God to the soul, but in the pleasure which God has in the soul . . . not desiring satisfaction for herself but for Him ' (Ven. Frère Jean de St. Sampson, *Vray Esprit du Carmel*, chap. xvi.).

For ' progress in the spiritual life does not consist so much in having the grace of consolation, as in bearing the withdrawal of it with humility, self-denial and patience ; so as not then to grow slack in the exercise of prayer, nor to suffer thyself to relax from any of thy accustomed good works, but according to thy ability and understanding to do willingly what lieth in thee, and not, through any dryness or anxiety of mind which thou feelest, wholly to neglect thyself ' (*Imitation*, Bk. III. vii. 1).

So St. Teresa teaches the soul should come to prayer

with a great courage, not ' expecting to reap a reward at the beginning,' for ' the sole aim of one beginning to practise prayer should be to endure trials, and to resolve to the utmost of her power to conform her own will to the will of God,' in which our whole welfare consists (*Inter. Castle*, M. II., chap. i. 13, 15). This is the constant teaching of the Saints ; true devotion is not a matter of the feelings, emotions, sentiments, but simply a readiness to conform our will to God's will in all things.

In the *Interior Castle* St. Teresa says : ' There may *appear* no difference except in name between sensible devotion and consolations : I think there is a very great difference . . . it appears to me that we may term " sweetness in devotion " that which we acquire for ourselves in meditations and petitions to our Lord. It is natural, although, ultimately, it comes from the grace of God.' Such sweetness is of the same character as the pleasure we derive from some good fortune which may befall us. ' Spiritual consolations, on the contrary, arise from God.' The first we gain ' by our thoughts, by meditating on created things . . . it is the result of our endeavours ' ; the second is a supernatural favour, produced in the depth of our souls, which cannot be gained by our wishing for it or by any act of our own (except so far as all fidelity, etc., prepares us for the reception of grace), for ' it does not rise from the base coin of human nature, but from the most pure gold of Divine Wisdom ' (M. III., chap. ii. 13 ; M. IV., chap. i. 4–6 ; M. IV., chap. ii. 4–5). ' Sensible devotion is very desirable ; if the soul is humble enough to understand that it is not better on account of these sentiments, which cannot with certainty always be ascribed to charity, and even if they are, they are the gift of God.' That ' if ' should be emphasised, lest such sensible feeling be mistaken for Divine graces, which are seldom, if ever, bestowed upon beginners, and so excite spiritual pride.[1] They are, as St. John of the Cross points out, but destined to help us in the beginning of the spiritual life – ' milk for babes ' – and may easily lead us astray. We must not be disappointed, or imagine that all is going wrong when we do not have them, for the loss of them may, on the one hand, be due to some natural cause, or, on the other, if it is the act of God, ' the more our Lord subtracts His sensible consolations the more perfections He prepares for us, provided that we humble ourselves before Him, and cast all our hope upon Him ' (St. François de Sales, *Letters to Persons in Religion*, xviii.).

' Touching meditation, I pray you not to distress yourself, if sometimes, and even very often, you do not find consolation in it ; go quietly on, with humility and patience, not on this account doing violence to your spirit. . . . Take it as a rule that the grace of meditation cannot be gained by any effort of the mind ; but there must be a gentle and earnest perseverance " (*ibid.*, *Letter* ix.). He advises that at such times we should follow the practice of St. Teresa, which was also his own, of taking a book and alternating reading with meditation until our time is up. St. Teresa also recommends the use of pictures, etc. ' Do you know when the gazing on a representation of Christ is a good and holy practice in which I take great pleasure ? It is when our Lord is absent, and makes us feel His loss by aridities. . . . To gaze on His picture rouses the soul to fervour ' (*Way of Perfection*, cxxxiv. 10). Or we may quietly and slowly recite well-known vocal prayers – the Paternoster, Ave Maria, Anima Christi, etc. – in the way St. Ignatius suggests, ' by rhythmical beats,' saying one word only between one breath and another,

---

[1] It is not unnecessary to warn beginners not to read spiritual books treating of the higher states of prayer. There are few which are not liable to misunderstanding by those who have little knowledge of both theology and the spiritual life, and such may easily fall into delusions about their state. Experience shows that, even in some religious houses, insufficient discrimination is exercised in this matter.

' and in the length of time between, one is to look chiefly to the meaning of such word, or to the person to whom one recites it, or to one's own lowly estate, or to the difference between such high estate and such lowliness of my own ' (*Spiritual Exercises : Third Method of Prayer*).   In cases where the aridity is complete and one cannot think at all, vocal prayers may be recited by a sheer act of will, but remember St. Teresa's advice as to what should be done when ' God permits a tempest of difficulties to assault His servants for their greater good.'   We should not trouble about it, nor tire ourselves trying to get rid of the evil by force, but pray as best we can, or leave off praying and rest our brains as if in illness, doing some other good work (*Way*, xxiv. 3).   Care, however, must be exercised about this, lest whenever prayer is found difficult or dry, we hastily abandon it for active work.   For, as St. Teresa adds, ' This advice applies to persons who watch carefully over themselves, and who grasp the truth that they cannot speak both to God and to the world at the same time.'

Those who are yet in the early stages of prayer will need usually to follow the advice given by St. Ignatius in the thirteenth Annotation to the *Spiritual Exercises*, that when we find it hard to complete our time of prayer we should ' act against the desolation ' and extend the time for a little in order to gain the habit, not only of resisting, but of overcoming the enemy.

In another letter (ii.) he gives certain signs by which we may know whether these feelings come from the evil or the good spirit.   It is a good sign when we do not rest in and simply enjoy them, but use them as a recreation to enable us to do our work better ; if they make us more humble, for if they come from the evil one they would cause us to think that we deserved them as a reward ; if, when they depart, we are not discouraged but strengthened, whereas those that are not of

God give us a little joy only to leave us cast down ; if they cause us to love God more, and not merely these feelings in themselves. ' Receive them with this sole condition, that you be ready not to receive them . . . and are ready to live without them, when God shall consider you worthy and able.' For, as Fr. Sebastian Bowden says : ' It is when we are in darkness and solitude – when God seems not to be there – when we are without devotion –*frozen*, we may say – when there seems not a word or a sigh to help us – that we learn our utter nothingness before God, and that we are also making progress and being purified in a way we know not ' (*Spiritual Teaching*, p. 112).

There is yet another reason why we should have a clear estimate of the true place of sensible devotion in the spiritual life. These feelings affect both soul and body, with the not infrequent result that, unless they are rightly understood and used, they may plunge the latter into the most grievous sin. ' For when sense and spirit are both delighted together, the whole nature of man is moved to that delectation according to its measure and character. For then the spirit, that is the higher part of our nature, is moved to delight itself in God ; and sensuality, which is the lower part, is moved towards sensible gratification, because it knows and admits no other ' (St. John of the Cross, *The Dark Night of the Soul*, Bk. I., chap. iv.). Hence arises the phenomenon of apparently devout men and women, whose lives are a constant alternation between prayer and passion, who on one day are wrapped in pious emotions and the next in the satisfaction of physical desires. We talk of such as leading a double life, but in reality it is but one, now directed toward God, now turned toward the creature, and this is to a large extent due to a wrong estimation and use of the emotions. Professor Thouless has pointed out that ' mysticism seems to result from the utilisation for higher ends of energy derived from the lowest instincts ' (*The Lady Julian*, p. 11) ; and if this is so, it means that the whole of our nature, not merely the higher part of it, must be directed to one end. A religion of ' feelings ' is always danger- ous, as the records of many ' revivals ' show, and those who are naturally emotional, who tend easily to sensible devotion, need particularly to guard themselves from that reaction, in which the physical nature asserts itself, which is so common. A thorough conversion of the will is necessary in such cases, together with sound teaching and reflection upon the true nature of devotion accom- panied by real mortification. ' It does not take much of a man to be a Christian,' said Huxley, ' but it takes all there is of him.' It is the failure to recognise this which is the cause of so many breakdowns of those who seem most in earnest. The fact is that their efforts are but sectional and largely emotional ; only part of them moves forward, leaving the lower instincts behind untouched, with the result that by and by these come hurrying up, intensified rather than calmed by the efforts made, and easily overtake and drag down the soul.

Aridity in the early stages of the Christian life principally arises from three causes : first, lukewarm- ness ; second, various natural circumstances ; third, from God.

St. John of the Cross gives three tests by which we are to know whether aridity comes from God, from sins and imperfections, lukewarmness or some physical indisposition. The first is ' that we find no comfort in the things of God, and none also in created things.' It is not only that prayer does not attract or satisfy us, but also that nothing else does, whereas if the aridity were caused by sin or carelessness, we should probably find pleasure in creatures. But since all this may have a physical cause, we must seek for a second test. This is found in the fact that the soul is alarmed at its state, the absence of any delight in prayer causing it to think that it is going back. This would be a sign that the aridity is not caused by lukewarmness, for, if this were so, there would not be this anxiety. The third sign is 'an inability to meditate and make reflections, and to excite the imagination as before, notwithstanding all the efforts we make.' The existence of three signs taken together show that the aridity is a gift of God destined to lead us to a higher state of prayer.

(1) 'What a farce it is! Here we are, with a thousand obstacles, drawbacks and imperfections in ourselves, our virtues so newly-born that they have scarcely the strength to act (and God grant that they exist at all!), yet we are not ashamed to expect sweetness in prayer, and to complain of feeling dryness in prayer' (*Interior Castle*, M. II., chap. i. 14). How shall we expect to be anything but 'bored' in our time of prayer if our real interests and inclinations are elsewhere, if there is no real mortification of our passions and will, no studied detachment from creatures, if our whole love and service of God are but mediocre and lukewarm? It is little short of astonishing, save that one knows the capacity for self-deception we possess, that, of all sins, we do not fly from that one which God has declared so pre-eminently hateful to Him – lukewarmness. To be, as so many are, content with mediocrity in that which demands all! And then to wonder why prayer is so difficult, meditation so dry, our desire for the things of God so weak! A dissipated, unmortified life, a life of half-service, a life where religion is but one of many interests, can only find aridity in prayer. There is but one cure – a thorough conversion to God. Let the soul who finds prayer dull, arid, distasteful, examine itself as to the wholeheartedness of its love for God ; let it begin at once to practise detachment, mortification, penance ; let its prayer be centred on the thought of who and what God is, Whom it has dared to treat in such a manner. Let it consider

that ' the highest point of life is thought, the deepest root of life is likewise thought, the eternal life is thought, but in this mortal life we must strive through act to fit ourselves for highest thought, and the fruitful in thought are the ascetic in life, the servants girded in spirit, who watch for their Lord, who passes hidden and unseen ' (Mother Stuart, *Highways and Byways in the Spiritual Life*, p. 144).

(2) Aridity may arise from natural causes – e.g. bad health (indigestion and kindred troubles are not infrequently the source of what people imagine are ' spiritual ' difficulties), the weather, conditions and circumstances of life. ' As long as thou livest thou art subject to change, even against thy will ; so as to be sometimes joyful, sometimes sad ; now at peace, again troubled ; at one time devout, at another indevout ; sometimes fervent, at other times sluggish ; one day heavy, another elated ' (*Imitation* III. xxxiii. 1). It may be something great – a serious illness or some deep sorrow – or very little – a slight physical derangement, a word, a look ; little things affect little people, and it takes but little to set in motion feelings of pride, vanity, envy, depression, sulkiness, impatience, etc., which will inevitably have an effect on our prayer. For physical ills physical remedies must be used, although we shall do well to remember that a little extra mortification is often the best cure ; ' prayer and self-indulgence will not go together,' insists St. Teresa ; ' little indispositions . . . are often only fancies suggested by the Devil, which come and go . . . the body possesses this defect – the more you give it the more it requires . . . when once we begin to subdue our wretched bodies, they do not trouble us so much ' (*Way of Perfection*, chap. xi.). In all other troubles which threaten to disturb our prayer we must abandon ourselves more completely to God, renewing our confidence that, to them that love Him, ' all things work together for good.'

(3) We have seen already how we may form an idea as to the cause of aridity ; it now remains to be seen why God often plunges the soul into this state and how we should act when He does so. It is, indeed, one of the most necessary lessons of the spiritual life, nowhere better elucidated than by St. John of the Cross in the opening chapters of *The Dark Night of the Soul*. He tells that God treats beginners as children who need to be ' spiritually nursed and caressed ' so that they may be drawn to the practice of prayer and of the virtues, and may ' taste and see that the Lord is gracious.' But since they are yet weak and imperfect these very spiritual delights may easily become a danger by their being ' drawn to these things and to their spiritual exercises by the comfort and satisfaction they find therein,' which leads them to regard them as ends rather than as means, and to love the gifts more than the Giver. Then God withdraws these consolations, partly because the soul is becoming too centred upon them and they are in danger of becoming sources of pride, vanity, etc., or because He wishes to lead us to a higher state of prayer for which it is necessary that our humility and the sense of our nothingness should be deepened, that we should be more detached, learning not to depend upon sensible impressions, led to a more spiritual appreciation of Divine things, and to a greater desire and more real endeavour to seek God for Himself alone. These consolations are not gone for good, but in order that we may ask why, may realise how much there is yet of self-satisfaction to be got rid of, that we may learn ' not to leave the Giver in order to regard and amuse ourselves with His gifts ' (St. Jane Chantal, *Œuvres*, Tome III., p. 268). This withdrawal on God's part is not a punishment, though even His punishments are always acts of love, but an invitation to enter that dark night of faith in which the soul is purified and detached from creatures, and so progress through the

Night of Sense to the *Night of Spirit* in which the soul forsakes all to find God the All. Here are heights we need but know exist, we who are yet in the plains, or, at best, amongst the foothills, but we do need to realise that the greatest part of the journey is yet before us, and that the withdrawal of consolations and the state of dryness which results mean that we are on the way, not that we have lost it. There is cause for thankfulness, not for discouragement, for this is the school of the friends and apostles of God.

How, then, are we to behave when we are reasonably conscious that aridity is not due to any at least deliberate fault of our own or to merely natural conditions? We are apt to think that the first thing to do is to discover the cause, but this often leads us into seeking consolation from creatures, and so defeats the end we are aiming at. Actually, a time of dryness is also a time of darkness in which we are scarcely able to see what is wrong with us, much less to know why, and to throw ourselves into an energetic self-examination will probably do more harm than good. We must, if necessary, consult our director, provided that we know him to be possessed of the requisite knowledge to diagnose our case and help us. But an ignorant director is worse than none. The signs already given will help us, but above all it is necessary to realise that dryness is an ordinary feature in the spiritual life, not an alarming symptom peculiar to ourselves, and that it is always of far greater advantage to the soul than consolation. So we should meet aridity with calmness, patience and confidence in our Lord, Who in His own time will show us whence it comes and why. We must go on faithfully with our ordinary exercises even though we *feel* not the slightest benefit from them. ' The longing of a loving heart for God and its endurance of unwelcome difficulties is one of the most perfect prayers . . . when we pray we should be as empty vessels before God, into which His grace may be poured drop by drop if He so wills, and we should be as ready to go home with our vessel empty as if it had been filled to the brim ' (St. Jane Chantal, *Entretien* xxx). Again she says, ' In aridity it is possible to make all the acts of prayer, and if it is without taste or sentiment, it will not be without utility and profit. For the prayer of patience, of submission, and of abandonment to the good pleasure of God, which should be practised on these occasions, is not less agreeable to His Divine Majesty ' (*R.* 515).

To a religious suffering from ill health and much disquietude of spirit, Père Ginhac writes : ' Your incapacity to taste anything in prayer does not prevent your being dear to Jesus, of making progress in virtue, or of contributing to the glory of God . . . you want to serve God in your own way, that is to say, without distractions, dispensations, interruptions or bodily indispositions. If it could be so, all would be according to your own desires ; but you would not die to self, to your own will and judgment ; you would seem to be very virtuous, but it would only be, at the bottom, a seeming virtue, whilst, on receiving from the hand of our Lord all that afflicts your nature, you really do what advances you most in true and solid sanctity ' (*Choix de Lettres de Direction*, cxvi., p. 172).

There is much of real help in the advice which a Dominican, Fr. Raymond Hocking, gave to young Baron von Hügel. ' You want to grow in virtue, to serve God, to love Christ ? Well, you will grow in and attain to these things if you will make them a slow and sure, an utterly real, a mountain step-plod and ascent, willing to have to camp for weeks or months in spiritual desolation, darkness and emptiness at different stages in your march and growth' (*Selected Letters*, January 26th, 1919, p. 266). In another letter he writes, ' The stress of darkness and dryness . . . peculiarly trying . . .

but *irreplaceably profitable*.' He goes on to give three examples or ' images which have helped me along many a flinty furlong.' First, the climbing of a mountain, enveloped in mist for days on end, in which the mountaineer halts and camps, quietly waiting until it has cleared away. Second, that the spiritual life is like a long sea voyage, for which one must choose some few and appropriate things, selected in view of ' dirty ' weather. Third, travelling across a desert. On windless days all is well, but when the sirocco blows there is only one thing to do – dismount, lie down in the sand, cover your head and wait until the storm is over. And whatever it be, ' whether cloud-mists on the mountain-side, or huge, mountain-high waves on the ocean, or blinding sandstorms in the desert ; there is each time one crucial point – to form no conclusions, to take no decisions, to change nothing during such crises and, especially at such times, not to force any particularly religious mood or idea in oneself. To turn gently to other things, to maintain a vague, general attitude of resignation – to be very meek, with oneself and with others ; the crisis goes by, thus, with great fruit ' (*Selected Letters*, pp. 304–305).

Especial note should be taken of the advice that we must never make any changes when in a state of aridity. ' One ought never to make a change in time of desolation, but to stand firm and steady in the resolutions and determination in which one was on the day previous to such desolation, or in the determination in which one was in the previous consolation (*Spiritual Exercises : Sixth Rule for the Discernment of Spirits*). But, continues St. Ignatius, ' it is very helpful heartily to change ourselves in the contrary direction, by insisting more on prayer, meditation, much examination, and putting out our strength in some suitable manner of doing penance.' Yet the saint, who was so careful in leaving souls the fullest liberty, knowing the difference which exists between them, would not, we may be sure, always apply this latter rule, but would at times advise that gentle quiet resignation of which Baron von Hügel, following many approved teachers, speaks.

It would be impossible to sum up, in fewer or more incisive words, the whole traditions of the spiritual masters on this matter. Quiet, patient, humble, confident, persevering, waiting upon God, this is the one attitude of the soul in dryness and desolation, wherein we may gain comfort from the thought that, while we may not see or feel any good, God our Lord does see and is glorified, and that some day, by that mercy which is the fount of all He does, we shall see the progress that was made when, to our blinded eyes, we only seemed to be sitting still and wasting our time.

One fact emerges from all that has been said about the difficulties to be met with in mental prayer, and that is that it is impossible without mortification. ' To pray without mortification is simply to amuse oneself,' says Père Eymard. Fr. Baker makes all the practice of the Christian life consist in two acts, of which he says, ' Mortification without prayer will be but superficial, or, it is to be feared, hypocritical ; and prayer with a neglect of mortification will be heartless, distracted and of small virtue ' (*Holy Wisdom* II. i. 1, 9.).

St. Jane Chantal says that ' the measure of our perfection is the measure of our mortification ' (*Exhort.* xiv.), and it cannot be otherwise, since our Lord explicitly tells us that if we would follow Him the first condition is that we deny ourselves. ' Perfection does not consist in taste or sentiment but in an entire mortification and a firm and unalterable resolution to be all for God ' (St. Jane Chantal, *Entretien* xxxiv.).

To imagine that we can live an interior life of prayer and union with God without mortification, interior and exterior, is to expose ourselves to the gravest dangers. For nowhere is a double life more easily led. It is

possible to spend much time in prayer, to have a taste
for spiritual things, to experience a great deal of sensible
consolation in prayer and to imagine ourselves half-way
up the steps of Carmel, whilst, in sober reality, we are
living self-centred, dissipated and even grossly sinful
lives.   A good deal of present-day religious and
devotional life is nothing but self-deception, a mere
pandering to sensation and feelings, for it lacks that
contra agere without which all religion becomes but a
worship of self.   Our spiritual life is suffering – as
indeed is our whole life – from moral, mental and
spiritual flabbiness, the result of that worship of comfort
and ease, that avoidance of all that calls for real effort
and the denial of self, that discounting of the Gospel
of the Crucified which is preached on all sides, that
endeavour to make the best of both worlds which St.
Teresa ridicules as ' a general disposition to reconcile
soul and body together, that we may not miss our ease
in this world, and yet have the fruition of God in the
next . . . the pace of a hen.'

We have but to recur to the object of prayer to see
the necessity of mortification.   To come into union with
God we must go by the way, that is, by Jesus Christ ;
we must ' put on Christ,' and there is no other Christ
than Him Whose whole life was a putting away, not of
sin, but of self, a willing, joyful, entire submission of His
whole being, mind and will, to the will of God.   It is to
put on the Christ Who ' pleased not Himself,' ' sought
not His own will,' chose poverty, humility, obedience,
suffering for Himself, and demanded them from all
who would follow Him.

CHAPTER II

The Ascetic and Spiritual Preparation for Prayer

THE title of this chapter must not be regarded as implying that the practices and virtues named in it are to be acquired before we begin to pray. On the contrary, we shall never attain to them without prayer. Prayer is the first act to which the converted soul must turn, no matter what his life has been. ' Look that no man think it presumption, that he that is the wretchedest sinner of this life dare take upon him after the time that he have lawfully amended him . . . to proffer a meek stirring of love to his God . . . for not what thou art, nor what thou hast been, seeth God with His merciful eyes, but what thou wouldest be ' (*Cloud of Unknowing*, chaps. xvi., lxxv.).

If we want to turn a piece of waste, weed-choked land into a garden we begin by digging it up and destroying as many of the weeds as we can. But because we know that it will probably be a long time before they are all eradicated, we do not leave it bare and content ourselves with a continual warfare against them ; on the contrary, we sow our seeds and cultivate the soil ; knowing that only so shall we ever get a garden, and that with a little care the weeds will be got rid of in time. The same plan must be adopted in the spiritual life.

The purpose of this chapter is to show what are the necessary conditions for prayer, the dispositions which are required, the attitude of soul with which we must come to prayer. For, as Dom Lehodey writes, ' there will always be a rather strict proportion between holiness of life and the degree of mental prayer one has arrived at. These two things run parallel, and give each other mutual support ; they progress together or they fall away together ' (Lehodey, *Les Voies de l'Oraison mentale*, Pt. I., chap. iv.).

Père Desurmont lays down three necessary conditions of prayer – that it should be real, very simple, and adapted to our actual state ; we must come as we are. ' The greatest of sinners can and ought to pray ; the one thing necessary is that he should pray as a sinner. The man of evil will, can, and ought to pray ; but he must pray according to the state of his soul, speaking to God as he is, a man of evil will. The lukewarm must pray as he is, the just with the prayer of the just ; each one must come to God as he is in reality ' (*Retour continuel à Dieu*, p. 103).

The ascetical preparation for prayer consists of three fundamental and necessary practices :

(1) The renunciation of sin.

(2) The mortification of self.

(3) The purification of the heart.

I. The desire to pray implies the desire for God, however ignorant and weak that desire may be, and this, in turn, implies an entire renunciation of sin, for God and sin cannot co-exist in the soul. It is always from this point of view that the sinner should be directed. Conversion must be seen, not primarily as a turning away from sin, a giving up of this or that, but a turning of the desiring self to God. It is true that sometimes a conversion is the result of a profound disgust for sin, which makes renunciation easy ; but more often the soul, drawn by God to desire Him, is yet still drawn to sin, and an over-emphasis on the renunciation required may only cause the snapping of the fresh and tender link with God. It is this last which has to be strengthened and developed, for it is the thought of God, the desire for God alone, which supplies the motive power required to break with old-established habits of sin. Evil can only be cast out by good, an unworthy passion eliminated by a nobler and stronger one. And in the majority of cases this is not an instantaneous act, but a slow, uphill progress. ' We cannot become perfect in a day,' says St. Teresa. This fact needs emphasis and attention. Nothing is commoner than discouragement arising from repeated failures and slowness of progress. But, as St. François de Sales writes, ' The ordinary purgation and healing, whether of body or soul, is only brought about by little and little, by progressing from improvement to improvement, with effort and by slow degrees. . . . Let us not be troubled, then, because of our imperfections, for our perfection consists in fighting against them, and we cannot fight against them if we do not see them, nor conquer them unless we meet them ' (*Devout Life*, Pt. I., chap. v.). The only remedy for our failures is humility, penitence, and to rise from them and go on again as if they had not been. What it is necessary to see first is what St. Ignatius calls the ' first mode of humility, that for love of God a man resolves to abase and humble himself in obedience to the law of God, so that for no thing whatever, even in order to gain any temporal good or to save his life, will he commit mortal sin. This ' mode of humility,' Fr. Rickaby says, ' does not consist in never committing mortal sin, but in a serious purpose never to commit mortal sin as a means to any advantage or a way out of any difficulty.' It ' is not an act, but an habitual purpose – a standing order, as it were, framed, glazed and hung up in the council chamber of the soul . . . standing orders get violated, and yet remain standing orders ; they are ' not set aside by action to the contrary, but by a resolution rescinding the order emanating from the same authority which originally framed it ' (Rickaby, *Waters that go Softly*, chap. viii. 57).

Thus after having, in all sincerity, made such a resolution, a man may fall into sin, but unless he remains in sin, and gives up his purpose of seeking God, he has not fallen from this mode of humility, nor must he cease his prayer. This is most important, for the common result of failure to keep such a resolution is discouragement, in which the soul is tempted to think the task hopeless and to give up his prayer from the mistaken idea either that God is now angry with him or that to go on praying would be hypocritical. Neither is true. ' I am not angry with My servants when they fall,' showed our Lord to Dame Julian. ' Lo, lo, my loved servant, what harm he hath taken in My service for My love, yea, and for his goodwill ' (*Revelations of Divine Love*, chap. li.). ' Full preciously our Lord keepeth us when it seemeth to us that we are near forsaken and cast away for our sin, and because we have deserved it. . . . By contrition we are made clean, by compassion we are made ready, and by true longing toward God we are made worthy . . . our courteous Lord willeth not that His servants despair, for often nor for grievous falling ; for our falling hindereth Him not from loving us ' (*ibid.*, chap. xxxix.) Nor, as St. François de Sales teaches, do falls, even into mortal sin, hinder our prayer, provided that we turn to our Lord in contrition when we perceive our state and renew our purpose of serving Him. The fact is that the weaker we are, the more prone to fall, the more we need to pray ; our sinful state is never a barrier between our Lord and our souls. ' It is self-importance, not our misery, that gets in His way ' (Fr. Considine, *Delight in the Lord*, p. 24).

But our renunciation of sin must be more than a bare keeping within a narrow margin of safety ; it must extend to the second mode of humility so that ' not for all creation, nor for a threat to take my life, would I seriously contemplate the commission of a venial sin.'

St. François de Sales is the best commentator on these words of St. Ignatius : ' We must purify our souls from all affection to venial sins – that is to say, we must not deliberately harbour the will to continue and persevere in any kind of venial sin, for it would be too great a baseness to resolve, quite wittingly, to keep in our consciences a thing so displeasing to God, as is the willingness to displease Him ' (*Devout Life*, Pt. I. cxxii.). Here again it is not a resolve never to commit venial sin which is expected, for, as St. François says, ' We can never be altogether free from venial sins,' but the resolve not ' to contemplate seriously ' and ' harbour deliberately the will ' to sin venially. For although venial sin does not deprive us of the grace of God, it does hinder the work of grace in our soul and ' hamper the powers of the soul with bad habits and inclinations ' so that she cannot exercise ' that promptitude of charity in which devotion consists.'

And if the resolve to renounce all sin is a necessary condition of prayer, no less is it true that this resolution cannot be carried out without prayer, for ' inasmuch as prayer places our understanding in the clearness of Divine light, and exposes our will to the warmth of heavenly love, there is nothing which so purges our understanding of its ignorance and our will of its depraved inclinations ' (*Devout Life*, Pt. II., chap. i.).

' For when a spiritually-minded person rises from deep devout prayer, then straightway all his good resolutions are renewed, together with fervour and determination to do well ' (St. Pedro de Alcantara, *On Prayer & Meditation*, chap. i.).

II. *The Mortification of Self.* Under this head must be included all that is implied in the death to self of which the Apostle speaks, the conquest or redirection of the passions, detachment from creatures, the guard of the senses, the ' making ourselves indifferent ' of St. Ignatius, and the constant warfare on our strongest

NP

enemy – self-will. ' Fight self,' said St. Catherine of
Genoa, ' and you need fear no other foe.' ' The
Christian life is nothing else but a continual cross and a
continual prayer. The cross is necessary for the whole
of man, and all his parts, since all are, through sin,
diseased, and all need the operating-knife and
remedy. . . . Without this cross all our prayers avail
nothing, save to cause us to live lives of still deeper
deception' (*On Prayer & Meditation: Of Three Things*, p.
179). Since in prayer we draw near to God in order to
contemplate Him, to speak to and hear Him, and to
possess Him, it is necessary that the soul should be at
peace. Now ' peace is the tranquillity of order '
(St. Augustine : *De Civ. Dei*, LXIX., chap. xiii.). And
there can only be peace in this disunited nature of ours
when our passions and inclinations, our desires and
aims, have all been ' brought into captivity to the mind
of Christ,' ' *in sua voluntade è nostra pace* ' – ' in whose will
is our peace.'

All our attitude toward, and our practice of, mortification must keep in view the end to which it is only the
means ; that is, not to cramp or mutilate our nature,
but to free it from all which would hinder our search for
God, to make us both pure and strong, as says Abbot
Vonier. It is to detach ourselves from all inordinate
affection for external things, to subdue our flesh to the
spirit, to let the peace of God rule our hearts so that we
may attain that ' certain privilege of a detached mind,'
which enables us to attend to ' heavenly things and
amidst many cares pass on without care ' (*Imitation*
iii. 26).

' There are,' writes Fr. Baker, ' two general impedi-
ments that nature lays in our way to hinder us from
attending to God. The first is distracting images ; the
second, unquiet passions. The remedy against the first
is abstraction of life, a not engaging in business which
belongs not to us ; the mortifying of the curiosity of

knowing or hearing strange or new things not pertinent to our profession ; the tempering of our tongues from vain and unprofitable conversations ; the reducing our thoughts, as much as may be, from multiplicity to unity by fixing them continually on the Divine love ... against the second, the mortification of all inordinate affection to creatures . . . especially of that most dangerous, because most intimate and spiritual, thirst of unnecessary knowledge, and of all ambition to get victory or glory by disputing, writing, etc., as likewise of all anger, impatience, melancholy, fear, scrupulosity, etc. ; a studious care to help our souls in all the peace, tranquillity and cheerfulness possible . . . avoiding all violence and impetuous hastiness in performing our best and most necessary duties ' (*Holy Wisdom,* Sect. II., chap. v.).

Mortification is not easy. Like St. Augustine in the hour of his conversion, we find how ' the very toys of toys and vanities of vanities, my ancient mistresses, still held me ; they plucked the garment of my flesh, and whispered softly, " Dost thou cast us off ? " ' (*Conf.* VIII. xi.). But what so often makes it harder is that we look more upon what we deem we are losing than upon what we shall gain, upon what we give up rather than upon what shall be given to us.

All which I took from thee I did but take
Not for thy harms
But just that thou mightest seek it in my arms.
All which thy child's mistake
Fancies as lost, I have stored for thee at home ;
Rise, clasp my hand and come.

To ' die to self ' that we may live in and for Christ, to forsake the lower for the higher, the passing for the eternal, shadows for realities, self for God – this is the meaning of mortification. ' To count all things but

loss for the excellency of the knowledge of Christ Jesus
my Lord . . . that I may win Christ and be found in
Him ' (Phil. iii.).

' Would that I could persuade spiritual persons that
the way of God consisteth not in the multiplicity of
meditations, ways of devotion or sweetness, though
these may be necessary for beginners, but in one
necessary thing only, in knowing how to deny themselves in earnest, inwardly and outwardly. . . . And if
he be deficient in this exercise, which is the sum and root
of all virtue, all he may do will be but beating the air ;
utterly profitless, notwithstanding great meditations
and communications. There is no progress but in the
following of Christ ' (St. John of the Cross, *The Ascent
of Mount Carmel*, Bk. II., chap. vii. 7).

III. *Purity of Heart.* ' Keep thy heart with all diligence ; for out of it are the issues of life ' (Prov. iv. 23).
' The primary means of attaining to perfection is purity
of heart, which consists in not having anything in our
heart the least contrary to God and the operation of
His grace' (Lallemant, *La Doctrine spirituelle*, Prin. III.,
chap. i.). So St. John of the Cross teaches that
' we must not hinder God's work within us, nor resist
His Majesty,' ' but give ourselves freely,' and ' content
ourselves with God alone,' ' willing to be divinely filled
with the spirit of God.' The Fathers of the desert made
this the first and constant aim of the soul who would
aspire to a life of prayer. ' The end of our profession,'
says the Abbot Moses, ' consists in the Kingdom of God,
it is true ; but our aim is purity of heart, without which
it is impossible to attain that end ' (Cassian, *Conferences*, I. i. 4). ' It is for this that we ought to seek
solitude, to fast, watch, work, give ourselves to reading
and the practice of other virtues, having no other
intention than of guarding our heart securely from
all evil passions, and to progress, step by step, toward
the perfection of charity ' (*ibid.* I. i. 7).

Upon the degree of purity of heart which we have attained will our prayer depend, for ' where our treasure is, there will our heart be also,' our Lord tells us. So far as our heart is divided between God and creatures, so far our prayer will be lacking in that purity of intention which seeks only His glory and His will. Slowly it may be, but yet surely and persistently, we must strive to purify our hearts, our affections, our inclinations, from all that is not of God ; from venial sins and imperfections, from wayward thoughts, especially of vanity and curiosity, all attachment to useless occupations, of disquietude born of care of the opinions of men or of solicitude for our temporal interests, of pre-occupation with self, of seeking the gratification of self in our actions, of all that dims that singleness of vision by which God alone is seen. For it is ' the pure in heart that shall see God.'

Without constant introspection or nervous watching of ourselves – for all must be done quietly and peacefully in the spiritual life – we must seek to evict from our hearts and to prevent the return of all those memories, imaginations, vain and foolish thoughts, which seek to occupy so much of our waking hours and dissipate the grace of God in our souls. And we shall do this all the more easily by filling our minds with good thoughts than by a constant endeavour to avoid bad and useless ones. ' Set your affections on things above ' – that is, have those things in mind, pay attention to them, so that you are ever occupied with things that matter. A great deal of the waste of our spiritual life comes from sheer laziness of mind, for, since we must ever be thinking of something, if our thoughts are not occupied with what is good and useful they will be occupied with what is vain and useless. Thus St. François de Sales's ' Spiritual Nosegay ' is no mere pretty conceit, but an intensely valuable practice, since to keep in mind some leading thought of our

morning prayer will again and again save us from
occupying our minds with things of no value. ' Whilst
you are at prayer or when you are recollected . . . your
soul finds itself in a certain interior position before God ;
it takes a certain direction. This interior attitude is
always the same, as you will note if you carefully
consider it ; and it is this attitude which is called a
state of prayer . . . and it is this you should keep in all
your actions during the day' (Libermann, *Lettres*, i. 401).

' We should hunger,' writes Baron von Hügel, ' not
for the knowledge of things to avoid, but for the future
revelation of realities to love ' (*Letters to a Niece*, p. 38).
' Holiness consists primarily not in the absence of faults,
but in the presence of spiritual forces, in love creative,
love triumphant – the soul becoming flame rather than
snow, and dwelling upon what to do, give and be
rather than upon what to shun' (*The Mystical Element
in Religion*, ii. p. 238).

So he who would desire to pray well, to gain that
knowledge which is eternal life, must not only erect
fences and set guards to protect the house of his soul ;
he must at the same time adorn that house with the
virtues which make it the kind of dwelling God loves.
Indeed, as I have already implied, this must be our
chief concern, for the active desire for good is the most
potent weapon against evil. What, then, are the
principal virtues which conduce to good prayer ?

I. *Humility*. ' The prayer of the humble pierceth the
clouds' (Ecclus. xxxv. 17). Humility, which consists
in a true knowledge and acknowledgement of what
one is, would seem to be the favourite virtue of God,
for He not only commends it and is attracted by it –
' He hath regarded the lowliness of His handmaiden '–
but chose it as the most complete manifestation of
Himself (Phil. ii), and bids us learn of Him, 'for I am
meek and humble of heart.'

Nothing is more necessary to prayer than humility,

as our Lord teaches in the parable of the Pharisee and the Publican. The latter had but one virtue – the knowledge that he was a sinner, totally unworthy of entering the Divine Presence. The whole virtue of our prayer consists in our coming to God as we are. It doesn't matter *what* we are, whether we be as David or Mary Magdalene, but it does matter that we pretend to be something we are not. For the one impossible state is that of the soul blind to itself, lacking that honesty, that truthfulness, which alone enables it to be made other than what it is.

Further, we come to prayer in order to seek and find God. But how shall we see God if we are looking at ourselves? Unless we are convinced that there is nothing in ourselves worth looking at, and that the only thing which is truly our own is the sin we avoid looking at. To find God we must go out of ourselves, regarding ourselves as that nothingness which we are, emptying ourselves of all self-regard and self-seeking in order that we may be filled with the Spirit of God. Only to the humble does God bestow His gifts, much more Himself; 'the rich He hath sent empty away.' Our only merit, our only claim upon Him, is that we are beggars who have nothing of our own.

There are two principal ways of gaining humility.

(1) We must look for it, look at it and seek it from Jesus Christ. No mere consideration of humility as an abstract virtue will make us humble; we must see it and seek it in the Sacred Heart, for, as St. John Eudes writes, our Lord 'communicates His own virtues to His members who are docile to His influence, for He is the vital principle Who implants in them the Divine seed of His grace, making them participate in His merits, so that the virtues of the faithful are nothing else but the continuation and extension in them of the virtues of Jesus Christ.'

'Now this same humility is to be exercised, not so

much in considering thine own self, thy sinfulness and misery (though to do this at the first is very good and profitable), but rather in a quiet, loving sight of the infinite endless Being and goodness of Jesus ; the which beholding of Jesus must be either through grace in a savorous feeling knowledge of Him, or at least in a full and firm faith in Him ' (Baker, *Holy Wisdom*, Sect. I., chap. vi. 5).

' Remaining little means to recognise one's nothingness, to await everything from the goodness of God, to avoid being too much troubled at our faults, not to worry over amassing spiritual riches, nor to be solicitous about anything ' (St. Thérèse of Lisieux, p. 227).

(2) By the acceptance of humiliations. I say the acceptance of humiliations rather than the practice of humility, because it is chiefly in the former that the latter consists. The surest and quickest way of becoming humble is to receive and welcome the humiliations which God sends to us. ' Observe that we gain more in a single day by trials which come to us from God and our neighbour than we would in ten thousand years by penances and exercises we take upon ourselves ' (St. Teresa).

We know this is true, and it sounds simple enough, but it is actually one of the hardest lessons we have to learn. One of the commonest faults of the spiritual life is the attempt to go to God in our own way. It is one of the chief causes of our failures and our slow progress. We desire to be humble, but we want to pick and choose the means of becoming so for ourselves, which only means that our supposed humility is nothing else but self in a new disguise. The only sure way of becoming humble is the training of ourselves to say ' Deo gratias ' for the daily inconveniences, difficulties, slights, unpleasant tasks, imperfections and failures, reproofs, etc., the acceptance of all those things which ' go against the grain ' and which are the real test of whether we do know ourselves to be deserving of nothing before God. To seek humility in extraordinary ways is all contrary to the example of Jesus Christ, Who ' humbled Himself ' by submitting to the common ways and conditions of human life, Who humbled Himself in His passion because He had humbled Himself in the womb of Mary, in the manger of Bethlehem, in the Hidden Life, in all His relationship with men.

II. *Charity*. There must be the intention and the desire to love God above all things ; that is, to *prefer* God before all creatures, and to love our neighbour as ourselves, for God's sake. We must see that love of God is not any vague, sentimental feeling, aroused at particular moments, but a constant act of the will choosing God before anything else. There will be times when that love calls for emotional expression, and we must not be afraid of telling our Lord, ' Thou knowest that I love Thee.' For we are to love God ' with all our hearts,' and the repetition of acts of love and desire in our prayer is one of the best ways of increasing and deepening our love for God. But it is a greater act of love, because more an act of our whole nature as well as being more difficult when' we resist and endure, if we cannot banish, some temptation from within or without, deliberately, in the face of all opposition, whatever it may be, preferring God to sin. So is it that martyrdom is the greatest act of love, as our Lord said (St. John xv. 13).

And our love of God must be a love of God Himself, not merely for His gifts or for what He is to us, but because He is Himself infinitely lovable and deserving of love. So often our spiritual life is impoverished and weakened because it lacks this love of God for Himself. True love loves not for its own gain, but because it perceives someone most lovable. Such love desires to give more than to receive, to forget and put self on one side for the sake of the beloved ; it manifests itself in the desire to be with the one loved, to please, to give to, to make sacrifices for, to be utterly generous to, to be one with the beloved. These are aspirations and desires which should always bring us to, and animate, our prayers.

Nor must we ever forget that our Lord has mad charity toward our neighbour one of the foremost conditions of prayer, that there are no limits to the exercise of this charity. " There is a limit to human charity," said Lady Outram. " There is," said Father Brown drily, " and that is the real difference between human and Divine charity."

Fundamentally, it means, and can only be produced by our looking at our neighbour ' as a subject enclosed within the Divine Providence for His glory, and as an hierarchy of heaven and earth . . . and since the misery of this world and our blindness does not raise our minds to these thoughts, we ought to elevate our spirits to such an estimation by the power of faith and consider each soul as a work of God hidden in earth, a great work, yet buried in a perishable body and in the peculiar imperfections of nature and sin which hide from us its value and worth, known to God and His angels ' (Bérulle, *Direction Spirituelle*, chap. iii.). For we come to our prayer, not as individuals, but ever as members of the Body of Christ, so that anything which hinders our perfect union with that Body, or any member of it, hinders that union with God sought in our prayer. St. Teresa is very emphatic in her teaching that no progress in, or favours received in, prayer are worth anything unless they deepen charity for others within us. ' If these effects are not found, and are not greatly increased by prayer, we must conclude that this was no Divine favour, but a delusion of the Devil sent to increase our self-esteem ' (*Way of Perfection*, chap. xxxvi. 9).

III. *Simplicity.* ' Except ye become as little children, you cannot enter into the Kingdom of Heaven.' There has scarcely been an age when it was more difficult to attain simplicity of heart than our own, and it is probably one of the reasons why God raised up and gave to the world such a Saint as Sœur Thérèse of the Holy Child Jesus, the Little Flower, teacher of the ' way of spiritual childhood, the way of trust and absolute self-surrender.'

' To simplify things as much as possible is a great principle of the spiritual life ; the more our conduct is simple and uniform, the more perfect is it and the more easily we persevere in it ' (Libermann, *Lettres* I., lxxxvii. 419). ' Simplicity is the virtue of the perfect. It draws down upon us the greatest favours and lights from God, since he who possesses it, thinks not, wills not, loves not any but God, for God and in God's way ' (*ibid.*, Lettre xliii.).

How shall we gain simplicity ? By having our will ' anchored in the will of God ' ; by a constant renewal of our intention to do all for God and in God's way ; by a more and more complete forgetfulness of self. ' It is absolutely necessary to shun as the most pernicious vice the reflex action of the mind, the tendency to come back upon ourselves ' (Maritain : *Prayer and Intelligence*). By a holy and quiet contempt for what the world thinks and says, by doing what we do calmly and as perfectly as possible, yet without any anxiety as to *how* we do it, or wanting to do things too perfectly ; by learning to do one thing and one thing only at a time ; by training ourselves to be slow – all hurry, impatience, over-anxiety destroy the spiritual life ; by moderating our affections and desires ; by much silence ; by always humbly following our grace, not trying to do more than our Lord wills and enables us to do at the present moment ; by living in the present moment, which is all we have and upon which our salvation depends ; by an entire and generous abandonment of ourselves into the hand of God, ' casting all your care upon Him, for He careth for you,' content, as a blind man, to be led by His Spirit, for ' as many as are led by the Spirit of God, they are the sons of God ' ; living ever in the spirit of David : ' Delight thou in the Lord, and He shall give thee thy heart's desires.'

How many things are here, we might say, how shall we ever learn them all ? Never, perhaps, if they were to be taken one by one as progressive lessons in some language or science. But all we need is to see, in a broad glance, as it were, the outstanding characteristics of simplicity, and then fix upon one or two which we perceive to be our most real need. For in the spiritual life virtues are never gained singly, but to have gained one is to have gained many. For indeed they are not won by our efforts, but by our placing ourselves in the position where our Lord is able to give them to us. We cannot, by observing rules, make ourselves simple ; all we can do is to show our desire, to remove the hindrances in our Lord's way, to empty ourselves so that we may be filled with the simplicity which is in Christ Jesus.

IV. The life of prayer must be begun and permeated with a rich generosity, the spirit of the Sacred Heart ' Who loved me and gave Himself for me ' ; the spirit of the *Suscipe* of St. Ignatius, of that glad giving which has marked all the Saints. ' Give, and it shall be given you,' and one of the chief reasons of the poverty of our spiritual life is that we are for ever ' keeping back part of the price.' ' We pass entire years and often all our life,' says Père Rigoluec, reproducing the teaching of his beloved master, Lallemant, ' hesitating as to whether we shall give ourselves entirely to God. We cannot persuade ourselves to make an entire sacrifice. We reserve to ourselves many affections, desires, plans, hopes, pretensions, of which we are unwilling to deprive ourselves, in order to gain that perfect nakedness of spirit which disposes us to be fully possessed by God . . .

encumbered by self-love, ashamed of our ignorance, held by false fears, we do not dare to take the step, and from fear of being miserable are always miserable ' (*La Doctrine Spirituelle* du P. Louis Lallemant, pp. 65, 66).

' We think so much of ourselves, and are so dilatory in giving ourselves wholly to God, that, as His Majesty will not let us have the fruition of that which is so precious but at a great cost, so neither do we prepare ourselves perfectly for it . . . we think we are giving all to God, but, in reality, we are offering only the rent or produce, while we retain the fee simple of the land in our possession . . . a pleasant way this of seeking the love of God ! ' (St. Teresa, *Life*, chap. xi.).

It is this lack of entire generosity which makes it impossible for God to give us His best gifts – 'Open thy mouth wide and I will fill it ' ; which prevents the freedom and facility of our prayer ; which holds us back from the attainment of that peace which is so essential to the interior life, which binds our soul to creatures, and so prevents the clear vision of the Creator. ' Blessed are the poor, for theirs is the Kingdom of Heaven.' ' Blessed are they who hunger and thirst after righteousness, for they shall be filled.' Blessed is he who, having found the pearl of good price, sells all that he has in order to possess it. ' Give and it shall be given you.'

It must not be forgotten that the price is not paid once for all, but by instalments. We pay it in will and intention at our conversion, and that will is accepted, but the actual payment has to be made as our Lord demands it day by day, just as the cross has to be borne, not as a whole in one single glorious act, but piecemeal, bit by bit, and each so small, so common and ordinary, that faith and love alone discern in them veritable relics of the true Cross. Only by a constant generosity, a giving of what is asked when it is asked and in the way it is asked, do we keep our souls open to the receiving of God's gifts.

V. *Courage.* St. Teresa tells us how, in her early life, she required all the courage she had to force herself to prayer, but that ' when I had done this violence to myself, I found greater peace and joy than I sometimes had when I felt a desire to pray' (*Life*, chap. viii.). ' His Majesty seeks and loves courageous souls, but they must be humble in their ways, and have no confidence in themselves ' (*ibid.*, chap. xiii. 3).

To enter upon a life of prayer and, much more, to persevere in it, demands a firm determination, a resolute will and a great confidence in God. For whilst a life of prayer brings enduring joy, yet it has not the attraction or the reward which active works give to nature and self-love. Here, all is hidden, slow, contrary to nature, so that, as St. John of the Cross teaches in *The Spiritual Canticle*, the soul needs ' a firm resolution not to gather flowers by the way, courage not to fear the wild beasts, and strength to pass by the mighty and the frontiers.' To gather flowers by the way may be taken to mean the resting on the enjoyment of consolation and delights in prayer, ' amusing ourselves,' taking for our own pleasure a satisfaction that is meant to lead us to God ; not to fear the wild beasts ; to resist manfully, yet confidently and quietly, all the attacks which the Devil, self and the world make upon us ; strength to pass the mighty and the frontiers, to persevere in overcoming all the obstacles which we meet with, in a deliberate and sustained faith in God, to Whom ' all things are possible.'

If we consider the lives of the Saints, and ask what was the secret of that indomitable courage by which they persevered unto the end, a courage always accompanied with a deep and solid joy, we shall find it in the singleness of their aim and the constant thought of their eternal reward – two things conspicuously absent in the lives of most Christians of to-day. ' They endured, as seeing Him Who is invisible.' God Himself was the one object of their whole life ; all their energies were directed into a single channel, toward a single end. It was for this they had been created, called, endowed with grace, for this that all around them existed. What compared with this were all the difficulties, temptations, trials of the journey ? Were they not pilgrims – the world but a night in an inn – life but a journey in which the one necessary thing was a courageous perseverance? It was God they sought, Him alone, and He would not fail them. Inspired by this conviction, they ' reckoned that the sufferings of this present time are not worthy to be compared to the glory which shall be revealed in us.' Heaven, which was to them pre-eminently the sight and possession of God, not a mere going on of life under superior conditions – heaven was a reality of which they had already received a foretaste in their prayer. To be with God, one with God, to ' see the King in His beauty ' and to ' wake up after His like-ness,' to enjoy God in the dear company of Mary and the Saints – who would not be full of courage in pressing on to such an end ?

Thus in our day, all enwrapt as we are in the actual present, Shakespeareans[1] rather than Christians, what we need in order to inspire a real courage within us is more thought of and seeking of God Himself – God as All-Adorable, All-Lovable, All-Desirable in Himself. We are too content with the means, too intent on the way, too occupied with the seen, and so, when the means do not afford us sensible comfort, when the way becomes difficult and the seen is found to be so empty, our courage has nothing solid upon which to rest.

[1] Shakespeare ' has not got that sense – not merely of life's mystery, etc., but of the supernatural, of the other life, of God, our Thirst and our Home . . . no dying figure in Shakespeare looks *forward* ; they all look *backward* ; none thirst for the otherness of God, they all enjoy, or suffer in, and with, and for, the visible, or at least the immanent, alone ' (Von Hügel, *Letters to a Niece*, p. 36).

And since we do not habitually so think of and seek
God, we think little of Heaven and thus lose the
attracting force which would do so much to reinforce
our failing courage. A 'glory for me' religion will
never create a thirst for the living God, that desire to
be one with Him which, the stronger it grows, the more
it accentuates the pain of separation from Him and
intensifies the generous courage of the soul which seeks
Heaven only because Heaven is naught else but the
seen, known, loved and enjoyed Presence of God. No
one, as a matter of fact, desires Heaven for itself, and,
unless we have learnt and tasted in our own experience
'that the Lord is gracious,' we shall have but little
courage to follow the narrow path which leads thereto.
So if indeed courage is needed to begin a life of prayer,
much more will our prayer aid our courage as we go on,
learning more and more of our own weakness, and
leaning more and more on 'the strength which God
supplies.'

VI. *Patience.* 'In humility,' said Blessed Giles, 'the
mind is set at rest and peace ; patience is her daughter.'
Every spiritual writer insists that all eagerness, impatience, anxiety, haste, impetuousness, are destructive of
prayer and the spiritual life. St. François de Sales calls
impatience 'the mother imperfection of all imperfections ' – ' we must possess our hearts in longanimity ;
great designs are not effected save by virtue of patience
and duration of time ' (*Letters to Persons in Religion*, vi.).
' We must in all things and everywhere live peacefully.
If trouble, exterior or interior, come upon us, we must
receive it peacefully.   If joy come, we must receive it
peacefully and without throbbings of heart. Have we
to avoid evil ?   We must do so peacefully, without
disquieting ourselves ; for otherwise we may fall as we
run away, and give time to our enemy to kill us.   Is
there some good to be done ? We must do it peacefully ;
otherwise we should commit many faults in our hurry.

Even our repentance must itself be made peacefully : *Behold in peace is my bitterness most bitter,* said the penitent' (Letter viii.). Impatience dissipates our life, wastes our energy, displays a lack of faith and confidence in God, leads us to act at the wrong time and in the wrong way, provokes us to say things that we do not really mean, prevents our seeing clearly, exaggerates things out of all proportion, throws us off our balance, all of which is implied in our Lord's words, ' In your patience ye shall possess your souls,' and in the fact that in nearly all languages the word for impatience means ' to be beside oneself.' ' Woe unto you that have lost patience,' for it is the way to moral, spiritual, and, not infrequently, physical suicide. No good ever comes of an impatient thought, word or act, only, at the least, a multitude of venial sins, and always a general lowering of the spiritual temperature, depression, disgust and a distaste for holy things. As to prayer, how indeed shall we pray if we come to God in a spirit of dissatisfaction and impatience with Him and His ways, forgetting ourselves and our place in petulance, sulkiness and irritability, daring, in manner at least, to blame Him for the way He acts, or, more often, because, as we foolishly imagine, He doesn't act ?

We have to learn patience with ourselves, with others and with God, lessons only learnt by continual repetition and practice. ' We cannot become perfect in a day.' With ourselves, our ignorance, our slowness, our broken resolutions, our mistakes and failures, all impatience with which is only the result of our natural vanity and self-love, wounded and hurt by the sight of our imperfection. ' I am convinced,' writes Fr. Doyle, ' from a pretty big experience, that perfection is only won by repeated failures,' and St. Jane Frances de Chantal tells us that ' the best practice of the virtue of patience is bearing with oneself in failure and feebleness of will.'

OP

Impatience with others, which in beginners in the spiritual life often excites an indiscreet zeal for their reformation, is fraught with danger to the soul. The only way of reforming others is to begin with ourselves. ' For their sakes I sanctify myself.' Our impatient zeal is too often no more than the product of self-love, which is hurt because others do not go by our way or come up to our standard.

The Devil, says St. Teresa, works like a file, and one of his wiles is to turn our zeal for perfection into a watch upon others, with the result not only that we become blind to our own shortcomings, but vitiate and harm those who resent our behaviour (*The Interior Castle*, M. I., chap. ii. 20, 21).

It would seem almost impossible that we should be impatient with God, yet it is very common. We get tired of walking by faith ; ' impatience for vision,' says Coventry Patmore, ' is one of the last faults to be cured ' ; we complain because our prayers are not answered to the minute, or that our finely woven schemes do not attain their purpose ; we lapse into despondency because God acts so slowly, and seems so often to take little notice of our feverish activity, except to reveal its sterility.

No virtue is more necessary both to our interior life and to our exterior activity than patience, and we shall only gain it from much dwelling in the quietness of the presence of the ' God of Patience.' ' Rest in the Lord, wait patiently for Him.' ' For the vision is yet for an appointed time, but at the last it shall speak and not lie ; though it tarry, wait for it.' Nature is all for seeing, doing, accomplishing, but ' My ways are not your ways ' is one of the first necessary lessons of the spiritual life, and ' he that believeth shall not make haste ' ; ' they that wait upon the Lord shall renew their strength.'. Impatience is ever a shirking of the real thing, a getting out of tune with the purposes of

God, a missing of the beat, which all comes, as says Plotinus, ' from not looking at the Conductor in the midst and keeping time with Him,' for ' He shall keep him in perfect peace, whose mind is stayed on Thee.'

VII. *Desire.* ' Blessed are they that hunger and thirst after righteousness ; for they shall be filled.' ' Open thy mouth wide, and I will fill it.' Nothing is more necessary to good prayer than humble, confident, loving desire for God. ' As the hart panteth after the water-brooks, so longeth my soul after Thee, my God.' A spiritual writer says, ' God's free gifts are generally proportioned to our desires. We get what we *really* desire in our spiritual life.' ' Prayer,' says St. Thomas, ' is the interpreter of a desire ' (*Summa Theol.* II. ii., q. clxxxiii., a. 1, ad. 1). The more we desire the better will our prayer be, and the more we pray with desire the more our desire will grow. So writes St. Augustine to Proba : ' We pray always by continually desiring in faith, hope and charity. . . . And since the care of temporal things cools our desire, at certain hours we put them on one side in order to attend especially to prayer, so that by the words we pronounce we admonish ourselves of that which we desire, and by repeated desires prevent the flame from being extinguished within us ' (Ep. cxxx. 18).

The desire for God is indeed His gift, and a great sign of our predestination to be cultivated to the utmost. It is the desire, the vehement thirst of the Sacred Heart for us which enkindles a responsive desire in us, and this will grow as we yield ourselves to it. There are times when we feel acutely our coldness and lack of progress, and our hearts go out in strong beseeching : ' Hear my prayer, O Lord, and consider my desire,' and yet there seems to be no reply. But that very desire burning in our hearts *is* the reply : ' Thou wouldst not have sought Me hadst thou not already found Me.' ' Your ardent desire to love God,' says Fr. Doyle, ' is the best proof of a real love for Him.'

It is both true psychology and true spirituality to cultivate our highest desires and aspirations by expressing them in acts of the will, for by this means we root them in our innermost self. Any desire which is kept in mind, frequently reverted to and expressed is, says Baudouin, a command, a prophecy, which will probably manifest itself in full vigour. Timid souls are sometimes afraid of such expression, fearing to give voice to what seems to be, and is, so far above their actual practice. But without such expression we shall make little progress, for whilst on the one hand we must not be content with the gulf between our desires and our accomplishment never becoming narrower, on the other, we must not be content with desires which are matched by execution, for this will be to remain in mediocrity. If it be hard at times to keep going at all, what shall it be if we cease to desire ? Our only safety lies in fervour, in a continual reaching forward to what appears to be far beyond our reach ; ' our Lord does not ask for success, but for infinite desire,' and there will be little real endeavour where there is little desire. Who tries to obtain what he does not desire ?

' Is this pure love really in my heart ? Are not my boundless desires but dreams – but foolishness ? If this be so, I beseech Thee to enlighten me ; Thou knowest I seek but the truth. If my desires be rash, then deliver me from them, and from this most grievous of all martyrdoms. And yet I confess, if I reach not those heights to which my soul aspires, this very martyrdom, this foolishness, will have been sweeter to me than eternal bliss will be, unless by a miracle Thou shouldst take from me all memory of the hopes I entertained on earth. Jesus, Jesus, if the mere desire of Thy love awakens such delight, what will it be to possess it, to enjoy it for ever ! ' (St. Thérèse de Lisieux, chap. xi.).

The masters of the Oratorian school of spirituality insist very strongly on the fact that our acquisition of the virtues depends less upon our own efforts than upon gently yielding ourselves to the action of Divine grace within our souls, and this will be found to be true for all, but especially for those whose temperament and character are such that their efforts are too often rendered sterile by their very violence and activity. Bérulle constantly speaks of the need of exposing ourselves to the influence of Jesus. We should ' present ourselves before His humility, His charity, His benignity, and open our hearts that they may imprint themselves there ' (*Œuvres*, 1393).

' All the mysteries of Jesus Christ,' writes P. Bourgoing, ' His words, thoughts, desires, movements, and all His holy operations, interior and exterior, are as rays having their influence upon us . . . and imprint their virtues upon us without other effort on our part and without acts of virtue formally produced . . . we have but to look at them simply and fixedly with all humility and respect, waiting their influence upon us . . . I do not say this in order to abolish the exercise and practice of interior acts and the seeking and asking for virtues . . . but . . . to introduce souls into a way of interior prayer, by manner of regard, exposition, esteem, honour, reverence, admiration and adoration of Jesus ' (*Les Vérités*, Avis xii.). Like the Saints, we are ' to attempt an humble, creaturely imitation of the Eternal, Spaceless Creator, under the deliberately accepted conditions of time and space,' and this has been made possible to us by the fact that the Divine Life itself has actually been lived under those conditions, so that we may, as St. Dominic used to bid his companions, ' think a little of our Lord Jesus Christ,' and, ' looking unto Jesus,' catch the spirit of His Heart.

CHAPTER III

Progress in the Life of Prayer

A CAREFUL study and analysis of the various states or degrees of prayer as given by spiritual writers enables us, avoiding subtle and, for practical purposes, unnecessary distinctions, to define three main steps by which the soul progresses toward a more perfect prayer.

(1) Mental or Discursive Prayer.

(2) Affective Prayer, or the Prayer of Simplicity.

(3) Active or Acquired Contemplation.

The essential note of progress in prayer is simplification. Beginning with mental prayer, in which there is a large use of the understanding, having as its end the motiving of the will, the soul, more or less unconsciously and by virtue of its fidelity, passes to a prayer in which the understanding moves the will much more rapidly, one thought, and that more and more single and simple, actuating to acts of prayer. This, in turn, leads to a state in which recollection is almost constant, and the soul's prayer is but a more deliberate and direct centring of itself upon God at special times. Whereas, in mental prayer, careful and deliberate attention had, as it were, to be forced upon Divine realities, and the will moved to act by definite and prolonged reasoning, in the prayer of simplicity, acts follow thought without any appreciable interval, until in acquired contemplation the multiplicity of acts give way to a single direction of the soul toward God in which acts of prayer, as hitherto practised, are merged in an intuitive sight in which the soul no longer meditates upon God, nor addresses Him in varied acts, but simply, adoringly and lovingly contemplates Him as its Supreme Good.

In his admirable treatise *Divine Contemplation for All*, Dom Louismet describes the three stages of ordinary prayer very clearly. ' *Discursive prayer* is the mental prayer in which the Holy Ghost moves the mind of a fervent Christian to many considerations concerning the Divine Essence of the Blessed Trinity, or the mysteries of our Blessed Lord.

' *Affective Prayer* takes place when the Holy Ghost puts a stop to the arguments of the mind, and acts directly on the sensitive faculties and on the will, drawing the soul towards God, with great sweetness and vehemence.

' *The Prayer of Quiet* is when the Holy Ghost stays even the multiplicity of the affective movements of the soul, and reduces it to silence, but a silence pregnant with unutterable love, in presence of the Divine Majesty.'

Fr. Augustine Baker also makes a threefold division : (1) Discursive prayer or meditation. (2) The prayer of forced acts or affections of the will. (3) Active contemplation of aspirations flowing naturally from the soul under the immediate direction of the Holy Spirit (*Holy Wisdom*, Sect. II., chap. i.).

In Chapter III. I have given reasons for what I believe is the great need of to-day – the practice of methodical, mental prayer – since so large a number of Catholics are woefully ignorant of the fundamental truths of their religion, and can in no other way gain that kind of knowledge which unites them to God. But this is far from saying that there are not many who, if they are rightly directed, will not quickly reach a more perfect state of prayer. In fact, those who will apply themselves faithfully to the practice of the interior life, who set their prayer in its rightful place and are prudently zealous in the matter of mortification, especially of self-will, ought to arrive in a comparatively short time at affective prayer. This is particularly true of those, e.g. priests, religious and lay people with a certain amount of time and aptitude for spiritual reading, who, having their minds more constantly fixed upon Divine things, do a large part of their meditation in advance, as it were, and so come to their prayer with much material which the ordinary Christian has to find at the time of prayer. But no particular period can be laid down in general. It is not true, for instance, as I have heard a Retreat conductor say, that religious should arrive at affective prayer in six weeks.

I have already emphasised the fact that all souls are called to perfection, and this implies a more or less steady progress in the life of prayer, which, without any forcing, tends to seek that acquired contemplation which is the highest state possible to the soul's efforts aided by Divine grace. 'Contemplation,' says St. Thomas, ' is for man the end of human life. Wherefore Augustine says, in his first volume on the Trinity, that the contemplation of God is promised us as the end of all our actions and the eternal completion of our joys, which in the next life shall indeed be complete, for we shall see Him face to face. It is this vision that fulfils every function of the blessed ; here on earth we contemplate Divine truth imperfectly, " darkly, through a mirror," but this itself is the beginning of the Beatific Vision, begun here and completed hereafter ' (*Summa Theol.*, Pars II. ii., q. clxxx. 4. 4).

The witness to the possibility of contemplation for all faithful souls runs through all the ages, as may be seen in St. Augustine's ' If we be faithful we have already arrived at the way of faith, and if we do not abandon it, we shall without doubt arrive . . . to the height of contemplation which the Apostle calls face to face !

For some of the least ones, who yet walk perseveringly in the path of faith, come to most that blessed
contemplation ' (*Ep*. cxx. 4) ; St. Gregory's ' There
is no state of life of the faithful from which the
grace of contemplation can be excluded ; anyone who
keeps his heart within him, may be illumined by the
light of contemplation ' ; Fr. Baker's words already
quoted ; the common teaching of the Counter-
Reformers as exemplified in such a popular preacher as
the Carmelite, Père Leon, ' There is no Christian who,
by the obligation of his profession made in Holy
Baptism, is not called to the study and practice of
mystical theology ' (he uses the term in the more
ancient sense, not as modern writers would rightly now
restrict it to those higher states of prayer which are not
attainable by any human efforts) – all those admirable
sentiments, nearly always confined to the monastic
state, primitively and literally apply to all Christians.
' Ye are not of the world,' 'You are dead, and your life
is hid in God.'   ' To whom, my Master, dost Thou
pronounce these words ?   To the cloistered ?   Not at
all, but to the whole Church.   To whom and of whom
speakest thou, O great St. Paul ?   Of solitaries, of
religious, of Benedictines ?   No !   No !   Of whom,
then ?   Of the baptised, of the faithful, of Christians '
(*Sermons prêchés à Montmartre en* 1661), down to Bishop
Hedley's ' It is the very aim of the teaching of Fr. Baker
and his school that extraordinary prayer, contemplation, should be an ordinary state for Christian souls,'
and the Abbot of Pershore's ' In point of fact, some of
the best mystics and contemplatives are to be found
in the world.'

That this truth is so little recognised is largely due
not only to the prevailing ignorance about any prayer
except vocal prayer, intercessions and the like, but also
because any mention of the higher states usually
connotes to the mind such extraordinary phenomena

as visions, locutions, raptures, ecstasy, which are comparatively rare and are not to be sought for or expected
by any soul. Undoubtedly existent and deeply valuable
as they may be where God vouchsafes them, there is
much to be pondered over in the words of R. P. L.
Grandmaison (*Études*, May 1913) on this difficult
subject. ' It is unnecessary to concur in the common
opinion that the ecstatic phenomena constitute the
essential of the mystic state and call for our admiration;
they are nothing more than its concomitants, consequences and effects, due to the weakness, the imperfection, the insufficient spiritualisation of the human
instrument, which diminish with its progress in the
spiritual life. Ecstasy – I here reserve the term to the
phenomena of inhibition, temporary insensibility – is
not an honour nor a power ; but a tribute paid by the
mystics to the humanness of their nature.'

Further, many are held back by the thought that
any advance would be only a mark of presumption in
one so imperfect and full of failure. They are obsessed
by the common error which seeks a self-made goodness
as a condition for receiving the gifts of God, and give
all their attention to efforts of their own when they
should be simply abandoning themselves to the
guidance of the Holy Spirit. The experience of St. Teresa
is so common that we may well listen to her description
of a personal struggle which is so like our own.

She had entered a convent which was somewhat
relaxed ; there was a great deal of intercourse with
relations and friends, and the young novice found
herself drifting toward a mere exterior observance of
the religious life. ' My soul was so distracted by many
vanities that I was ashamed to draw near to God in an
act of such special friendship as prayer . . . it was the
most frightful delusion into which Satan could plunge
me – to give up prayer under the pretence of humility.
. . . I thought it would be better for me, seeing that in

my wickedness I was one of the most wicked, to live like the multitude, saying the prayers I was bound to (i.e. by the Rule) and that vocally, not to practise mental prayer nor commune with God so much.' She was tormented by the gulf between her prayer and her life, accentuated as it was by the good opinion all had of her ; she had great desires to further the progress of others, ' a most common temptation of beginners.' ' I have been a year or more without praying, thinking it an act of greater humility not to do so. This was the greatest temptation I ever had and very nearly wrought my utter ruin ; for when I used to pray, if I offended God one day, on the following days I would recollect myself and withdraw further from the occasion of sin.' About this time she received great help from a Dominican priest, who advised more frequent Communion and charged her never to omit her prayer, for ' it would not do me anything but good.' Yet no less than eighteen years passed ' in that strife of soul which arose out of my attempts to reconcile God and the world . . . the reason of my telling this at so great a length is that men may understand how great is the good which God works in a soul when He gives it a disposition to pray in earnest, though it may not be so well prepared as it ought to be. If that soul perseveres in spite of sins, temptations, relapses, brought about in a thousand ways by Satan, our Lord will bring it at last–I am certain of it – to the haven of salvation ... I may speak of that which I know by experience, and so I say let him never cease from prayer who has once begun it, be his life ever so wicked ; for prayer is the way to amend it, and without prayer such amendment will be much more difficult ' (*Life*, chap. vii.).

Another difficulty often arising in the minds of those who find themselves giving much more time to affective acts of the will, to the reiteration of a few acts or even one act of adoration, etc., than to actual meditation, or

who remain motionless before God contemplating the
Divine Majesty and Beauty, is the fear that they are
' doing nothing.'   There is, of course, a danger of the
soul drifting into a mere dreamy reverie in which
nothing is done, and this must be checked at once by
a return to considerations, acts or resolutions, but
when the eye of faith is riveted on God, the memory,
imagination and will possessed by and drawn to Him,
there is nothing to fear, for this is a state of prayer
commended by all the Saints.   Thus St. J. F. de
Chantal writes to St. François de Sales, ' My spirit in
its extreme summit is in a very simple unity ; it does
not unite, for when it desires to make acts of union,
which it too often wishes to do on certain occasions,
it feels a strain and perceives clearly that it cannot
unite itself, but only remain united ; the soul would
not willingly stir thence.   She neither thinks nor does
anything, unless it be a certain deepening of her desire,
which goes on, as it were, imperceptibly, that God
should do with her and with all creatures, in all things,
as He wills ' ; and again she says : ' In this state of
holy indolence our capacity for love grows greater, and
the shafts of Divine love strike far more deeply ; our
own activity keeps the soul chained, it is in stillness
that it grows.'

Père Surin says that there are three signs by which
we may know that this kind of prayer, which Bossuet
describes as ' one simple look of ours, one loving attention on our part, towards some Divine object – either
God in some of His infinite perfections, or Jesus Christ
in some of His mysteries, or some of the Christian
virtues,' a prayer in which there are no distinct reflections, is good and should be adhered to.   First, that
during the prayer the soul is in peace without any
sense of weariness or *ennui* ; second, that it goes forth
from prayer with a great resolution to persevere in
good ; third, that during the day it sees clearly how to

conduct itself and has much strength in the practice of virtue (*Cat. Spirit*, Pt. I., chap. iii.).

There is much need to remember that the Christian life is a unity and a continued, ordered progress, though, as Fr. Martindale has said, it is a progress up an inclined spiral, so that at times the going on is apparently on a lower plane. St. John of the Cross has left an exact and vivid description of the soul's passage from the darkness of sin to the heights of Carmel, showing us how the soul is gradually liberated from its lower self by the practice of active mortification and meditation, then led through the Dark Night of the Spirit in which it surrenders all dependence on external and even on spiritual things, mortifying the understanding, the memory and the will, passing through and beyond the use of all intermediate images to direct union with God Himself. He further emphasises the unity of progress by his teaching, which is also that of St. Catherine of Genoa, in her treatise on Purgatory (*vide* chap. xvii.), that the pains of Purgatory are a continuation of that purification of the soul by Divine love which begins in this life, as the final vision of God is but the fulness of that sight of Him in contemplation, in which, as St. Augustine says, we see ' in such a way as the heart sees, when it is said, He is Truth,' but cannot here abide in that seeing, but 'glide back into usual and earthly things'(*De Trinitate*, Tome viii., chap. ii.).

In this connection, too, we are enabled to see that all our exercises of prayer are not meant to end in themselves (' he who prays only on his knees, prays but little ' – Cassian, *Confer*. X. xiv.), but are designed to create and foster within us that life of prayer of which the Apostle speaks, that life which is lived ' in Christ,' sharing in His virtues, animated by His Spirit, guided by His principles, inspired by His mind, a life, not now and then, here or there, turned to God, but all and always turned to Him, lived in a continual, abiding recollection of His Presence, 'in Whom we live and move and have our being,' given over to His interests and inclinations, governed at all points by Divine, super-natural, Christ-like views, dispositions and standards.

A further point is of importance. St. John of the Cross, who describes so fully that 'strait and narrow way' of the 'Nada, Nada, Nada y in monte nada,' the way of universal and complete renunciation by which the All is to be found by the loss of all, yet says that 'God does not raise to perfect contemplation everyone that is tried in the way of the Spirit, not even half of them : the reason, He knows' (*Dark Night*, Bk. I., chap. ix.).[1] And, indeed, in his map or diagram of the ascent of Mt. Carmel he shows another path leading upward but not actually reaching the summit, i.e. the perfection of union with God so far as it is possible in this life. This is, indeed, the path of the many who ascend to God, not by the way of renun-ciation of all creatures, even the most spiritual, but by the right use of creatures who, without inordinate attachment to the gifts of God, yet never cease to be in some way dependent on them, finding in them, as Saint Robert Bellarmin teaches in his *De Ascensione Mentis*, steps in a 'ladder of created things.' Not all souls, then, are to be expected to follow St. John of the Cross all the way, nor, indeed, unless God wills, can they

---

[1] As this sentence is often mistranslated, 'lleva' being rendered 'called' instead of 'raised' and 'el por qué él se lo sabe' by 'God *alone* knows why,' both of which do violence to the Saint's meaning, I give the original. 'No á todos los que se ejercitan de propósito en el camino del espiritu lleva Dios á contemplacion ni aun á la mitad : el por qué, él se lo sabe.'

The point is that all are 'called' but not all are 'raised' to the highest state of contemplation owing, not to something known to God alone, but as St. John teaches in *The Living Flame* (Stanza II. 28. English of David Lewis), to the fact that he finds so few who have the patience, courage and resolution to endure the least hardness or mortification by which God wills to detach them from creatures and lead them into the dark night of pure faith (Edit. espagnole, Tomo ii. p. 640–641).

do so. For the majority the other path opens out and must be trodden with all the generosity possible, and with the utmost confidence that so long as the soul follows the Divine leading humbly and faithfully, it shall find rest ' in the haven where it would be.'[1]

How are we to know whether a soul is in the state of prayer which God wills for it ? What are the normal signs which mark the transition from one stage to another ? Actually, two moments have to be considered ; first, the passage from the ordinary mental prayer of beginners to affective prayer, and second, that from affective prayer to ordinary, acquired contemplation. In the first case, there is a gradual but increasing ability to pass more rapidly from considerations and the use of the imagination to acts of prayer. The soul finds in a single thought, or even in the act of placing herself in the presence of God, a desire and a facility to pour herself out in affective acts of prayer – catches fire, as it were, at once, without the labour of reflection hitherto necessary. It is not so much that meditation becomes more difficult as that it becomes less necessary. In this stage the acts of prayer may be spontaneous, or use may be made, especially where a certain aridity is experienced, of such acts and aspirations as those given by Father Baker at the end of his *Holy Wisdom*, or in Dom Rutherford's *Acts of Mental Prayer*. The test which determines the need and the time of making this advance in the prayer-life is the attraction the soul feels toward a more actual prayer, as contrasted with the exercise of the mind, etc., which leads to prayer, *and* the fact that it moves the will to at least as

[1] Cf. the conclusion reached at the second Spanish Congress on ascetism and mysticism organised by the Carmelites of the Province of Castille at Madrid in 1926. ' The mortification taught by St. John of the Cross is principally interior . . . the practice of his doctrine of *Nada* (entire renunciation) ought to be ruled according to the general condition of human nature and to the particular dispositions of the individual. The doctrine of total negation concerns all contemplative souls.'

great a desire and endeavour after the solid and common virtues as did the previous prayer. The latter may, and probably will, be slow in appearance ; indeed, as all real progress in prayer must bring increased light and purity of heart, the soul will see its defects and imperfections more clearly, and may be tempted to think that she is going back. Further, this strengthening of the union of the soul with God results in a keener sight of the existence of exterior faults, e.g. lack of humility and charity in regard of one's neighbour, which had hitherto been overlooked, partly from the appreciation of, and attention to, the needs of the interior life. Thus, it is the best of signs that the soul is walking in the path marked out by God for her, and that real, if little, seen progress is being made, if she goes out of prayer not only possessed with an interior peace in ' the fine point of the soul,' but also with a greater desire to exercise those virtues which concern her relation to others.

In the second case, that of the passage from affective prayer to the beginning of contemplation, all our guides follow the teaching of St. John of the Cross, although in some there may be found a lack of clarity in their exposition resulting from a failure to grasp that the Saint does recognise the distinction between acquired contemplation and that infused contemplation which belongs to the mystical life properly so-called, and to which not all are called. It is true that St. John is not always easy to follow, and that more than one reading is necessary if one would sound the depths of his doctrine. But it is, I think, clear that in *The Ascent of Mount Carmel* he speaks of a state of prayer which the soul arrives at and enters upon by its own activity, aided by grace, and that this state is what is now commonly known as acquired contemplation. The signs which he gives in chapters xiii. and xiv. of the *Ascent* as denoting the time when the soul should pass to contemplation are not identical with those mentioned in *The Dark Night of the Soul*, and should not be applied to the higher state of infused passive contemplation.

In the *Ascent*, then, St. John is treating of acquired contemplation and of the signs by which the soul may know when to abandon the latter stages of mental prayer, affective acts produced by few considerations, and go on to the first rungs of the ladder of contemplation. That this is acquired, active contemplation may be gathered from his own words : ' The end of meditation and reflections on the things of God is to have the knowledge and love of Him as its fruit. Each time this is done, it is an act, and as acts often repeated produce habits, so many acts of loving knowledge continuously made by the soul beget the habit thereof in the course of time. God is wont at times to effect this without these acts of meditation – at least without many of them – leading souls at once into a state of contemplation. Thus what the soul obtained before, at intervals, by dint of meditation, in particular acts of knowledge, is now by practice converted into habit and substance of knowledge, loving, general, not distinct, particular, as before ' (*Ascent*, Bk. II., chap. xiv. 2). Now all this is an active response of the soul to the attraction and grace of God, gradually leading to a more complete unification of its powers and to a closer union with Him, whereas infused contemplation is a pure gift of God, which the soul can do nothing to attain to and which is not bestowed, according to St. John, but to a few. But that there is a form of contemplation which is open to all is, as we have seen, the common tradition of the Church.

The signs which the Saint gives of the arrival of the soul at this state are three in number :

(1) An inability to make reflections or to exercise the imagination upon Divine truths, coupled with an aridity resulting from the endeavour to make such

Pp

acts wherein previously light and consolation were present. So long as meditation is fruitful it should be persevered in nor must it be supposed, that the entry upon contemplation precludes any return to formal meditation, for, as the Saint says, until the new state has become habitual, ' sometimes one, sometimes the other, occurs in this time of proficiency in such a way that very often the soul finds itself in this loving or peaceful attendance upon God, with all its faculties in repose ; and very often also will find it necessary, for that end, to have recourse to meditation, calmly and with moderation' (*Ascent*, Bk. II., chap. xv. 1). Here, again, the phrase 'for that end' indicates a form of contemplation attainable by the soul's fidelity to mental prayer.

(2) The second sign manifests itself in a growing detachment from creatures, not only of the natural but of the supernatural order. It is true that the imagination may still wander toward them, ' for it is disorderly even in the most complete self-recollection,' but the will is more firmly rooted in God, and the desire of the soul is for God Himself more than for His gifts or consolations. It sees more clearly that thoughts about God and the means by which He is apprehended and approached are not God ; that they are to be used, not rested in or enjoyed in themselves ; that, as St. Augustine says, ' the things of the world are for our use, not for our enjoyment. That which is for our enjoyment is the Father, the Son and the Holy Ghost.' There is an increasing transcendence of particular thoughts of God which are replaced by a general, confused, loving knowledge and perception of Him.

(3) The third sign, ' which is the most certain of the three,' consists in the fact that the soul finds itself at peace in this prayer, delighting ' to be alone, waiting lovingly upon God without any particular considerations, in interior peace, quiet and repose,' occupied in

a general knowledge and loving attention to God, undisturbed by any scruples that it is doing nothing, or that it is losing ground. Any fears of this nature which result in forced efforts to produce reflections, or to seek for a more particular knowledge in place of this 'general loving knowledge,' a state 'confused, loving, peaceful and tranquil wherein is drunk wisdom, love and sweetness,' are to be resisted as tending to deprive the soul of the higher gifts God now wishes to bestow upon it.

It is important to note that all three signs must be present before the soul may safely give up the practice of ordinary mental prayer. For the inability to meditate alone may be due to one's own fault, to lack of preparation, dryness or to conditions of physical health. Added to this inability there must be a positive lack of desire to occupy oneself with other things, a more pronounced detachment from creatures. Yet even these two signs are insufficient in themselves, for both may be the effect of some mental disorder, 'melancholy or some other oppression of the brain or heart' which creates a morbid disinclination for things in general. But the third sign sets its seal upon the others, providing the soul with an assurance that, despite the subtilty and delicacy of this new state, it has begun to find the fruit sought in the labour of mental prayer.

'It is by the bodily senses that the soul is able to reflect, search out, and come to the knowledge of things ; and by the spiritual sense to rejoice in the knowledge thus attained without further labour, search or reflection. The difference between these two conditions of the soul is like the difference between working, and enjoyment of the fruit of our work ; between receiving a gift, and profiting by it ; between the toil of travelling, and the rest at our journey's end.'

This state of ordinary, acquired contemplation marks a real advance from the way of sense to the way of spirit, an intense deepening of the soul's union with

God. It is the end – itself unending (for there can be no end in the sense of a full stop to the soul's growth in the loving knowledge of God) – of the journey of those whom God does not raise to the highest stages of the spiritual life. The soul, having ' found Him whom her soul loveth,' rests in peaceful contemplation at the feet of her Divine Lord, ' listening to His word ' and ' with joy drawing water out of the wells of salvation.'

CHAPTER IV

Direction of Souls in the Life of Prayer

IT is hardly possible to speak of spiritual direction in its relation to prayer without some preliminary consideration of the whole purpose and scope of the office of a director. This, indeed, is the more necessary from the fact that the few works in English on this subject are more occupied with the treatment of sin than with advance in virtue, and also that some of them appear to have been written with an almost total disregard of the teaching and methods of the great spiritual directors. ' Anglo-Saxon common sense ' and ' my experience,' mingled with the often debatable and sometimes already exploded theories of psychoanalysis, are not such safe guides to spiritual direction as some modern writers seem to believe. Of the great need there is of a sound knowledge of dogmatic, moral and ascetical theology, coupled with a constant study of the writings of the great spiritual masters, whom I shall enumerate particularly later, one cannot speak too strongly. I should not care to estimate the percentage of confessors whose direction often betrays a gross ignorance of the difficult and delicate task they have undertaken.[1] No man would dare to practise as a physician or lawyer with so inadequate an equipment. It is true that the clergy with few exceptions have little training worth the name, but this only makes it the more incumbent that they should train themselves with the aids which are now abundantly

---

[1] Such ignorance is not confined to our own time or country. Both St. Teresa and St. John of the Cross witness to it in their day, and similar criticisms of bad or inefficient directors might be quoted in later writers down to our own day.

to hand.   And, unless a priest will do this, he had better confine himself to spheres of work in which, to say the least, he may do less harm to souls.

The director of souls in the spiritual life must have a very clear, definite and convinced knowledge (1) of the scope and limitations of his office; (2) the end which is to be sought; (3) the means to be used; (4) the manner of applying those means to various classes of souls.

(1) The office of a director is a subordinate, dependent one; he is no more than an instrument of the one Director, Jesus Christ. His sole work is to wait upon God, to seek to discern the Divine will for each soul, to follow the *attraits* and graces which God bestows upon souls, to co-operate with the Divine leading by aiding the soul to see, understand and follow it. Direction is not our own work upon which we invoke the help of God; it is His work which He calls us to aid Him in accomplishing. ' I have nothing of my own to put in souls,' says Père Condren. ' In the direction of souls we must place ourselves in the hands of our Lord as instruments which He chooses to use in order to make His will known to them, to make them walk freely in the way of perfection, to strengthen them in their weaknesses, to encourage them in their discouragement, to deliver them from the snares of their enemies, and to conduct them by a sure way to Heaven. In order to do this we must direct them by the light of our Lord not by our own; and this must be done by annihilating ourselves in order that we may be entirely filled with the spirit of the Son of God, being intimately and inseparably united to Him, that we may enter into the ways by which He wills to conduct souls, never directing them by our own ways, which will assuredly be of great harm to them. . . . For in the Church there is but one priest . . . one sole director, Jesus Christ, Who wills Himself to conduct all the faithful by the ministry of His priests, and to be in all

directors in order to govern all whom He has confided to them' (M. Olier, *Esprit d'un Directeur des Âmes*, chap. i.). ' To direct a soul is to lead it in the ways of God ; it is to teach the soul to listen for the Divine inspiration, and to respond to it ; it is to suggest to the soul the practice of all the virtues proper for its particular state ; it is not only to preserve that soul in purity and innocence, but to make it advance toward perfection : in a word, it is to contribute as much as possibly may be in raising that soul to the degree of sanctity which God has destined for it. . . . It is necessary that the confessor should be, as it were, the voice of God, the instrument of Divine grace, the co-operator with the work of the Holy Spirit, and, consequently, that he should be an interior man, a man of prayer, a man well versed in spiritual things, as much by his own experience as by study and reading ; that he should have no purely natural designs, either of vanity or self-interest, but that he should only consider the glory of God and the good of souls ; that he should never act according to the leadings of his own spirit, but that he should judge of the things of God by the spirit of God ' (Grou, *Manual for Interior Souls*, p. 128).

The director, then, must have a high regard and deep reverence for souls, and for the designs of God for each soul. ' To direct a soul is to direct a world which has more secrets and diversities, more perfections and rarities, than the material universe, and a more perfect relation to the archetypal world, that is, to Him Who is both the Creator and the Idea of all that which exists outside the Divine Essence ; so that God regards a soul in a manner far different from that with which He regards the rest of His creation. And we ought to honour, follow and imitate that regard so holy, so pure and Divine, looking upon God's work as He looks upon it ' (Bérulle, *La Direction Spirituelle*, chap. i.).

This is as essential as it is not uncommonly forgotten.

Directors too often fall into the temptation of forcing souls according to their own predilections, of domineering and dictating, assuming a personal authority which is quite unjustifiable. 'There are,' says Père Surin, 'directors who get an idea and a plan into their heads, which they think much of, and apply to all the souls who come to them, thinking that they will accomplish something great if they bring them into line with it. So they have no other object than of carrying out what they have imagined like one who should wish all to wear the same clothes' (*Spiritual Catechism*, II. iii. 2). 'Let spiritual directors . . . remember that the Holy Ghost is the principal agent here, and the real guide of souls ; that He never ceases to take care of them and never neglects any means by which they may profit and draw near to God as quickly as possible and in the best way. Let them remember that they are not the agents, but instruments only, to guide souls by the rule of faith and the law of God. . . . Their aim should be, then, not to guide souls by a way of their own suitable to themselves, but to ascertain, if they can, the way by which God Himself is guiding them. If they cannot ascertain it, let them leave these souls alone and not disquiet them' (St. John of the Cross, *The Living Flame*, Stanza iii.). Mgr. Gay, whom Mgr. d'Hulst calls 'the master of spiritual direction in the nineteenth century,' writes to a penitent who desired to follow his direction with the exact obedience of a servant to a master : ' I shall not employ, at least habitually, in spite of your desire, the imperative formulas of which you speak. It seems to you that so you would find peace. Yes, but a natural peace which is not what I wish. Such commands would relieve you of the burdens of life, but it is not good that you should not feel the weight of them. I will be to you as the Cyrenian, nothing more. I would help you, not substitute myself for you. Strong natures

have need of obedience ; weak ones, such as yours, have
a gentleness which inclines to idleness. It is necessary
to give to each according to their needs. I do not want
you to be a slave – the word is your own – a word excessive and reprehensible. I wish you to be a son, and a son
reasonable, enlightened by the counsels of his father . . .
but walking as a man, not as a child ' (*Lettres*, iv. 10).

It necessarily follows that a soul cannot be directed
until it is known, and that what is principally to be
known is the particular will of God for it, which is to
be discerned in the vocation, graces and *attraits*. He
has bestowed upon it and in its circumstances, conditions, character, temperament and so on, all of which
are parts of God's designs for it. ' In the direction of a
soul it is necessary to begin, and this is all-important,
with an understanding of its interior, supernatural
state, the state of grace and the action of grace in that
soul ; seeing how far the soul is responding to its
grace, to what degree the life of our Lord, Divine grace,
is dominant in the soul and its works. This first consideration is of the highest importance. If you know
well the state of a soul, the operation of God and the
action of grace within it, you have gained a very clear
knowledge of the designs of God for it. But that is not
all ; the obstacles which grace finds there must also be
seen, the action of the soul and its character, the vices
and faults which exist. . . . Further, to cause a soul to
advance it must be brought back to the principle of
sanctity within it, to Divine grace, that it may become
docile to it and enabled to triumph more and more by
its power ' (Libermann, *Lettres*, Tome iii., Letter
cclviii., p. 97). In a later letter to a priest on the same
subject he writes, ' Recognise as a fundamental principle of direction that the person directed must not be
cramped or restricted ; too many rules must not be
prescribed ; a too rigid system must not be followed, or
harm may be done. If a director conducts and restricts

you overmuch, holding too closely to principles, much evil may come. I regard it as essential in direction that one shall allow grace to act with a great freedom, seek to distinguish false *attraits* from the true, and prevent souls from wandering from, or going beyond, the limits of such *attraits*.'

(2) The end to be sought. This is nothing less than the end for which man was created, to seek, find, know, praise, reverence and serve God, and by this means to save his soul and to possess God in Heaven. The director's whole efforts are to be aimed at bringing souls to see this, at creating in them a desire for and an intention to seek this end, and of aiding them by all the means in their power. It matters not what state the soul is in, how far away from its end it may be, how little its comprehension and desire, there must never be any doubt in the director's mind as to whither the soul is to be led, no compromising or minimising of the Divine precept, ' Be ye therefore perfect.' It will be true that we shall often only succeed in obtaining a very low and mediocre degree of perfection, but it is essential to remember that we shall not even attain to that unless we see in each soul a potential Saint, one whom our Lord has called to perfection. ' Each soul . . . ought to be considered with humility as the work of the Divine power which created it, as an object of the Divine wisdom which conducts it, as a subject of the Divine sanctity, shining and operating in it by grace . . . as enclosed in the Divine providence, for His glory, as a hierarchy of Heaven and earth, which ought to be established in God ' (Cardinal Bérulle, *La Direction Spirituelle*, chap. iii.).

Now this emphatically does not mean that we set before our eyes a certain ideal of sanctity and endeavour to force all souls into the paths by which that ideal was attained, for, although the end is one, it has to be reached in the particular way desired by our Lord.

The way of St. Augustine is not the way of St. Dominic ;
St. Teresa is very unlike St. Margaret Mary ; St.
Philip Neri treads another path from St. Paul of the
Cross. The whole setting of a soul has to be considered,
and what needs far more insistence upon than it
commonly gets is the truth that the sanctification of a
soul depends upon its fulfilling the duties of its state as
perfectly as possible with the aid of grace. St. François
de Sales makes this one of the capital points of all his
direction, and amongst later directors who owe so
much to the saintly bishop, Père Ravignan may be
quoted. ' A wife, a mother, the mistress of a house
have their perfection in their own hands. Prayer and
piety will bear no better fruits than the attention to
performing well of ordinary actions and the sanctification of the domestic life. It is there that we shall find
precious occasions of abnegation, patience, devotion
and zeal.' Only by recognising this truth can we make
people see how it is possible for them to attain to
perfection and enable them to practise perfection in
the way God has designed for them. Without this the
apparent gap between ordinary life and the life of
worship, prayer and Sacraments will become real and
no progress will be made.

Further, we must beware of demanding too much, of
expecting from one soul what we should have a right
to expect from another, owing to its very different
circumstances, grace, etc. ; of undervaluing the worth
of what seem to be but feeble efforts and slow progress.
We have to learn to be content at the moment with the
least things, the faintest response to grace, the scarcely
awakened comprehension of and desire for the one end.
For so it is that God is often content with us, and always
sees more of good in souls than do we, nor ' ever breaks
the bruised reed or quenches the smoking flax.' That
poor, struggling soul we so often despair of is very dear
to the Sacred Heart, that ' hopeless ' case may be one

day raised to the altars of the Church.   Thomas of
Jesus, speaking of the way our Lord ' took to cure the
weakness and frailties of His Apostles,' bids us note how
He took care to ' suit the remedy and its degree to what
He knew they could at the moment receive, never
going beyond that, lest they should be made worse
rather than better, and leaving their after-improvement
and perfecting to the operation of the Holy Ghost.'
So we must often, he says, pass over those imperfections
of which sinners are themselves unconscious, gently
and quietly leading them on to think more and more
highly of virtue, without showing any disgust and
contempt for their frailty and weakness.   This is the
best way to open their eyes, and dispose them to receive
the grace of enlightenment ' (*Sufferings of Jesus*, p. 350).

   (3) The means to be used.   Since man was created
for a Divine and supernatural end, the means by which
he is to attain that end must be Divine and supernatural.   For He Who is the End is also the Way, and
the Life of the Way ; it is by His Way that souls must
travel, by His Life they live in the Way.   Direction,
then, must be entirely supernatural, founded not ' on
the things of men, but of God.'   In the service of our
neighbour we should abandon ourselves to the disposition of God, the times, the means and the manner of
doing that good which He wills to accomplish by our
ministry.   He alone knows the manner in which His
designs will best be furthered ; He is the Master of the
work and of its direction ; He is Himself the accom-
plisher of His work ; we are but the instruments.   We
are not to direct of ourselves, but to leave ourselves to
be directed and conducted by Him.   ' If any speak,'
says the Apostle St. Peter, ' let him speak the words of
God ; if anyone minister, let him minister of the power
God giveth, that in all things God may be glorified
through Jesus Christ.'   So is it necessary that Jesus
Christ should do all things in the order of grace by His

spirit, as He has done all in the order of nature, and that He should be the soul and the life of all things. If we speak we should speak in Him and by Him ; ... with an entire confidence in His assistance, submitting ourselves in all things to be conducted by Him alone, in order that we may act in His time and in the manner which pleases Him, according to His good pleasure and for His glory ' (M. Olier, *Esprit d'un Directeur*, Art. i.).

The true direction of souls requires a conviction that the end sought is more easily attained by training them to desire and practise virtue than in directing all their energies towards the overcoming of temptation. Too much direction is moral rather than spiritual, more concerned with sin than with God, with self-examination and self-improvement rather than with the search for God. For God, Who is alone our End, can never be attained by merely negative means ; ' it is the appreciation of good rather than the dread of evil which makes a soul advance toward perfection' (Janet Stuart, *Society of the Sacred Heart*, p. 50). Much more is done by teaching souls to think upon the Divine realities, to meditate upon the great Christian truths, to look at Jesus in the arms of Mary or upon the Cross, than by confining our advice to the need of avoiding sin, of fighting temptation and of making vocal prayer. This applies to gross sinners no less than to the more refined (and more guilty) ; that which drew Mary Magdalene and Dismas is always more efficacious than any mere exhortations to moral effort. ' It is a great grace from God to practise self-examination, but *too much is as bad as too little*, as they say, believe me, by God's help, we shall advance more by contemplating His divinity than by keeping our eyes fixed on ourselves ' (St. Teresa, *Interior Castle*, M. I., chap. ii. 9).

Fr. Baker says that souls recently converted ought ' not to dwell long upon the exercises that concern remorse for sin, or other matters of fear, as death, judgment and hell, but rather to fix upon affections contrary to their present disposition'; such acts are, he concludes, more beneficial to the soul and more acceptable to God (*Holy Wisdom*, Sect. iii., chap. ii. 10).

One of the chief causes of the poverty and mediocrity of spiritual life in our day is the failure of the clergy to live, act and speak *supernaturally*, sometimes through ignorance or the lack of a true conversion, sometimes through timidity.   People of all classes are constantly suffering disappointment from this fact ; hungering for bread, they are offered a stone ; in place of the Gospel of Jesus Christ, they are given moral platitudes.   That we have not a revival of religion is not the fault of the laity, but of the clergy.   Let us but live, act and speak as ' ambassadors of Jesus Christ,' *alteri Christi*, priests in life as in name, filled, possessed and inebriated by the spirit of Jesus, and that revival would come to-morrow.

In this connection it should be noted that a director should always adopt a certain attitude of reserve toward those whom he directs. Frequent intercourse is undesirable ; long visits, conversations and profuse correspondence to be avoided ; the relation between director and directed should always be in the supernatural order, *in Christo*.

' Directors who attach themselves to souls are ordinarily the cause of far greater evil than they think ; they deprive God of that which He would have received by His Son in those souls if they had been perfectly established in grace. Finding them attached to earthly things, our Lord does not communicate Himself to them so abundantly ; and this is the reason we see so little progress in them, so few graces and solid virtues, so little union with God, but, on the contrary, so much inconstancy, lightness and self-love. Thus, directors who encourage such attachments, instead of being " men of God " are in reality " men of the

Devil," since in place of destroying the enemies of Jesus Christ in hearts that He may reign there, they diminish His royalty and increase that of His enemy, whose power over souls is always strengthened by these attachments ' (M. Olier, *Esprit d'un Directeur*, Art. ii.).

An equal danger is caused by those directors who forbid souls to seek another priest or show jealousy and anger when they do so. ' Thus,' says St. John of the Cross, ' thou art become a tyrant of souls, the robber of their liberties, claiming for thyself all the freedom of evangelical doctrine, and taking care that none of thy penitents leave thee – yea, still further, and much worse, should it come to thy knowledge that any of them have gone elsewhere for direction, or to discuss a question which it was not convenient to submit to thee, or if God hath led them for the purpose of learning what thou teachest not – I say it with shame – thou art jealous, like a husband of his wife. This is not zeal for the honour of God, but the zeal which cometh of thine own pride and presumption ' (St. John of the Cross, *The Living Flame*, Stanza iii.).

Far from attaching souls to himself, the director must do all that lies in his power to enable them to walk in entire dependence upon the guidance and in the power of the Holy Spirit. Far from always telling them what to do, he should exhort them to choose for themselves under the leading of the same Spirit, assured that if they are earnestly and desiringly seeking to do God's will they will receive the light necessary. People will ask, for instance, what particular mortification they should undertake, and it is often better to answer by pointing out that, the end of all mortification being the bringing of our will into union with the Divine Will, they can probably think of something which they have not yet done, and which they need to do, to effect this more completely. Such mortification will nearly always be allied to the subject of their particular examen. This throwing them back upon themselves, as it were, not only strengthens the will, but will often reveal to them the fact that, in asking advice, they were, in reality, endeavouring to evade what our Lord had already demanded of them. Behind the question there lay, perhaps unconsciously, the hope that something more pleasing to self would be imposed. ' I am not,' wrote Dom C. Marmion, ' a great partisan of much direction. I feel that the Holy Spirit is the unique Director capable of giving true light and inspiration. Yet it is God's way to direct us by His ministers . . . it is necessary that the director should know the soul *perfectly*, and this once done, he ought to indicate the way to be followed and then leave her to the Holy Spirit. From time to time, at long intervals, he should control her progress, and if anything arises outside the ordinary way he ought to know it, but, to my mind, long and *frequent* letters of direction do more harm than good ' (Dom R. Thibaut, *Un Maître de la Vie Spirituelle*, p. 264).

In order that a soul should not only begin well, but also advance in the way of perfection, there are certain essential points which directors should keep in mind. The first is the need of establishing the soul in a true peace. To this end not only is a general confession advisable, but also a full and frank account of one's life, circumstances, difficulties, graces received, etc. A soul cannot be directed, as I have said, unless it is known, and many go on making routine confessions for years without ever knowing themselves or making themselves known in such a way that any adequate direction can be given. There is always an unknown region in which, consciously or unconsciously, lie the roots of sins confessed again and again, and this suffices to prevent that peace without which no progress can be made.

Since the importance of this primary need of the soul seems to be so little understood, a little consideration of it is necessary. It is one of the continuous and repeated lessons of Holy Scripture and of the Saints that peace of soul is essential to any true, deep intimacy with God. 'Dominus non in commotione.' 'Be still, then, and know that I am God.' 'In returning and rest shall ye be saved ; in quietness and confidence shall be your strength.' 'Commit thy way unto the Lord, and He shall bring it to pass.' 'He that believeth shall not make haste' – shall not fuss, is the nearer meaning. The constant prayer of St. Paul for his converts is that the peace of God may dwell in their hearts. It is one of the chief gifts our Lord makes to His Apostles in His Passion, 'Peace I leave with you, my peace give I unto you.'

All disquiet, fear, impatience, violence, haste, excitement, scrupulosity sap the energies of the soul. 'We must in all things and everywhere live peacefully. If trouble, exterior or interior, comes upon us, we must receive it peacefully. If joy comes, we must receive it peacefully, and without throbbings of heart. Have we to avoid evil ? – we must do so peacefully, without disquieting ourselves ; for otherwise we may fall as we run away and give time to our enemy to kill us. Is there some good to be done ? – we must do it peacefully, otherwise we should commit many faults in our hurry. Even our repentance must be made peaceful' (St. François de Sales, *Letters to Persons in Religion*, I. viii.). In the same letter the Saint says that peace is to be gained by our having a thoroughly pure intention of willing in all things the glory of God ; by doing the little we can to that end under the advice of our spiritual father, and by leaving all the rest to God. 'Accept with a great heart,' writes Père Ginhac to Mother Mary of St. Francis Borgia, 'the truth that you are nothing and can do nothing, that you are possessed only of misery and incapacity. But, at the same time, rejoice that God our Lord is all, has all perfections and

Q P

a power without limits . . . peace is the possession of the soul which endeavours in all things to do the will of God, giving itself without reserve and refusing nothing to grace ' (*Choix de Lettres de Direction*, xvii., p. 29). Père Grou teaches that ' this peace is the effect of the presence of God in the soul . . . the principle of our advancement.' In order to preserve and increase it we must act towards it as we do with good health – enjoy it without thinking about it ; do all our actions with simplicity, without anxiety or trouble as to *how* we have done them (this is a characteristic of Père Libermann, who also insists that we must not worry ourselves about doing them too well : ' It is no doubt necessary to do things as well as we can ; but without torturing oneself or being in a perpetual qui vive ') ; we must put away all vain fears as to our state, for these never come from God, but only from our imagination ; God never troubles a soul which is sincere. He may reprove or warn it, and that severely, but all agitated or troubled thoughts come of the imagination or the Devil (cf. 'Rules for the Discernment of Spirits,' Ignatian *Exercises*) ; that when troubled in mind we must never change our conduct ; that we must never go against our director, but always live in obedience (*Manual for Interior Souls*, xlvii.).

In our prayer, says St. Nilus, we must not wish that our petitions should be answered in the way which seems good to us, but ' follow the good pleasure of God ; then thy prayer will ever be made in tranquillity and thanksgiving.'

This interior peace, then, which enables the soul to remain calm and tranquil, even when the lower part is moved by the passions, is founded in an entire renouncement of self, in detachment from creatures, in a care to moderate all interior movements and imaginations, in avoiding all solicitude and precipitation, and in an unbounded confidence in God. Interior as all this is, it will not be accomplished without attention to the exterior, and there is great virtue in seemingly small acts which tend to restrain natural tendencies to haste, excitement and so on.

Second, the director's work being to further the will of God in souls, he must, whilst making all due allowances for the state, circumstances, etc., of each, never allow any considerations of human prudence, calculation or compromise to obscure either the supernatural end which is to be sought, or the need of entire, courageous use of the necessary means. He must seek to inspire them with the desire of surrendering themselves entirely to our Lord, he must make them see the personal nature of religion, personal love, devotion and service for God in Jesus Christ ; not a mere tame acquiescence in a moral code, but a burning enthusiasm for a Master, a passion of the lover for the beloved. For – strange as it may sound in our unsupernatural days and ways – the Christian religion *is* this, the joyous, heroic, magnificent thing the Saints have seen and lived, not the dull, cold, safe, respectable and comfortable travesty to which the English eighteenth and nineteenth centuries reduced it. Directors should steep themselves in the spirit of the Ignatian exercises, especially those of the Second Week, as well as in the lives and writings of the great spiritual directors, for that enthusiasm and passion may only be communicated by those who, at least in some small way, have experienced it for and in themselves.

Particularly should they respect and develop the early aspirations of the young. There has been, and there is, far too much ' throwing cold water ' upon the fires kindled by the Holy Ghost in the hearts of children. A lack of supernatural vision in priests (and parents) is one of the main causes of the loss of vocations to the priesthood and the religious life as of the fact that so many churches are sparsely filled with the old and middle-aged, youth being conspicuously absent. The desire for God and special vocations normally manifests itself in early years, and needs watching and directing instead of, as is too common, being smiled at as childish dreams which the years will dispel, or, at the most, dismissed with the injunction to wait until one has grown up, seen the world, etc. It is not knowledge of the world, or the clouded vision of a later age, that is needed, but the knowledge of God and of Divine realities, more often 'revealed to babes' than to our dull, commonsense and utterly unsupernatural eyes.

At the same time, whilst welcoming and encouraging the generous desires of beginners, young or old, the director must see that these are exercised with discretion. In the first fervours of conversion, everything seems not only desirable but possible, and souls often lade themselves with a number of practices which tend to assume the nature of obligations and, sooner or later, become a drag upon the soul's progress. With the more or less uninstructed, it is always well to point out how few – and how stringent – are the actual *obligations* which the Church imposes upon her children, for people only too easily come to regard certain practices they take up – e.g. confraternity rules and prayers – as 'obligations' comparable with hearing Mass on Sunday or performing their Easter duties. The common desire, too, to immerse themselves in active works should be closely watched, for their chief concern at first must be with their own souls, their most necessary practices, prayer and mortification. If some active work seems to be desirable, it should be of as hard and as hidden a nature as possible. There are already too many unspiritual amateurs doing 'parochial work'; priests will be well advised to see that *any* work done for God and for souls can only be done by humble, obedient, loving, practising Christians, and to spend some of the time in producing such, being content to wait, seeing many things left undone, until he has

trained souls who are in some degree capable of being
the instruments of Divine grace. Third, to establish a
true peace in souls and to nourish their good desires
means that their prayer-life must be the director's first
and continuous concern. Unless such are taught to
pray, they are taught nothing. To inspire a soul with
the true idea of prayer, to get it interested in its prayer,
is the greatest thing we can do for it. The director,
then, must inquire as to the knowledge of the end,
value and practice of prayer possessed, the kind of
prayer made, the particular difficulties encountered,
the *attraits* and special devotions to which the soul is
led, and, where necessary, he must choose for and direct
the soul in such methods of prayer as seem most suitable.

Now nothing of this can be done unless the director
is himself convinced of the necessity and value of
prayer, and *this will be in proportion to his own practice and
experience of prayer.* Study of the science of prayer, of
methods, of the great guides in the paths of prayer, is
most necessary, as necessary as it is wanting, but no
degree of study alone will give that sense of conviction
which is needed in order to be convincing. ' Without
prayer, our work will be sterile, our words dry, our
direction altogether unfruitful. Without prayer we
shall never be able to support souls in their weaknesses. They have given themselves to us as those upon
whom they may rest, but without prayer we shall but
be the cause of their falls, since they will not find in us
the power and light they need. Being of ourselves but
darkness and weakness, it is only by the means of
prayer (*oraison*) that we can be enlightened and made
strong in Christ Jesus. All the faults which arise in
the direction of souls come from the fact that directors
do not apply themselves to the holy exercise of prayer '
(M. Olier, *op. cit.*, Art. i.).

The fourth point is the need of renunciation of self
in every form. ' Fight self, and you need fear nothing

else,' says St. Catherine of Genoa, and directors should constantly underline this. Too often directors are content with teaching the need of fighting temptation, with the result that souls carry on a long, weary warfare without ever attacking the real citadel of evil – the will. In the first seven chapters of *The Dark Night of the Soul*, St. John of the Cross ruthlessly exposes the ways in which self intrudes into and spoils the early stages of the spiritual life, and it is against this most dangerous enemy that the *contra agere* must be waged continuously. The state of a soul once known, at any rate in its broad outlines, the director will be able to advise how best the battle must be fought, and here his direction must be precise, definite and practical. All cannot be done at once, nor must he be in a hurry. The regular practice of the particular examen, in which one fault is taken at a time, resolved against on rising, and then taken as the subject of an examen at noon and again in the evening, is most valuable. One experienced director goes so far as to say that without it ' we shall be in twenty years what we are to-day, not one vice the less, not one virtue more.' The further suggestion which St. Ignatius makes – that a book ruled with two lines for each day of the week, on which are marked the results of the two examens, should be used – may be helpful to some, but is not advisable for all.

But behind this attack upon our faults must lie the constant daily, hourly abnegation and renunciation of self, practised, for most souls, in little ways and little things. ' Nothing is so opposed to spiritual advancement and to union with God than attachment to oneself, to one's own will, one's own mind, one's interests, one's goods. It is for that reason that our Saviour counsels us, ' If anyone will come after Me, let him deny himself.' Renunciation and abnegation is a vast field of battle, where there is a long combat against many enemies ; a combat much more important and difficult than that against exterior foes' (Père Ginhac, *Lettre* lix.).

A point very necessary to be emphasised is that all this takes time, ' we cannot be made saints in a day,' that all true progress is slow and almost imperceptible at the time.   It is enough that a soul keep on in the right direction, steadily, with resolution and generosity, content to be fed by the Holy Spirit.   We must not desire to see and understand our progress, but walk in faith and confidence.   ' Leave yourself to Jesus Christ and to His holy leading in the spirit of faith, detached from all adherence to your feelings and impressions, without ever dwelling on that which passes within you. . . . We cannot see or know that natural and animal life we live in the body, and yet we often desire to see and know that spiritual and incomprehensible life which God lives by grace in our souls ; all this must be avoided ; we must not seek to know, by any interior experience, the movements of the life of grace in the soul ' (Condren, *Lettres* ccxxxiv., ccxxxv.).   To a Superioress of the Visitation order St. François de Sales writes, ' You go considering your steps too much, for fear of falling.   You make too much reflection on the movements of your self-love, which are doubtless frequent, but which will never be dangerous so long as, tranquilly, not letting yourself be annoyed by their importunity nor alarmed by their number, you say no. Walk simply, do not desire repose of spirit too earnestly, and you will have the more of it ' (*Letters*, Bk. III. xvi.).

Discouragement arising from slow progress or from failures should be seen as the greatest of evils in the spiritual life.   John of Bonella, in his *Pax Animæ*, but echoes what every spiritual writer has said since Cassian : ' Take, then, this rule and method in all the falls you shall make, be they great or little ; yes, though ten thousand times in the same day you shall have committed the same fault, and that not unwillingly, but voluntarily and deliberately ; observe, I say, this advice : that as soon as you see your fault, instantly, without troubling or disquieting yourself, as soon as you realise what you have done, turn in humility and confidence towards God, beholding your own weakness, and, fixing your love upon Him, say with heart and mouth, " Lord, I have done that which is like what I am, nor can anything be expected at my hands but these and the like transgressions. . . . Pardon me for Thine own sake, and for what Thou art, and give me grace not to offend Thee again, but admit me once more to the favour of Thy friendship " . . . Note this well, it is the key to all spiritual advancement' (*Pax Animæ*, chap. xv.).

The truth is that sins do not hinder our spiritual progress so long as we do not remain in them for long. The true remedy for sin is not disquietude, but contrition, and the right way to treat our sins is to make an act of contrition, beg for grace and go on again as if nothing had happened. This is one of the most necessary lessons to be learnt.

' Be diligent and careful to set thy heart upon one thing, and that is naught else but a spiritual desire after God, how to please Him, love Him, know Him and see Him, and to enjoy this by grace here in a little feeling and in the bliss of Heaven in a full being. This desire – if thou keep it – will tell thee what is sin and what is not ; and what thing is good and what better ; and if thou wilt but fasten thy thoughts to this same desire, it shall teach thee all thou needest and it shall procure thee all thou wantest. Therefore, when thou risest against the ground of sin in general, or against the ground of any particular sin, hang fast upon this desire, and set the point of thy thoughts more upon God whom thou desirest than upon the sin which thou abhorrest ; for, if thou do so, then God fighteth for thee and will destroy sin within thee. And thou shalt much sooner come to thy purpose if thou doest this, than if thou shouldst leave thy humble desire after God and set thy heart only against the striving of sin, as though thou wouldst destroy it by thine own mastering, but thou shalt never so bring it to pass ' (Hilton, *Scale of Perfection*).

So from another age and land comes the same teaching : ' The Spouse . . . loves well their falls – not as falls – but because of what they practise, profound humility, abnegation, rectitude, stability and a simple and loving union with Him, and we must believe that He would not allow them to fall were it not for this. . . . The faithful soul, then, who desires uniquely to please Him, of giving Him that contentment so desired, will raise himself from those falls with the same love as if he had not fallen ; and go on again as if nothing had happened ' (Ven. Frère Jean de Saint-Samson, *Vray Esprit du Carmel*).

The director should never tend to rigorism. The Saints, ever hard upon themselves, were ever tender towards others. St. Francis of Assisi, St. Dominic, St. Alphonsus, St. Paul of the Cross, noted for the severity of their austerities, had the greatest compassion for sinners, using all their efforts to comfort and encourage their penitents. In the *Sommaire des Procès Apostoliques* of the latter, one of the witnesses records that the Saint once said to him, ' It is necessary to hearten and encourage souls and to make them walk with confidence in God ; without this they will never advance in the way of perfection,' and St. Paul's letters are full of such encouragement. ' Treat sinners with the greatest sweetness and tenderness, nothing of hardness or stiffness, make them feel the evil they have done, but without wounding them ; never reprove with severity. Pray to God, have recourse to Mary, that they may touch the hearts of sinners. Do not teach a severe doctrine. I am not a theologian and ought not to speak of that. But I dare to assure you that severe principles are ruinous to souls. Follow St. Liguori boldly' (Libermann, *Lettres*, vol. iii. cclii.).

So also Mgr. Segur : ' Severity is never necessary ; it is impossible to try and produce goodness except by kindness.' He held that rigour may be able to extort promises from souls, but it will never give them that love for God which, more powerful than fear, causes them to be kept. Our Lord does not wish souls to be fed by such means ; we must overcome them by charity and patience and by leaving much to the Divine mercy. Segur, it is worth remembering, spoke from an experience gained in dealing with the lowest classes, numbers of whom were converted by his zeal during the terrible days of the revolution of 1848.

A later director, noted for his life of severe mortification and penance, Père Ginhac, S.J., says, ' Severe directors teach virtue rather than perfection. To acquire virtue, fear is useful, but to progress toward perfection, love is necessary. Fear makes servants, love the children of God ' (Cagnac, *Lettres Spirituelles en France*, II. 262).

Of the most important questions concerning direction in prayer the following need attention :

(1) Beginners must be taught to see that mental prayer is but the first step, yet a first step upon which further advance depends. Only by discursive prayer will souls learn to pray well. Prayer is an art and a science, and the rules cannot be dispensed with until, by knowledge and use of them, we have passed beyond the need of them. Some method is then necessary both for the reasons already given and to train the soul how to pray. It will be noticed that of the methods given in Part II. each contains all the essential parts of prayer as well as employing all the various faculties of the soul. This is important, for just as where, for instance, creeds are abolished or made little of there soon emerges an over-emphasis on one doctrine and a

minimising of another, so, without a method, there will be a tendency for prayer to become one-sided, e.g. as in the present day, in which prayer practically means intercession and petition.[1]

The question of 'what method' depends upon the particular conditions and circumstances of each soul, and a director should spare no pains to see that each one has the method most suitable for it in every way.

(2) The director must watch the progress made so as to be able to give aid when necessary ; he must know his subject well, so as to be able to answer questions, often of the most unexpected kind. He will be careful not to confine himself to one guide or one

[1] The fundamental truth underlying the practice of intercessory prayer is that of the personal union and identification of the soul with Christ from which springs the desire to share in and advance His interests. ' If ye abide in Me and My words abide in you, ye shall ask what ye will, and it shall be done unto you ' (St. John xv. 7). ' For,' asks St. Augustine, ' abiding in Christ, how can they wish for anything but what befits Christ ? ' Our intercession is none other than that of our Lord : ' Who ever liveth to make intercession for us,' and, like His must be one primarily of life, not of words; an act or state of being, not a list of needs. Indeed, we can only rightly and fruitfully intercede when we have made some progress in the earlier stages of prayer, ' for we know not what to pray for as we ought : but the Spirit Himself maketh intercession for us . . . according to the will of God ' (Romans viii. 26, 27).

The common idea that intercession is an elementary stage of prayer in which anyone may join is completely alien to that of the New Testament. Confronted with the many needs of the Church and of the world, the first impulse of to-day is to fly to intercession, public and private. The real remedy is the deepening of the soul's union with God, so that ' in My Name ' may have its actual meaning ' in My Person.' God does not see less than we do, nor has He need of being told of what is lacking in the world, as teaches St. Augustine. ' Similiter et nos cum oramus, non Deum docemus, quasi nesciat quid velimus, et quo indigeamus : sed necesse habet rationalis creatura temporales causas ad aeternam veritatem referre, sive petendo quid erga se fiat, sive consulendo quid faciat ' (De diligendo Deo, ed. Mauri, 1240), and St. Thomas, ' We need to pray to God, not in order to make known to Him our needs or desires, but that we ourselves may be reminded of the necessity of having recourse to God's help in these matters.' (Summa Theol. II. ii., Q. lxxxiii, A. 2, Obj. 1). What God does need, not from any necessity in Himself, but because He has so willed to act in human affairs, is instruments through whom He can act. Hence, before intercession must come the prayer which establishes the soul in union with God and so makes it an instrument of His Will. ' Prayer which is mainly occupied with a result to be obtained is comparatively powerless to obtain results ' (Archbishop W. Temple, Christus Veritas, p. 40). Ever we must come back to ' Seek ye first the Kingdom of God ' and ' Delight thou in the Lord, and He shall give thee thy heart's desire.'

school of spirituality, but know something of them all, so as to be able to deal with the diversity of souls who come to him. In no case is it truer, 'A little knowledge is a dangerous thing.'

(3) In directing persons living in the world, the question of the amount of time actually available for mental prayer has to be considered. There are often real difficulties here, though seldom any that cannot be met by a director who clearly sees the end to be sought. With the ordinary person in the world, we cannot go far wrong in demanding a minimum of fifteen minutes daily. Daily, I say, for it is absolutely necessary that a definite period of time should be prescribed, and that daily. Any general rule; as, for instance, 'two hours a week,' which one has heard of being advised by directors, is obviously useless, and always proves to be so. Even a quarter of an hour daily may mean real and persevering effort and sacrifice to many in these strenuous days, but directors must insist on sacrifice as an essential element of Christian practice. When there is lack of time, vocal prayers, intercessions, particular devotions and the like may give way to, or be merged in, mental prayer, the soul's intimate intercourse with its God. There will be, too, moments during the day when such matters can be attended to, if one is alert to seize them. Much should be made of the fact that those fifteen minutes with God at the beginning of each day set the scene in which the soul is to dwell during the hours which succeed, so that, however one may be immersed in the necessary activity of a busy life, one's 'conversation is in Heaven.' Those fifteen minutes, together with our other spiritual exercises, especially ejaculatory prayers and aspirations, serve toward that prayer 'without ceasing' which is nothing else but the retaining and keeping up of that attitude deliberately taken in our mental prayer. And nothing will be found more

valuable than this for ensuring the guard of the senses, and that instant resistance to temptation which is so necessary. Clad in this armour, the soul may safely pass through busy distracting days, hearing without hearing, seeing without seeing, since its gaze and its attention are fixed on God.[1]

The method of prayer prescribed for such persons will necessarily be of the simplest, with but the barest time given to the exercise of the understanding. Let the essentials suffice ; the Act of Faith and Adoration ; a brief glance at the subject, sufficient to move the soul to acts of prayer ; the general and particular resolution, as in the Liguorian method, and a thanksgiving. Priests and lay persons of some leisure should give *at least* half an hour daily to mental prayer. The more active a priest's life is, the more he needs resolutely to keep to his prayer. Every priest should possess, read and re-read, Dom Chautard's *L'Âme de Tout Apostolat*, in which are exposed with clarity and vigour the sterility, perils and ultimate failure of all work not rooted in and proceeding from an interior life of prayer.

(4) What knowledge does the soul possess ? Has it any true conception of God, Jesus Christ, the end of man ? Are its conceptions clear, or only vague

[1] Spiritual writers all insist on the need of keeping exactly to the allotted time of prayer, especially when it is seemingly less fruitful. St. Ignatius bids us even lengthen it a little on such occasions. The often-felt difficulty of spending our time of prayer to advantage is greatly lessened by a punctual adherence to a method. Half an hour without a method may seem intolerably long; with one it passes rapidly. The same applies to thanksgiving after Communion, where it is often accentuated both by a natural and a spiritual fatigue. A good plan is to divide the quarter of an hour, say, of one's thanksgiving, into five three-minute acts, which may vary on different days. Thus,

Sunday : Adoration ; Thanksgiving ; Oblation ; Desire ; Petition.
Monday : Adoration ; Gratitude ; Humility ; Imitation ; Petition.
And so on – the first and last acts being invariable and the other three according to one's own feelings and needs. The liturgical thanksgiving should not, of course, be omitted, but it is desirable that in the first moments after Communion we should not 'lose this golden opportunity,' as St. Teresa calls it, ' but remain in His company . . . for this hour is of the utmost value to your soul, and the good Jesus desires you to spend it with Him : take great care not to waste it ' (*Way*, xxxiv.).

and general? Is it capable of much use of the understanding?

These are some fundamental questions which, especially in these days, the director must ask. People are profoundly lacking in any true conception of God and of their relation to Him. The truth that He is all and man is nothing is almost unknown. St. Paul's ' ut simus in laudem gloriæ ejus nos,' re-echoed in the Church's ' per ipsum et cum ipso et in ipso,' comes as a shock to them. There is need of insisting repeatedly on the facts that we need God, not that God needs us, that ' religion is adoration,' that ' man was created to praise, reverence and serve God,' for our servers, M.C.s and devout women are often ignorant of them.

As to the Incarnation, one may find every heresy ever propounded believed in by regular communicants. I have had to convince a religious that 'the Word was made flesh ' did not mean ' God was changed into a man.' Errors concerning the Sacred Humanity, the union of the Divine and the human natures in one Person, of the inseparable nature of that union, etc., all of which are truths affecting the bases of the Christian life, are common. The Catholic faith as to the position of Mary in the economy of redemption, her relation to her Son, and, through Him, to us, is rarely understood. Even Bishops and priests are guilty of statements which a reading of the treatises *De Deo* and *De Incarnatione* would have rendered impossible.

With regard to the idea and practice of the Christian life, one meets with little better than a morality with pious additions. Great use needs to be made of the distinctive features of the Oratorian spirituality, deeply rooted as it is in Pauline and Johannine teaching. The conception of ' intercessions ' as the main work of prayer should be eliminated. The fact is that intercession can only be made by souls in union with our Lord, and that, as a matter of experience, only after education in mental prayer is it possible to perceive one's particular *attraits* in this matter and really to begin to intercede in the real sense of the word. ' In My Name ' does not mean long lists of intercessions ending with a collect ' through Jesus Christ our Lord,' but 'in Me,' in My person, My mind, My will, My way.

Further, we must not forget, either in practice or teaching, that prayer will accomplish little without mortification. There must always be the element of sacrifice in our prayer. Is there not something of the truth of this in St. James's ' Ye ask and receive not, because ye ask amiss, to consume it upon your pleasures.' Prayer may become little more than a spiritual picnic, an ' amusing oneself,' as more than one writer terms it, and it will always be shallow in the proportion that it lacks that spirit of mortification which alone renders it worthy. St. Ignatius constantly insists upon mortification, true sign of generosity, as the base of all prayer. ' For a man truly mortified,' he said, ' a quarter of an hour is sufficient to unite himself to God in prayer.' Fr. Gonsales da Camara says of him, ' Whenever the father spoke of prayer he always supposed the passions subdued and mortified. Speaking to him of a good religious whom he knew, I said, " He is a man of great prayer." He corrected me, saying, " He is a man truly mortified " ' (*Scripta de Sancto Ignatio*, vol. i., p. 250).

(5) The question of the reading of spiritual books – and, indeed, of all reading – is so closely related to prayer that it cannot safely be neglected or ignored. It is not too much to say that, *with necessary exceptions*, the incessant reading of newspapers, ephemeral magazines and journals (even, or especially, ' religious ' ones) makes impossible any real life of prayer. Not only are so many of them absolutely worthless, both as to matter and form, so that the reading of them is the worst possible waste of time, but, being what they are,

they tend to weaken the mind, distract the imagination and render any real application to things that matter more and more difficult. Modern civilisation presents hardly any more pitiable sight than the absorption displayed in the pages of the daily Press, an absorption which might be excusable if it pointed to – as normally it does not – an intelligent interest in matters of real moment. I do not claim that the practising Christian should confine his reading to 'spiritual' books or magazines, far from it, but that he should read books of worth, of permanent value, books which tend to form and inform the mind and to stimulate thought. For in all such reading, which may be as wide as life's interests, the mind will gain material which will often become fruitful in prayer.

With regard to spiritual reading, one great function of which is to supply material for our prayer, Holy Scripture must be brought back to its rightful position. These ' letters from our heavenly country,' as one of the Fathers calls them, need to be rescued from the hands of critics and commentators and used once more for the purpose they were primarily given for. Direction should be given as to the reading of the Gospels, Psalter, such books as Wisdom and Ecclesiasticus, the Epistles, etc., without commentaries, ' those parasitical glosses which hide the Word of the Master,' difficult passages being passed over or referred to the director for explanation. For here, as nowhere else, will the soul ' tasting and savouring the Divine Food ' – for, as à Kempis says, there are two tables in the house of God, not merely one – find that which will nourish the Divine life within him.

Then *one* spiritual book, suited to the soul's needs, and kept continually at hand, as St. François de Sales kept the *Spiritual Combat* for fifteen years. For most people this book, the *Introduction to a Devout Life* of St. François de Sales, the *Confessions of St. Augustine* (not, perhaps, the most suitable for young people), the *Imitation*, Fr. Baker's *Holy Wisdom* (for the more educated in spiritual things), St. John Eudes's *Reign of Jesus*, and Walter Hilton's *Scale of Perfection*, will be found most useful, especially the first two. As a guide to prayer for ordinary folk the *Treatise on Prayer and Meditation* of St. Pedro of Alcantara is unsurpassed.

Modern books, with few exceptions, especially those purporting to deal with mystic states of prayer, should be avoided, and many earlier ones need reading with caution. Such works as the *Exercises of St. Ignatius*, which, as I have said, is not a book to be read indiscriminately, but one to be used by directors, and the *Revelations of Divine Love* of Julian of Norwich, should not be recommended, except at least in editions which supply the necessary guidance to the ordinary reader, or by directors who know enough theology to supply it.

Many persons are more helped by lives of the Saints and biographies of holy souls than by books dealing with the spiritual life in general. Unfortunately, not many such are well written, and too often they lay overmuch stress on the extraordinary graces manifested. But there is a growing number of really admirable books of this class which are worthy of being even more known than they are. Amongst them I would particularly note Maud Monahan's *Life and Letters of Janet Stuart*, perhaps the most fascinating and helpful book of its kind there is ; Von Hügel's *Selected Letters* and *Letters to a Niece* – the former contains most of the letters reproduced in the latter, but not the introduction, which is well worth having ; Rahilly's *Life of Father Doyle* ; René Bazin's *Charles de Foucauld* ; Father Martindale's *Aloysius Gonzaga* ; Huvelin's *Some Spiritual Guides of the Seventeenth Century* ; Alice Curtayne's *St. Catherine of Siena* ; Ghéon's *Secret of the Curé d'Ars* ; Mackay's *Saints and Leaders* ; Chesterton's

RP

St. Francis of Assisi ; Fr. Burton's *St. Francis de Sales.*

Of recent books on the spiritual life there is nothing to equal the Abbot Marmion's *Christ the Life of the Soul* and *Christ in His Mysteries.* Exact theology, wide use of Holy Scripture and a deep devotion here combine to form real masterpieces of spiritual literature.

(6) Treatises on moral and ascetic theology alone are not sufficient for the director himself ; he should make himself familiar with the teaching given by à Kempis (*Imitation*, Bk. III., chaps. liv. and lv.) on the movements of nature and grace, with St. Ignatius's *Rules for the Discernment of Spirits* and *Rules for thinking with the Church*, as well as the *Annotations, Additions* and other suggestions scattered throughout the *Exercises* ; with the invaluable guidance given in *Scupoli's *Spiritual Combat*, St. François de Sales's *Devout Life* and his letters, with Fr. Baker's *Holy Wisdom*, with the spiritual teaching of *St. John of the Cross, especially in *The Dark Night* ; with everything that St. Teresa wrote, especially the *Way of Perfection* and *The Interior Castle*; with *St. Jane Frances de Chantal's writings ; the *Treatise on Meditation* of St. Pedro of Alcantara ; the *Direction Spirituelle* of Bérulle ; the letters of Père Libermann, Surin (to be read with caution in the critical edition by Michel and Cavallera) ; the *Doctrine Spirituelle* of Père Lallemant, *St. John Eudes, St. Vincent de Paul, M. Olier and *St. Alphonsus. The asterisks denote that some of the author's works are procurable in English. Mgr. Cagnac's *Les Lettres Spirituelles en France* is a valuable introduction to all the great French directors, from St. François to Mgr. Hulst.

Among more modern authors may be noted, in English, Saudreau's *Degrees of the Spiritual Life*, perhaps the best introduction to the whole subject one could have ; De Besse's *The Science of Prayer* and *Light on Mount Carmel ;* Lehodey's *The Ways of Mental Prayer*, exceptionally good ; Poulain's *Graces of Interior Prayer*, in which many valuable hints may be gained, even in the chapters dealing with the mystic states of prayer ; Fr. Morris's *Instructions for Novices* ; Tissot's *The Interior Life ;* Madame Bruyère's *The Spiritual Life and Prayer* ; a little book, *Prayer and Intelligence*, by Jacques Maritain, is a veritable treasure-house of thought and experience.

In French, the works of Père Desurmont, Redemptorist ; Letorneau, Sulpician ; Dom Chautard, Carmelite ; the *Lettres de Direction* of Père Ginhac ; Canon L. Beaudenom and other directors ; Père Grandmaison's *La Religion Personelle* ; Paulot's *L'Esprit de Sagesse*, and especially *La Véritable Disciple* by the Abbé Chevrier, invaluable for priests, may be mentioned from an abundance of spiritual literature which pours from the French press and a great part of which is intensely valuable. Such reviews, too, as *La Vie Spirituelle*, the *Revue d'Ascétique et de Mystique*, *L'Ami du Clergé*, the *Nouvelle Revue Théologique* are especially worthy of note.

In Italian, *Confessione e Direzione*, by Can. L. Boccardo, and in Spanish the third volume of P. Arintero's *Evolution Mistica*.

In order that the director should be able to guide souls when they come to the passage from ordinary mental prayer to affective prayer and contemplation, he should prepare himself by a careful study of the subject in such works as Saudreau's *Degrees of the Spiritual Life*, De Besse's *Science of Prayer* and *Light on Mount Carmel*, Lehodey's *Ways of Mental Prayer*, which are founded on and contain ample reference to the teaching of St. John of the Cross, who is the great authority in this matter, and to St. Teresa.

I have been asked whether children – the ordinary children of the Catechism – can be taught to practise mental prayer. Certainly, and they should be so taught ; a great deal of the failure of the Catechism method of St. Sulpice as adopted among us is due to the fact that whilst the dogmatic instruction has been all that could be desired, insufficient attention has been paid to the devotional side – the prayers, the homily and the teaching, public and private, of *ho*. to pray. The mere acceptance of dogma and the punctual fulfilling of obligations will never produce convinced, loving, humble souls. Nothing but prayer based on and proceeding from dogma will do this ; the Faith must be translated into living experience ; the Incarnation must not only be known, it must be lived.

Any priest who studies the methods will, no doubt, evolve his own way of teaching children how to make mental prayer, but the following suggestions may be useful. The true conception of prayer, the right idea of God, of what it means to be a creature, the need of adoration, of union with our Lord as the condition of prayer ' in My Name,' and so on, must be continuously inculcated, so that the child grows up in a supernatural atmosphere. It should be encouraged to pray in its own words, and, in using common forms of prayer, to do so slowly ; children are quite capable of understanding and practising the prayer by beats and pauses of St. Ignatius. The less they use books the better, for they tend to constrain the free and individual action of the soul. (So also are questions for self-examination and confession to be avoided ; they will be unnecessary if the priest take the trouble to instruct properly.) They should be taught to make short acts of prayer ; to practise kneeling in silence before God, the meaning and value of intentions, especially of the Morning Offering ; the practice of ejaculations and of offering their actions to God. All this helps to create an attitude of soul which will be receptive to higher things. A simple explanation of the meaning and object of mental prayer may be followed by a more scientific and precise description of a method, consisting of Preparation, Meditation, Conclusion, something as follows :

I. *Preparation.*
   The Act of Adoration.
   The Act of Humility.
   The Prayer for Help.

II. *Meditation.*
' Picturing out ' of the subject by the memory and imagination. Subjects might be given out in Catechism or class. The right and wrong use of the imagination explained. The visualisation of a Mystery may be done in much the same way that we can recall some scene we have witnessed, seeing it ' with our mind's eye.' Children's imaginations are usually vivid, and there will be little difficulty in teaching them how to see the subject ' as present before their eyes,' and putting themselves into it as actors as well as spectators. So looking, considering what they see, they will be taught to enter into it and take part in it by prayers and resolutions.

III. *Conclusion.*
The general and the particular resolution ' just for to-day.' The offering of their meditation to our Lord. A brief thanksgiving in the form of a colloquy or intimate talk with our Lord or His Mother, etc.

With teaching something on these lines and an occasional ' How are you getting on with your prayer ? ' which will afford opportunity for more individual aid, it is quite possible to train children to make mental prayer. And the results are more than worth the necessary care involved.

Finally, the question as to whether knowledge or sanctity is most necessary in a director may be answered by saying that he will accomplish little unless he is seeking both. ' We must acquire virtue,' says Père

Lallemant, ' before we can do much for others. . . . We shall have fruit to our labours only in proportion to our union with God and our detachment from self,' for spiritual direction is ' an art and a science, not of mind, but of spirit ; not of study, but of prayer ; not of preaching, but of practice ; not of contention, but of humility ; not of speculation, but of love ; of the love of Jesus, Who gives and abandons Himself, forgets and exhausts Himself for the salvation of souls,' (Bérulle, *La Direction Spirituelle*, chap. xi.). The Gospel must be lived before it can be preached or taught.

Finally, he whom God calls to direct souls must be prepared to experience in himself, not only many temptations, but in particular the severe trial of aridity in prayer and the suffering caused by the necessary exercise of pure faith unaided by consolation and that feeling of certitude which so buoys one up in the face of external difficulties. The apparent abandonment of the soul by God, at times accompanied by physical suffering, is one of the marked characteristics of the lives of the great directors of souls. They, more than others, dwell in the wilderness in silence, obscurity and suffering : of them Baron von Hügel's words are particularly true : ' In sufferings and dryness a more experienced soul can sustain the less. . . . All deepened life is deepened suffering, deepened dreariness, deepened joy. . . . Dulness, dreariness and loneliness. East winds always blowing : desolation, with certain lucid intervals and dim assurances ' (*Letters to a Niece*, p. xv.).

It must be so, for he who would direct a single soul enters upon a work of God, a work only to be done by him who is willing to share the Passion of the Divine Director Whose instrument, Whose hand, Whose voice, Whose heart he is. ' Cor mundum crea in me, Deus : et spiritum rectum innova in visceribus meis.' Only then may be said, ' Docebo iniquos vias tuas, et impii ad te convertentur.'

'An instant of pure love is more precious in the sight of God and more profitable to the Church than all other good works put together, though it may seem as if nothing were done. . . . Let those men of zeal who think by their preaching and exterior works to convert the world, consider that they would be much more pleasing to God – to say nothing of the example they would give – if they would spend at least one-half of their time in prayer, even though they may not have attained to unitive love. Certainly they would do more, and with less trouble, by one single good work than by a thousand ; because of the merit of their prayer, and the spiritual strength which it supplies' (St. John of the Cross, *The Spiritual Canticle*, Stanza xxviii., *note*.)

APPENDIX

An Analysis of the Teaching of St. John of the Cross on the State of Beginners

The Dark Night of the Soul

Book I. : The Night of Sense

Chapter I.

(1) The dark night is entered when God draws souls out of the state of beginners – of meditation – to the state of proficients, contemplatives, on the way to perfection – Divine union. Deals with the state of beginners that they

    (*a*) May perceive the weakness of the state they are in.

    (*b*) Take courage, and

    (*c*) Desire to enter the dark night.

(2) A soul, seriously converted, is, in general, spiritually nursed and caressed ;

(3) The grace of God gives it sweetness and delight in spiritual things and exercises, delight in prayer, joy in penance, consolation in the use of the Sacraments.

(4) Although the soul applies itself to devotion with resolution, earnestness and care – it is extremely weak and imperfect – for it is drawn to spiritual exercises by the comfort they give, and not being yet established in virtue, which is the work of the struggle it demands, it falls into many errors and imperfections.

(5) These I will point out and explain by reference to the seven Deadly Sins, considered in a spiritual

sense – this will show how like children they are and how great are the blessings of the dark night – seeing that it purifies the soul from these imperfections.

Chapter II. : On Pride

(1) Becoming aware of their fervour and diligence, beginners fall into spiritual pride. They look upon themselves and their works with a certain satisfaction. They display an empty eagerness in speaking of spiritual things – are tempted to be teachers rather than learners. (Common temptation of beginners. St. Teresa.) They condemn those who are not devout in their way.

(2) Their fervour and desire to do good works is frequently fed by Satan in order to increase their pride – some want no one else to be thought good but themselves : in word and deed they fall into condemnation and detraction (Matt. vii. 3, xxiii. 24).

(3) Sometimes when their spiritual directors do not approve of them – for they desire praise – they complain that they are not understood ; they seek others who will respect them, for they love to discuss their spiritual state. Presuming on their own strength, they make many resolutions and accomplish little. They are not above ' showing off.'

(4) Many seek to be favourites of their confessors, so are ashamed to confess their sins plainly, but palliate them, excusing rather than accusing themselves. They tell him of their goodness, in terms suggestive of more than is in them ; at the least they want their goodness to be appreciated, instead of wishing that no one should think it of the slightest importance.

(5) At times, they make light of their faults ; at others, indulge in immoderate grief because of them. They think they are saints, and so get angry and impatient with themselves when they fall – a great imperfection. They beg God to deliver them from faults, not for His sake, but for their own comfort – not

knowing that if He did they would become prouder than ever.

(6) Scarcely anyone can be found who, in some degree or another, in his first fervours, does not fall into some of these faults.

(7) But those who are going on to perfection grow and are built up in humility, looking on what they are and do as nothing, dissatisfied (but quietly) with themselves, looking on all others as better ; the keener their fervour the more they see how much they ought to do for God, how little is all they can do.

(8) All they do seems nothing – they are not anxious about others, they think little of themselves and wish others to do so also ; they think it strange that anyone should praise them.

(9) In great tranquillity and humility, they wish to learn from anyone, not to teach.

(10) Being far from wishing to instruct others, they willingly obey, for they never imagine they can be right in themselves. They rejoice when others are praised, do not wish to talk about their own state ; it seems so little and poor. They will speak of their sins and failures, and with those who have no great opinion of them. (But pride may come in even about our sins.)

(11) These will help any servant of God ; they bear falls with humility, meekness of spirit, in loving fear of God and confidence in Him. But such souls are very few, and we ought to be content when they do not rush into the opposite evils.

Chapter III. : *Avarice in the Spiritual Sense*

(1) Scarcely any beginner is contented with what God gives ; he is disconsolate and querulous because he does not find the comfort he desires in spiritual things. They listen to spiritual counsels, read books which treat of their state, spending more time on this than in doing their duty, neglect mortification and the perfecting of

an interior spirit of poverty. They love change – this image, that rosary, this book – like children with play-things.

(2) I condemn this attachment of the heart to the form, number and variety of these things, because in direct opposition to poverty of spirit, which looks only to the substance of devotion, using these things as means only.

(3) Two instances.

(4) They who would go on well do not rely on visible instruments, nor do they seek to know more than is necessary for right acting : their sole object is to please God. Generosity is theirs.

(5) The soul should labour so far as it can to purify and perfect itself – so that God may take it in hand and do what it cannot do for itself.

Chapter IV. : Luxury

(1) Putting aside the commission of this sin – my object being to speak of imperfections, which may be called spiritual luxury ; not that it is so in fact, but be-cause it proceeds from spiritual things – it is felt and experienced in the flesh because of its frailty, whilst it is the recipient of spiritual communications. Often, in the midst of spiritual exercises and when they can-not help themselves, impure movements of sensuality are felt, even when the mind is absorbed in prayer or receiving the Sacraments.

(2) This sometimes comes – but rarely – from sensible sweetness in spiritual things. Sense and spirit being de-lighted together, the whole nature is moved, according to its measure and character, the spirit to delight itself in God, and the lower part toward sensible gratifica-tion, because it knows no other, and therefore seeks what is nearest to it – sensual pleasure. So whilst the spirit prays, the senses are troubled with movements of the flesh passively : this often happens at the moment

of Communion . . . the sensual nature taking its share in its own manner. But as soul and body form but one subject, they share in their respective passions . . . for all that is received is received according to the condition of the recipient.

(4) This is the case with beginners, and even those who have made some progress – but in the purgation of the dark night it is no longer subject to these infirmities but possesses everything according to the measure of the spirit. ' Being in the spirit, ye are no longer led by the flesh.'

(5) Satan also causes these filthy movements of our lower nature, in order to disquiet the soul in prayer, and some relax or even abandon prayer because they are so liable to these assaults at this time.

(6) He causes vivid and foul images, even in close relation to spiritual persons and things – especially in those of a melancholy temperament. When the latter is the cause of these visitations, men in general cannot be delivered from them until their general health is improved, unless the dark night has overtaken the soul, gradually freeing it from all this trouble.

(7) The third source of these temptations is the fear of them, brought about by a sudden remembrance, a look, word or thought. Some souls never experience spiritual fervour without accompanying luxury, which sometimes succeeds in stirring the senses to rebellion. This because fragile and tender natures are susceptible to the slightest alteration of blood and humour whence these disturbances come, for the same thing happens when they are roused to anger or pain.

(8) So also, in speaking of or in doing spiritual works, some display energy and strength, considering persons present with a certain measure of vain joy. This also proceeds from spiritual luxury in the sense in which I use the word, and ordinarily is accompanied by complacency of the will.

(9) Spiritual friendships may have their source in this luxury. Does the thought of that affection increase our recollection and love for God, or bring remorse of conscience ?

(10) If the love of God grows, human love cools, the predominant one suppresses the other.

Chapter V. : Anger

(1) Beginners, when they find no consolation in spiritual things, become peevish, bitter of spirit ; trifles make them angry ; they are a burden to themselves and at times intolerable to all about them. This frequently happens after great sweetness in prayer ; as it passes, their natural temper becomes sour and morose.

(2) Some are angry with other people for their faults ; they watch and blame them with unquiet zeal, making themselves guardians of virtue.

(3) Others, seeing their own imperfections, become angry and impatient with themselves – want to be saints in a day ; they make many and grand resolutions, but, being self-confident, the more they resolve the more they fall and become angry. No perfect remedy for this but in the dark night. But some are so patient, and advance so slowly, that God wishes they were not so patient.

Chapter VI. : Gluttony

(1) Much to say – for scarcely one who does not fall.

(2) Many strive after spiritual sweetness rather than purity and discretion, and practise immoderate penances, take upon themselves more than they can bear, without rule or advice – unreasonable – undervaluing submission and obedience ; the penance of reason and judgment more acceptable to God than bodily penance. Bodily penance without the penance of the will

might as well be imposed on animals, for it is undertaken because liked and for consolation.

(3) All extremes being vicious – such grow in vice, not virtue – for they do not walk in the way of obedience ; all their satisfaction is in doing what pleases them.

(4) Many importune their directors that they may do their own will, and mope if they are refused, imagining their own will is the will of God ; if they are contradicted and told His will, they become fretful, faint-hearted and fall away.

(5) Others, ignorant of their real state and of the fear and respect due to God, ask to be allowed to confess and communicate often – worse, they communicate without permission. This eagerness for Communion makes them confess carelessly – being more anxious to communicate anyhow than worthily.

(6) Such strive after sensible sweetness at Communion instead of worshipping in humility and praising God within themselves. So when they have no sensible feeling of devotion, they think they have nothing, so meanly think they of God, not understanding that the least of the blessings of the Most Holy Sacrament is that which touches the senses, the invisible grace being far greater. God frequently withholds sensible favours that men may fix the eye of faith on Himself. It is a great imperfection against the purity of faith and the nature of God to desire always to feel and taste Him as palpable and accessible.

(7) So in prayer – they imagine that sensible devotion is all, and strive after it, wearying their brains and perplexing all their faculties. This destroys true devotion and spirituality, which consists in perseverance in prayer with patience, humility, distrust of self, solely to please God (*Ascent*, II. vii. 7).

(8) Like children, influenced by inclination, not reason, wasting their time in searching after spiritual

consolation, taking up one book after another. God refuses it, knowing this spiritual gluttony would grow to great evils.

(9) They are also very weak and remiss in following the Cross – refusing the pain of self-denial. But spiritual soberness and tenderness produce mortification, fear, submission, showing us that the value and perfection of things consist in our knowing how to deny ourselves in them.

Chapter VII. : Envy and Spiritual Sloth

(1) Vexed at others' goodness – progress – cannot bear to hear them praised – deprecate them as much as they can – wish to be more thought of themselves.

(2) As to sloth, the most spiritual exercises are found irksome ; they omit prayer because they have no sensible devotion ; they neglect the way of perfection, which is the denial of self-will and pleasure for God to do their own will.

(3) They want God to will what they will, and only reluctantly submit to His will. They measure Him by themselves.

(4) They find it hard to obey when commanded to do what they do not like : like delicately nurtured persons, they avoid with heavy hearts all that is hard, are offended at the Cross.

(5) Thus may be seen how necessary is the dark night, in which God weans souls from the breasts of sweetness, in pure aridities and interior darkness – cleanses them and makes them grow in virtue.

BIBLIOGRAPHY

(A * denotes works of special value)

ANON : *The Cloud of Unknowing*, ed. Dom J. McCann. 1943.
B.O.W.

ARINTERO, JUAN G. (O.P.) : **Evolucion Mistica*, Libro III. *De desenvolviemento y vitalidad de la Iglesia*, 2nd edit., Salamanca, 1921. A valuable treatise on the spiritual life.

AUGUSTINE, ST. : *Confessions.* New transl. F. J. Sheed, 1944.
Sand Ward
Letter to Proba (cxxx, Tome ii, *Omnia Opera*, Maurist edit.)
The Works of. Ed. Rev. Marcus Dods. 1873. T. & T. Clark

BAINVEL, J. V. : *Introduction à la 10ᵉ édition des Grâces d' Oraison du Père Poulain.* 1923. Paris : Beauchesne

BAKER, FR. AUGUSTINE (O.S.B.) : **Holy Wisdom.*
Burns, Oates & Washbourne
Confessions of . . . . . B.O.W.
The Inner Life of Dame Gertrude More. 1920. B.O.W.
Useful for directors of religious.

BAZIN, RENE : **Charles de Foucauld* . . . B.O.W.

BEAUDENOM, CHANOINE : *Pratique Progressive de la Confession et de la Direction* . . Paris : Librairie Saint-Paul
Lettres de Direction. 1919. Paris : Librairie Saint-Paul

BELLARMINE, ST. R. : *Ascent of the Mind to God* B.O.W.

BELLECIO, ALOYSIUS (S. J.) : *Spiritual Exercises according to the Mind of St. Ignatius* . . . . . B.O.W.

BELORGEY, DOM GODEFROID *La Pratique de l' Oraison Mentale.* tome i.*Oraisons Ordinaires.* ii. *Oraisons Mystiques.* 1945. Editions du Cerf Sens.
Sous le regard de Dieu. 1946. Same edition.... ..

BERULLE, CARD. : *Œuvres Complètes.* 1856. Paris : Migne
*La Direction Spirituelle. 1926 Librairie Desclée
Also see Bremond, *Histoire littéraire*, vol. ii., Pourrat, vol. iii., and Pottier.

BESSE, LUDOVIC DE : ** The Science of Prayer* B.O.W.
*Light on Mount Carmel. 1926. An introduction to the works of St. John of the Cross . . . B.O.W.
La Science du Pater pour faire suite à la Science de la Prière.
1929 . . . Paris : Librairie Saint-François

BLOSIUS : *A Book of Spiritual Instruction* . . B.O.W.
Comfort for the Faint-hearted . . . . B.O.W.
Works of. Ed. Wilberforce. 7 vols. 1925-30 B.O.W.

BLOUNT, C. F. (S.J.) : *Leading Meditations of the Spiritual Exercises* . . . . . . B.O.W.
Points for Mental Prayer . . . . . B.O.W.

BOCCARDO, LUIGI : *Confessions e direzione.* 2 vols. 1921.
Turino : Istituto per ceichi

BOSSUET, JACQUES BENIGNE : *Correspondance.* 15 vols.
Paris : Hachette

BOULLAYE. H. PINARD DE LA (S.J.) : *L'Oraison mentale à la portée de tous.* 1944 Albin Michel : Paris

BOURGOING, F. : *Les Vérités et Excellences de Jésus Christ Notre Seigneur.* 1636 . . . . . Paris

BOWDEN, FR. (S.J.) : *Spiritual Teaching.* 1921 . B.O.W.

BOYLAN. *Difficulties in Mental Prayer*

BREMOND, H. : *Histoire littéraire du Sentiment Religieux en France depuis la fin des Guerres de Religion jusqu' à nos Jours.* 1923-1929. 10 vols. . Paris : Librairie Bloud et Gay
S.P.C.K. have already published three vols. of this in English.

BRESCIANI, FR. (S.J.) : *Spiritual Exercises according to the Method of St. Ignatius* . . . . . . B.O.W.

BROU, A. (S.J.) : *La Spiritualité de Saint Ignace* Beauchesne
St. Ignace, Maître d'Oraison. ' Edition Spes.' 1925.
Paris : 17 Rue Soufflot (Vᵉ)

BRUNO DE JESUS MARIE (C.D.) : *Saint Jean de la Croix.* Preface de J. Maritain. 1929 . . . Paris : Plon.

BRUYERE, C. J. (Abbess of Solesme) : *Spiritual Life and Prayer.* 1922 . . . . B.O.W.

BUCKLER, R. (O.P.) : *A Spiritual Retreat* . . B.O.W.

BURTON, H. : *Life of St. François de Sales.* 2 vols.

CAGNAC, MGR. : *Les Lettres Spirituelles en France.* 1929.
2 vols. . . . . Paris : J. de Gigord
Deals with spiritual letters from St. François to our own times.

CASSIAN : *Conférences avec les Pères du Desert.* 3 vols.
Librairie St. Thomas d'Aquin, Saint-Maximin (Var.)
Also a selection from his works in English arranged by the late W. B. Trevelyan . Faith Press

CAVALLERA, F. (S.J.) : *Replies to and Criticism of M. Bremond's ' Ascèse ou Prière' and his Attack on Ignation Spirituality,* in *Revue d'Ascétique et de Mystique,* July 1928 and following numbers.

CHALLONER, BP. : *Meditations* . . . . B.O.W.

CHANTAL, ST. J. F. DE : *Selected Letters* B.O.W.
The Spirit of St. Jane Frances de Chantal shown by her Letters.
1922 . . . . . . Longmans

CHAPMAN, DOM JOHN (O.S.B.) : *Spiritual Letters.* 1935.
Sheed & Ward

CHARLES, PIERRE (S.J.) : *La Prière de Toutes les Heures. 1925. 3 vols. C. Beyaert, Bruges. English translation 1927. 3 vols. . . . . . Sands
Unusual and beautiful meditations.
La Prière de Toutes les Choses. 1947. Paris : Desclée

CHAUMONT, ABBE H. : Lettres Spirituelles. 2 vols. 1900.
Paris : Mersch

CHAUTARD, P. (O.R.C.) : L'Ame de Tout Apostolat. 1927. Tequi. American transl. 1943.
A book every priest should possess.

CHEVRIER, VEN ABBE : *Le Prêtre selon l'Evangile ou le Véritable Disciple de Jésus-Christ. 1922. Lyon : Vitte
Beyond all praise ; no other work on the priestly life is comparable with it.

CLAUDEL, P.; Seigneur, apprenez-nous à prier. 1943.
Paris : Gallimard

CLEMENTS, B. (O.S.B.) : *How to Pray. 1929. . S.P.C.K.

CLORIVIERE, P. PICOT DE : Considerations sur l'Exercise de la Prière et de l'Oraison. 1928. Paris : Beauchesne

COLOMBIERE, CLAUDE DE LA (S.J.) : Lettres Spirituelles
Paris : Haton

CONDREN, C. DE : Discours et Lettres. 1643 . . Paris
L'Idée du Sacerdoce et du Sacrifice de Jésus-Christ. Benedictine edition. 1901 . . . . . . Paris
Considérations sur les Mystères de Jésus-Christ. 1882. Paris
Also see Bremond, vol. ii.
Lettres du P. de Condren. 1943. Editions Auvray : Paris

CONSIDINE, D. (S.J.) : *Delight in the Lord. Notes of spiritual direction . . . . B.O.W.

COURBON : Familiar Instruction in Mental Prayer. 1871.
B.O.W.

CRASSET, FR. (S.J.) : A Key to Meditation . . B.O.W.

CUTHBERT, FR. (O.S.F.C.) : The Capuchins. 2 vols. 1928.
Sheed & Ward

DENYS LE CHARTREUX : De la Méditation : Editions de la Vie Spirituelle.

DENYS, First Abbot of Nashdom : Prayer and Contemplation. Laudate, Dec. 1944, 1945, June 1946.

DESURMONT, T. R. P. : *La Charité Sacerdotale. Leçons Elémentaires de Théologie Pastorale. 1925. 2 vols. Tequi
Deals with the principles and every phase of pastoral work : an invaluable book.
*Le Retour continuel à Dieu. 1 vol. . . . Tequi
Three sets of most valuable Retreat conferences.
*L'Art Divin de l'Oraison Mentale d'après St. Alphonse de Liguori. 1928.

D'HULST, MGR. : Lettres de Direction Paris : Poussielgue

DIDON, LE PERE (O.P.) : Lettres à Th. V. Paris : Plon
Spiritual Letters . . . London : Kegan Paul

DIGNAM, FR. (S.J.) : *Conferences* .   .   :   .   B.O.W.
          Retreats   .   .   .   .   .   .   B.O.W.

DIONYSIUS THE AREOPAGITE : *On the Divine Names and Mystical Theology.* G. E. Rolt. 1920.   .   ·.   S.P.C.K.

DOHET, P. (S.J.) : *Lumières sur la prière.* Editions Museum Lessianum   .   .   .   .   .   Desclée

DUPANLOUP, MGR. : *Lettres de Direction*   Paris : Lethielleux

ECOLES DE SPIRITUALITE CHRETIENNE, 1929.
                                        Librairie Giraudon
          Accounts of the various schools of spirituality by
          various authors.

EUDES, ST. JOHN : * *The Reign of Christ.* An admirable summary
          of his *Royaume de Jésus*   .   .   .   B.O.W.
          Les Œuvres Complètes. Dauphin et Le brun, 1905-1911.
                                                          Vannes
          Also see Bremond, vol. iii., and Pourrat, vol. iii.

FABER, F. : * *Growth in Holiness*
          * *The Creator and the Creature*
          And other works, uniform edition   .   .   .   B.O.W.

FENELON, FRANCOIS : *Œuvres Complètes*   Paris : Edition Gaume

FOCH, G. (S.J.) : *Spiritual Manual on the Interior Life*   B.O.W.

FROST, BEDE : *S. John of the Cross.*   1937.
                                        Hodder & Stoughton
          Priesthood and Prayer.   1933   .   .   .   Mowbrays
          In His Image.   1941   .   .   .   .   Mowbrays
          Prayer for All Christians.   1939   .   .   Mowbrays
          La Prière Chrétienne.   1945.   Editions du Cerf, Paris.

GABRIEL, FR. (O.D.C.) : *S. John of the Cross.*   English transl.
          1946   .   .   .   .   Mercier Press, Cork

GARRIGOU-LAGRANGE, P. REG. (O.P.); * *Perfection Chrétienne
          et Contemplation.*   1921...2 vols.   .   Desclée
          The Three Ways of the Spiritual Life.   1938.

GAY, MGR. : *Lettres de Direction Spirituelle.*   4 vols.
                                                  Paris : Oudin

GERARD DE ZUTPHEN : *The Spiritual Ascent*   .   B.O.W.

GHEON, H. : * *Secret of the Curé d'Ars.*   1929.   Sheed & Ward

GINHAC, PERE (S.J.) : *Choix des Lettres de Direction.*   1927.
          Apostolat de la Prière   .   .   .   .   Toulouse

GOODIER A. (S.J.) : *Some Hints on Prayer*   .   .   B.O.W.
          Also several books of meditations.

GRANDMAISON, LEONCE DE : * *La Religion Personelle.*   1927.
          Gabalda.   In English, 1929   .   Sheed & Ward
          ' Direction sur l'Oraison.'   *Revue d'Ascétique et de Mystique,*
          July 1929.

GROU, J. (S.J.) : *Manual for Interior Souls.*   1892   .   B.O.W.
          Thr School of Jesus Christ.   1932   .   .   B.O.W.

GUIGUES DE LA CHARTREUSE : *L'Echelle du Paradis.*   Editions
          de la Vie Spirituelle.   Saint-Maximin (Var.)

GUIGUES DU PONT: *De Contemplatione.* Article in *Revue d'Ascétique et de Mystique*, July 1929.

HAUSHERR, I. (S.J.): *Le traité de l'Oraison d'Evagre le Pontique* (pseudo Nil), traduction et commentaire. Editions de la Revue d'Ascetique et de Mystique, 9 rue Montplaisir, Toulouse.

HEDLEY, BP. (O.S.B.): *A Retreat* . . . B.O.W.
    Spiritual Retreat for Priests . . . B.O.W.
    Spiritual Retreat for Religious . . . B.O.W.

HERMAN, MRS.: *Creative Prayer* . . J. Clarke & Co.

HILTON, W.: *Scale of Perfection.* Edit. Dom. E. Nodinger.
    1927 . . . . . B.O.W.
    Minor Works . . . . . B.O.W.

HOWLEY, J.: *Psychology and Mystical Experience.* 1900.
    Kegan Paul

HUGEL, BARON VON: **Selected Letters.* 1928 . Dent
    *Lrtters to a Niece . . . . Gent
    *Essays and Addresses. 2 vols. . . . Dent
    *Eternal Life . . . . . T. T. Clark

HUVELIN, ABBE: **Some Spiritual Guides of the Seventeenth Century.* 1927 . . . . . B.O.W.

JAEGHER, PAUL DE (S.J.): *La Vie d'Identication au Christ Jesus.* 1943. Editions du Cerf.
    English Transl. *One with Jesus* B.O.W.

JOHN OF THE CROSS, ST.: **The Ascent of Mount Carmel.*
    *The Dark Night of the Soul.
    *The Spiritual Canticle.
    *The Living Flame.
    Definitive Spanish edition by P. Silverio de Santa Teresa (C.D.). 1930. Burgos, Tipografia de E. E. Monte Carmelo.
    English translation. Three vols. by E. Allison Peers. 1934 . . . . . B.O.W.

JULIAN OF NORWICH: **The Revelations of.* Orchard Books
    Edition . . . . . B.O.W.

KEUSCH, C. (C.S.R.): *La Spiritualité de St. Alphonse de Liguori*
    Paris : Desclée

KNOWLES, M. D. (O.S.B.): *The English Mystics* B.O.W.
    Good introductions to Hilton, Rolle, Julian, Baker, etc.

KNOX, W. L. (O.G.S.): *Meditation and Mental Prayer*
    Philip Allan

LACORDAIRE, R. (O.P.): *Lettres à des Jeunes Gens.* 1920.
    Paris : Tequi

LALLEMANT, PERE (S.J.): **La Doctrine Spirituelle.* Lecoffre
    Translation published . . . B.O.W.
    See Pottier and Bremond.

LANIER: *La Vie d'Oraison d'après St. François de Sales.* 1926.
    Tequi

LANSPERGIUS, J.: *An Epistle of Jesus Christ*   .   . B.O.W.

LEEN, E. (C.S. Sp.) :- *Progress through Mental Prayer.* 1935.
   And other Works .   .   Sheed & Ward

LEHODEY, V. (O.C.R.) : *The Ways of Mental Prayer.*
   Also an abridged edition   .   M. H. Gill & Son

LEHODEY, V. (O.C.R.) : *The Ways of Mental Prayer.* 1924.

LEONARD, J. (C.M.) : *S. Vincent de Paul and Mental Prayer.*
   1925   .   .   .   .   .   ., B.O.W.

LETORNEAU : *Lettres de Direction à un Elève de Grand Séminaire.*
   Guide du Prêtre dans ses Retraites Annuelles.
   Sous la Conduite de M. Olier.
   La Méthode d'Oraison mentale du Séminaire de Saint-Sulpice.
                     Paris : Librairie Victor Lecoffre

LIBERMANN, P. VEN. : *Lettres Spirituelles.* 3 vols.
                     Librairie Poussielque Frères

LIGUORI, ST. ALPHONSUS : *Duties and Dignities of a Priest* and
   other works in new edition published by B.O.W.

LILLEY, A. L. : *Prayer in Christian Theology.* 1924.   S.C.M.

LONGRIDGE, W. H. (S.S.J.E.) : *The Spiritual Exercises of St.
   Ignatius of Loyola,* translated from the Spanish with a
   Commentary and the *Directorium in Exercitia.* 1919.
                                                       R. Scott
   The Father-Rector of a Jesuit House told me that this
   was the best book on the *Exercises* in English.
   The Normal Development of Ordinary Mental Prayer. 1927.

L'ORAISON : Valuable essays by several writers. 1947. In
   Cahiers de la Vie Spirituelle, Editions du Cerf Paris-7e ;
   27 Boulevard Latour-Mauborg.

LOYOLA, ST. IGNATIUS : *Spiritual Exercises. Letters.* Catholic
   Library.
   Also see various authors on same.

LUIS DE LEON : *The Names of Christ*   .   .   . B.O.W.

LULL, RAMON : *The Art of Contemplation.* Tr. Allison Peers.
   1925   .   .   .   .   .   . S.P.C.K.

MARCHAND, J. B. LE :*Exercises Spirituels de St. Ignace.* 4 vols.
   1899   Letouzey et Ané

MARITAIN, J. : *Prayer and Intelligence*   Sheed & Ward

MARMION, ABBOT (O.S.B.) : *Le Christ, Vie de l'Ame.*
   Le Christ, dan ses Mystères.
   Le Christ, Idéal du Moine.
   Sponsa Verbi.
   Consecration à la Sainte Trinité, Texte et Commentaire. 1946.
      Maredsons,Abbaye.
         English translations publ. Sands & Co.
         Unrivalled for doctrine, spirituality, devotion.

MASSOULIE, R. P. ANTONIN : *Traité de la Véritable Oraison.*
   2 vols.   .   .   .   .   Paris : Lethielleux

McNABB, V. (O.P.) : *Path of Prayer*   .   .   . B.O.W.
   The Craft of Prayer .   .   . .   .   . B.O.W.

MERCIER, CARD. D.: *La Vie Intérieure. Retreat given to
priests. 1929 . . . . Louvian: Warny

MESCHLER, M. (S.J.): Le livre des Exercises de St. Ignace de
Loyola expliqué et présenté sous la forme de Considérations.
3 vols. 1929 . . . . Paris: Lethielleux

MEYNARD, A. M.: Traité de la Vie Intérieure ou petite somme de
Théologie Ascétique et Mystique. 2 vols. 1924.
Paris: Lethielleux

MEZARD: *Doctrine Spirituelle de St. Jeanne de Chantal
Paris: Lethielleux
Contains the teaching of the Saint arranged under
subjects.

MONOHAN, MAUD: *The Life and Letters of Janet Stuart, Fifth
Mother-General of the Congregation of the Sacred Heart. 1926.
Longmans
The most fascinating biography of our times.
Reprint now available.

MORRIS, J. (S.J.): Journals kept during Times of Retreat. 1896.
B.O.W.

Instructions for Novices. 1902. Mainly on mental prayer.
Manresa Press

MURAWSKI, F.: Die Aszetische Theologie. Ein systematischer
Grundriss. 1928. München: Kosel-Pustet

OLIER, JEAN-JACQUES: Œuvres Complètes. 1856. Migne
Vie de. 1914 . . . . . . Monier
Pensées Choisies. 1916 . . . . Letorneau
See also Bremond, vol. ii., Pourrat, vol. iii., and
Pottier, vol. iii.

PAULOT, L., MGR.: L'Esprit de Sagesse. 1926.
Paris: Librairie Desclée

PEDRO DE ALCANTARA, ST.: *On Prayer and Meditation
B.O.W.

PEERS: Spanish Mysticism. 1924 . . Methuen
*Spanish Mystics . . . . . Methuen
Studies of the Spanish Mystics. Vols. 1 and 2. S.P.C.K
Spirit of Flame. 1943 . . . . S.C.M.
Complete Works of St. John of the Cross. 1947. B.O.W.
Complete Works of S. Teresa. 1946 . . B.O.W.
The Poems of S. John of the Cross.
Letters of S. Teresa in preparation.

PERSHORE, ABBOT DENYS OF (O.S.B.): Articles and Reviews
in Laudate. 1923-1930. Quarterly publication at Nashdom Abbey, Burnham, Bucks.

PHILIPON, M. M. (O.P.): Sainte Thérèse de Lesieux. 1946.
Desclée

PLUS, R. (S.J.): How to Pray Always . . . B.O.W.
How to Pray Well . . . . . B.O.W.
and other works.

PONS, J. (S.J.): Meditaciones según el Método de S. Ignacio. 5th
edición. 3 vols. . Barcelona: Libreria Católica

POTTIER, P. A. (S.J.) : *La Père Lallemant et les Grands Spirituels de son Temps. 3 vols. . . . . Tequi
    Valuable and documented criticism of M. Bremond's theories on prayer and on the alleged dependence of later Jesuit writers on Bérulle.

*La Vie et la Doctrine Spirituelle du P. Louis Lallemant. Texte primitif revisé et annoté   Paris : Tequi
    The best edition of this valuable work.

Pour St. Ignace et les Exercises contre l'Offensive de M. Bremond
                                                Paris : Tequi

POPE, HUGH (O.P.) : On Prayer and the Contemplative Life. 1914. Commentary on Treatises of S. Thomas Aquinas   . B.O.W.

POULAIN : *The Graces of Interior Prayer. 1912.   Kegan Paul

POULLIER, P. (S.J.) : Reflexions sur la Semaine des Exercises
                                                    Toulouse

POURRAT, P. : *Christian Spirituality from the Earliest Times to the Present Day. 3 vols. The fourth not yet available in English. 1922-27. . . . . . B.O.W.
    A valuable summary covering the whole ground.

RAHILLY (S.J.) : *Life of Fr. Doyle   .   .   Longmans

RAPHAEL, MOTHER FRANCES (O.S.D.) : *A Memoir of . . . with spiritual note and letters. 1923. .   .   Longmans

RICKABY, J. (S'J.) : *Spiritual Exercises of St. Ignatius. Spanish text, translation and commentary   B.O.W.
*Waters that go Softly   .   .   .   .   . B.O.W.
    A companion to above ; both excellent.

RIDOLFI, N. (O.P.) : Short Method of Mental Prayer   B.O.W.

RODRIGUEZ, ALPH. (S.J.) : On Christian Perfection. 2 vols.
                                                    B.O.W.

ROLLE, R. : Amending of Life   .   .   .   . B.O.W.

ROOTHAN, J. (S.J.) : De Ratione Meditandi.   1947   Rome

ROSS, ALLAN (C.O.) : St. Francis de Sales and the Introduction to a Devout Life .   .   .   .   .   . B.O.W.

RUTHERFORD, A. (O.S.B.) : Acts of Mental Prayer.

SALES, ST. FRANÇOIS DE : *The Library of :
    contains translations of the following, based on the critical Annecy edition   .   .   .   . B.O.W.
Introduction to the Devout Life.
Conferences.
Letters to Persons Living in the World.
Letters to Persons in Religion.
Treatise on the Love of God.

SAUDREAU, A. : *Degrees of the Spiritual Life. 2 vols. 1907.
B.O.W.
Most valuable introduction to the science of the spiritual
life in all its stages, advice on direction, etc.
*Ideal of the Fervent Soul . . . . . B.O.W.
*Life of Union with God . . . . . B.O.W.
*The Way that leads to God . . . . B.O.W.
Mental Prayer according to St. François de Sales. 1929.
Sheed & Ward
Mental Prayer according to the Teaching of St. Jeanne Frances de
Chantal . . . . . Sheed & Ward
' Pour Fixer la Terminologie Mystique,' in La Vie Spirituelle,
October 1929 and following months.

SCARAMELLI, J. B. (S.J.) : Directorium Asceticum. 4 vols.
B.O.W.

SCUPOLI : *The Spiritual Combat.
In Series Orchard Books, publ. B.O.W.
Also recent transl. publ. Newman Book Shop, U.S.A.

SEGUR, MAR. DE : Lettres à ses Fils Spirituels.
Lettres à ses filles Spirituelles . . Paris : Retaux

SHAW, G. : Pilgrim Prayers. 1945 . . Mowbrays

SILVERIO DE SANTA TERESA (C.D.) : Obras de San Juan de la
Cruz, editadas y anotadas. Tomo I. Preliminares ;
Tomo II. Subida y Noche oscura. 1929.
Burgos : Monte Carmelo
Definitive Spanish edition Works of S. Teresa. 3 vols. Burgos

SMITH, ABBOT (O.S.B.) : The Ordinary of the Mass the Food of
Prayer . . . . B.O.W.

STEUART, R. H. (S.J.) : Map of Prayer . . B.O.W.

SURIN, JEAN-JOSEPH (S.J.) : *Lettres Spirituelles. Edition
critique par Louis Michel et Ferdinand Cavallera.
Toulouse
Also see Bremond, vol. v., and Pottier.

TANQUEREY : *Précis de théologique Ascétique et Mystique.
Desclée et Cie
Also in English under the title, The Spiritual Life.

TERESA, ST. : Translation of complete works. See Peers.

THEODORE DE SAINT-JOSEPH (C.D.) : L'Oraison d'après l'Ecole
Carmélitaine . . . . Bruges, Beyaert

THIBAUT, R. (O.S.B.) : Un Maître de la Vie Spirituelle, Dom
Columba Marmion. 1929. Paris : Desclée
L'Idée maîtresse de la Doctrine de Dom Marmion. 1947.
Editions de Maredsons.

THOMAS AQUINAS, ST. (O.P.) : *Summa Theologica.*
Summa contra Gentiles.
De Pontentia Dei.
English transl. publ. B.O.W.
Latin-French edition of *Summa Theologica* with valuable appendices and notes, about thirty pocket Vols. publ. in Editions de la Revue des Jeunes by Desclée.
On the Ways of God . . . . . B.O.W.
How to Study. Latin text, translation and exposition by Victor White (O.P.). 1947. Blackfriars : Oxford

THOMAS OF JESUS : *Little Book of Prayers* . . B.O.W.
Advice on Prayer . . . . . . B.O.W.
De Contemplatione Acquisita, et via brevis et plana Orationis Mentalis. 1922 Milan : Tipografia S. Lega Eucaristica

THOMAS A KEMPIS : *The Imitation of Christ.*
True Wisdom . . . . B.O.W.

TISSOT, J. : *The Interior Life* . . . . B.O.W.

VINCENT DE PAUL, ST. : See Leonard.

VONIER, ANSCAR (O.S.B.) : *The Art of Christ* . B.O.W.

WATKINS, E. : *The Philosophy of Mysticism* Thomas Baker
An advanced treatment from the philosophic side of St. John of the Cross. Valuable.

WATRIGANT, H. (S.J.) : *Des Méthodes d'Oraison dans notre Vie Apostolique.* 1906 et suiv. En Collection de la Bibliothèque des Exercises . . . Toulouse

WILBERFORCE, B. (O.P.) : *Memorabilia* . . B.O.W.

ZIMMERMAN, O. (S.J.) : *Lehrbuch der Aszetik.* 1929.
Freiburg im-Breisgau : Herder

INDEX OF NAMES

Principal references are in italics

GENERAL INDEX

Principal references are in italics

Date Due